1999

1999

Proprio Italiano II

II

Authentic Regional Italian Menus and Recipes

Lina Michi Coruccini

Other books by Lina Michi Coruccini:
    Proprio Italiano - Authentic Northern Italian Menus and Recipe

Additional copies of this book may be ordered from:
Lina Coruccini
P.O. Box 1342
San Mateo, CA 94401
Tel: (650) 344-5795 Fax: (650) 344-5378

Cover photography by Lina Coruccini
Cover design by Photoworks

Library of Congress Cataloging in Publication Data
ISBN 0-9639605-3-9

Corucinni, Lina Michi
    Proprio Italiano II, authentic regional Italian menus and recipes
    Includes index
    1. Cookery, Italian. 2. Menus and recipes

Printed in the United States

I dedicate this book with much love to my mother, Cesarina, my only teacher, and to my husband, Roberto, for his encouragement, love, and support as I wrote this book. Thank you so very much!

Contents

Introduction

Let's take a journey through Italy from north to south. We will cross many plains and hills, and mountains, some very rugged and steep. We will travel along picturesque coastlines. We will see many farm lands on the mountains, on rolling hills, or on flat land. We will visit the island of Sicily and Sardinia, tasting their wonderful fish dishes and drinking their famous limoncello liqueur and Marsala wine.

I took this journey to Italy with my husband. He said that he would gladly drive and carry my suitcase, just so he could eat his way through Italy. We rented a car for the whole trip, so that we could drive through each region and spend four to five days in each one. It was an incredible experience for both of us.

During this journey, I chose restaurants and trattorias that served authentic regional dishes. My husband and I would order as many different dishes as we could possibly eat in one meal. As we ate each dish, I would see if the dish could be reproduced and if the ingredients would be available in our country. Also I eliminated dishes that I felt Americans would not eat or tolerate.

While in each region I planned menus for the region and wrote down the different ingredients for each dish, so that I could make it leisurely when returning home.

As we toured each region, I visited friends of the old country wherever possible. I spent time in their kitchens with my notebook and pen. I listened and watched my friends' grandmothers cook and explain about the different dishes, their origin and why they are so special and still in use. Also in some cases, I helped friends cook regional recipes unknown to me before. I was born and grew up in a small town near Lucca in Tuscany and was most familiar with the cooking of that area and northern Italian cuisine, in general.

I bought many Italian books for each region and shipped them back home. Those books helped me very much in learning about the history of each region and, in many cases, who originated the different ways of cooking.

I have learned through my experiences that there is no such thing as a single style of Italian cooking. There are twenty different methods of cooking, one for each region. You have to take a culinary tour of the regions in order to see how different the cooking is from region-to-region.

In Italy regional cooking has made a comeback and is stronger than ever before, however, with a few changes. Olive oil has replaced lard in cooking, since the olive oil is readily available throughout Italy. Also the recipes now are leaner than before because people are paying more attention to their diets and health.

The Italians have started to go back to their individual heritages of everyday foods of the countryside. Poor pheasant dishes such as polenta, beans, and soups of all kinds are very popular again and are very healthy.

Italy also has fast food outlets such as MacDonald's, but they are different from ours. They serve hamburgers, but also lasagna and other Italian dishes. McDonald's is frequented by the young Italians who go there for a snack.

The Italians also have *panino (sandwich) and salad bars for those people that* are in a hurry or have only one hour for lunch. But on the whole, Italians love to sit for hours leisurely eating a lunch, drinking wine, and ending the meal with an espresso.

The reason for this book is to introduce you to the twenty (two are traditionally combined) regions of Italy and to the diversity of each region's cooking. I have assembled recipes from each region into menus. I selected what I believe you will enjoy cooking and what I liked about each region's cuisine.

Space does not permit me to include all of the wonderful dishes of each region, so I limited the recipes to two menus from each region. It was a hard task to decide what to choose. Some of the recipes I did not include in the book are either too fattening or take too long to prepare.

A prime reason for this book is to show you all the different types of cooking of Italy and to dispel the notion that Italian cooking is just pasta and tomato sauce. Not only is the cooking different in each region, but the people speak different dialects and even different languages.

From the many trips that I alone, or with my husband, consequently took to the regions of Italy, I have learned that Italian food is very simple, but full of rich flavors. This is true in all the regions.

In Italy cooking is an art. The essence of the food is the perfect blending of ingredients with sauces, spices, and herbs playing important roles. As my mother would say, it is not how many dishes you serve, but how well each one is prepared.

While I traveled through Italy and tasted the different desserts, I found out that the old Italian cakes were very rustic and dry. Traditionally pastries are made primarily for religious festivals.

The old-fashioned cakes used to be baked in forni (ovens). The ovens were made of bricks and cement. Most Italians had built them for baking breads. After the loafs of bread had been placed in the oven, the housewife frequently placed a cake or two just inside the opening where it was not so hot as to burn the cake. Italians in each region made cakes with what grew on their land and was available to them, thus the type of flour varied greatly among the regions.

If homemade, the traditional coarse and more rustic cakes are generally served with coffee for breakfast or with coffee during the day. If these cakes are served after dinner, they are accompanied by the liqueur or wine of that region, so that the cake can be dipped into it. Also a slice of cake can be served with Italian ice cream or with whipped cream over it.

Today the Italians prefer to buy their desserts (pastries) at the bakery. This is especially true for holiday desserts that celebrate Christmas, Easter, New Year, Carnival, the day of the dead, and Saint's day. For these occasions the bakeries make special pastries. Usually everyday meals are ended with fresh fruit in season and with some favorite cheese.

The success of any meal, whether Italian or otherwise, depends not only on the preparations of the food but on the composition of the menu. Every dish on a menu should complement the others. The menu should also take advantage of available seasonal ingredients.

Keeping in mind the traditional dishes of each region, the seasonal preferences, and the availability of ingredients, I have tried to create Italian menus to suit American occasions. I have focused on readily available ingredients, even though some of them may be seasonal.

For your convenience I have also included a preparation guide for each menu to enable you to schedule much of the cooking before the meals are to be served and allow you time with your guests.

I have kept to the original authentic way of preparing the dishes, but have made some improvements in making them. I reduced the amount of fat and have used olive oil when possible instead of butter.

In general, the cooking times of Italian dishes are shorter than they used to be. This is true especially for pasta sauces. The older Italians felt that the sauce had to cook all day. The vegetable cooking times are also much shorter than they once were, so that the vegetables are firmer and crisper. Also the meat and fish now are not overcooked. When I served fish in Italy to an old friend, she was surprised at how quickly I cooked the fish.

The Italians have learned some of the cooking techniques of nouvelle cuisine and also the importance of the presentation of a dish. They have a sense of taste and they use it in making the food taste and look fantastic.

In Italy the average consumption of bread is at least double that in the United States. The Italians eat bread with every dish, including with pasta.

Italians love to eat ice creams and ices all year long. They also like candies and pastries. Cappuccino, caffè latte (coffee and milk), espresso, and other types of coffee are served in Italy throughout the day.

The regions of Italy can be divided between those of the north and the south. Rome in the Lazio region is considered to be the dividing line. In northern Italy and Sardinia butter and flat pasta are primarily used. In southern Italy and Sicily, olive oil, salt pork (pancetta), and tube pasta are used. Rice is grown and used in northern Italy and polenta dishes are prevalent. In the south more pastas are used. In the north they raise beef and in the south they raise an abundance of vegetables, olives, nuts, and fruits. Consequently, more meat is consumed in the north and fish and vegetables are more popular in the south.

In the south more fresh cheese, such as ricotta, mozzarella and Provolone, is consumed. Hard-aged cheeses for grating, especially the famous Parmigiano-Reggiano or Parmesan, predominate in the north.

In the south more spices are used in making sausages and salumi (cold cuts) while in the north they are blander. In the north more butter, truffles, rice, and soups are a part of the cooking. In the south more olive oil, tomatoes, garlic, and pasta dishes are used. Many of the southern pasta dishes are made with vegetables and with different types of fish.

With the exception of a few dishes most Italian foods are cooked quickly. It shortens the time spent in the kitchen for our faster pace of today lifestyle

Bologna is known as the food capital of northern Italy and Naples that of southern Italy. More and more people are discovering the simple and elegant foods of Sicily. Because of their multi-cultural heritage the Sicilians have wonderful culinary traditions that have been handed down from family to family through the centuries.

Italy produces and exports a huge amount of wine, but many delicious smaller wines are known only locally. In Italy wine is used as food and is a part of the meal.

The Italians drink very little hard liquor. They frown on drunkenness and overindulgence. Early-on Italians expose their children to wine at meals. They add water to wine for little children. As they grow the ratio of wine to water is increased.

I hope I have given you enough ideas for cooking Italian regional dishes and helped you in deciding what you want to prepare for your family and guests.

Buon Appetito !

To all of my friends in Italy and also in the United States who helped me with recipes for this book I give my thanks and appreciation for all of your support and help.

I would like to express my appreciation to Frank Spadarella and Tom Vano for providing some of the pictures for this book.

I also want to give my thanks and gratitude to a special person, Hilde Lee, who advised me throughout this book project and who is also a very special friend.

The Typical Italian Meal

The typical Italian meal consists of various courses. Some meals may only have two courses — the main course and a salad or dessert — others may include five courses. The salad is often regarded as the main part of the meal, and cheese and fruit may be an interlude before a sweet dessert. Following are the courses in the order they are served. This is followed by a description of each course.

Antipasto
Appetizer

Il Primo
First Course

Il Secondo
Main Course

La Verdura
The Vegetables

Il Formaggio
The Cheese

La Frutta e il Dolce
Fruit and Dessert

Caffe
Coffee

Antipasto - Appetizer

The word antipasto means the course that is eaten before the meal begins. It literally means "before the pasta," since pasta is often served as a first course. The antipasto is supposed to stimulate the appetite and can be served either cold or hot. Antipasto varies from region to region. Many antipasto dishes could be eaten as a main course. The quantities of antipasto dishes should be small, since they are supposed to stimulate the appetite, not satisfy it. Appetizers are selected to complement the meal and not overpower it.

Il Primo - First Course

Often a plate of pasta or risotto is served as the first course. Many wonderful soups are also served as a first course — fish, vegetable, or bean soup. Polenta, a northern Italian dish, may also be served as a first course. It is either fried or baked and served with simple sauces, often accompanied by meat or poultry.

Il Secondo - The Main Course

The main course consist of meat, game, poultry or fish dishes. The meat and fish are prepared in many different ways — roasted, stewed, grilled, or fried. For special meals, two or three main courses are served.

La Verdura - The Vegetables

Vegetables are very important in Italy and must always be very fresh. Usually the vegetables that are served are the ones that are in season at the time. Italian salads are made of mixtures of cultivated and wild greens. They may contain many different types of greens and are served with simple dressing.

Il Formaggio - The Cheese

After the main course, cheese is often served. Many different kinds of cheese are made in Italy with many regional variations. Italian cheeses are made with cows', sheep's or goats' milk. There is even cheese made from buffalo milk — the famous buffalo mozzarella. In northern Italy the most famous cheeses are: Parmigiano Reggiano, (Parmesan cheese), pecorino cheese which is a more rustic cheese; Gorgonzola cheese, a creamy blue cheese; fontina cheese, which is semi-soft and used for cooking and fondue.

La Frutta e il Dolce - Fruit and Dessert

Fresh Fruit of the season is always served after a meal. Special desserts usually are served for special occasions, such as anniversary, birthdays, and Christmas and Easter dinners. Some of the fruit-based desserts are fruit tarts and pies; fruit sorbets and ice creams. Sweets and cakes are served usually at holiday dinners, for example: Panettone, Panforte, and Colomba cake.

Caffè - Coffee

Coffee is always served in Italy at the end of a meal, and it is always served black. The Italian coffee is called espresso, and it is served in small cups. Italians drink espresso anytime during the day, not just after a meal. In the morning they drink cappuccino, an espresso coffee with whipped milk on top which is served in a larger cup. Coffee is also used in Italy as an ingredient in many different kinds of dessert.

Some Unique Aspects of Italian Cuisine

Each region of Italy has its own unique dishes and methods of food preparation. In addition each cook has his or her own preferences for methods of food shopping, cooking, and food presentation. I am no exception, and I want to share with you some of my thoughts and ideas on various aspects and components of an Italian meal.

Soup

Homemade broth is an indispensable ingredient of good Italian cooking. I prepare big batches of it, which I freeze in plastic containers. I also keep odd chicken parts and beef bones in the freezer to make stock. Bones are as useful as meat because they give body as well as flavor to the stock.

Soup is often the first course in an Italian meal. It is frequently served once a day in Italy, mostly in the evening because it is very light. I have great childhood memories of my mother in the kitchen preparing our Sunday dinner. Sunday was the day when we would invite friends for dinner, and mother would prepare a beef soup for a first course. Our house was filled with the aroma of the broth simmering. Her soup would give a glow to our cheeks.

If you are making the soup because you want to eat the boiled meat or chicken, put the meat in water that is boiling. The boiling water seals in the flavor similar to the way browning meat does. If you want to make a rich broth to use for cooking, then place all the ingredients, meat bones and vegetables, in a stock pot and cover them with cold water. Cooking in cold water takes away the flavors of the ingredients and adds them to the stock, while boiling water seals the flavors into the meat. Always cook a broth over very low heat.

Bread

Bread is served with almost every Italian meal. Toasted bread is also the basis of *crostini* and *bruschetta*, which are served as appetizers.

Although stale bread is fed to the animals, it is also the basis of a number of famous Italian dishes. It is used in soup with beans, as the basis of a fruit pudding, and when soaked it is part of a delicious summer salad of tomatoes and cucumbers. Slices of bread and crumbs are used for stuffing meat, chicken, fowl, fish, and vegetables. Also the Italians make a bread cake from left-over bread and candied fruit.

Each region has its own bread specialties to accompany its own style of food. For example, in Tuscany a bread called *pan sciocco*, is made without salt.

It is served with salty, cured meats, such as prosciutto and different *salumi* (cold cuts). In southern Italy bread made with olive oil pairs well with tomatoes.

Nearly all of the Italian breads are firm textured with hard crusts. They vary in shape and size. One of the famous breads is *ciabatta*, which means slipper. It is a flat shaped loaf with a crisp crust and a hole inside. This bread is frequently cut in half and stuffed with a sandwich filling.

Focaccia is a flat bread that resemble pizza dough. Traditionally it is oiled and then baked in a wood oven. *Focaccia* often has different toppings. In Italy it is sold in pieces and by weight. Also different ingredients can be worked into the dough and then baked.

Grissini are thin long bread sticks that originated in Turin and are served in many Italian restaurants. Some of them are flavored with garlic or onion and some *grissini* are rolled in sesame or even poppy seeds.

Panini bread rolls are very popular throughout Italy. They are rounded or oblong, white in color with a soft inside and crusty outside. They are good for sandwiches.

Although baguettes are originally French in origin, they have become popular in Italy, particularly for crostini. The small slices of this bread with a topping are ideal to serve guests while they are having drinks before dinner.

Risotto

The basic method of making a risotto in Italy is as follows: The rice must first be sautéed in butter and olive oil or just butter, usually with onion but sometimes with other vegetables. Then simmering broth is added a little at a time, and additional simmering broth is added only when the rice has absorbed the liquid that was added before. The rice is cooked at an even heat, usually a low heat. At the end of the cooking time, more butter and some Parmesan cheese are always added. The risotto is left to rest fro a few minutes, then stirred, transferred to a dish, and eaten as soon as it is ready.

You will notice that in my risotto recipes I cook the rice with the entire broth, covered over low heat for 15 to 18 minutes, or until the rice is cooked through but still firm to the bite. I have found that this method works perfectly. The grains separate, yet they are bound together in a creamy consistency. This method leaves time to prepare other dishes while achieving the same results as the basic method.

Vegetables

You will notice as you read the recipes in this book, that vegetables, probably even more than pasta, are the main base of Italian cooking. Vegetables are mixed with rice or pasta, used as appetizers, in soups, and in elaborate main dishes. They are also served between courses as a part of a salad as a palate cleanser.

In Italy, the vegetables are always served on their own separate plate just like pasta or rice dishes. In the summer, when it gets very hot, the Italians live almost entirely on fresh vegetables. They are prepared in many ways, but are frequently very simply dressed with olive oil and lemon juice. Italians also love raw vegetables dipped in olive oil, pepper, and salt. Even today some of the best restaurants serve vegetables this way and this dish is called Pinzimonio.

One of the extraordinary sights that I love when I go to Italy, is an Italian open market full of vegetable stalls. This is called a *mercato*. In the *mercato* are colorful mounds of vegetables and fruit that were picked fresh that morning on the farm. The Italian housewife inspects all this abundance for a while. She touches, she smells, compares the produce from one stall with another and sometimes she also bargains.

Salads

In Italy salads are never served as a first course. They are always served after the main course, as they are supposed to cleanse and refresh the palate before the cheese, fruit, or dessert.

When serving a salad after a very special or heavy meal, it should be a light and simple one. A salad made with mixed cooked vegetables and cheese or eggs is perfect for lunch.

Italian salad dressings are very simple, but tasty. They consist of olive oil, salt and wine vinegar. The olive oil should be a fruity one and used generously. However, be stingy with the vinegar since too much can ruin a salad. Black pepper can be added and should always be ground fresh. Lemon juice may be substituted for the vinegar and is quite nice for summer salads.

Desserts

In Italy the pastry shops provide most of the sweets and desserts. The desserts that are prepared at home are very simple. More often after a meal, fresh seasonal fruit is served with a platter of different cheeses.

Most Italians would rather miss dessert than a first course, and I am one of them. I would rather have fruit anytime, than a fancy dessert. When a dessert is served at home, it is on a special occasion or on holidays. Pastries are sometimes served in the afternoon with espresso coffee. However, Italians prefer to go out to have coffee and pastry.

The Italian Pantry

The following are some of the basic ingredients you might want to have in your pantry for cooking Italian foods:

Italian Arborio rice to make risottos and to use in soups.

A few of your favorite dried pastas, so that you will have a variety to pair with different sauces.

Cornmeal for making polenta. I keep two kinds, a coarse cornmeal that needs to cook for 45 minutes and stirred constantly, and an instant 5-minute polenta for when I decide at the last minute that I want to serve polenta.

Dried beans (white cannellini and pink cranberry), lentils, and chickpeas.

Canned goods including Italian peeled tomatoes and tomato paste, cannellini, garbanzo, and kidney beans. Cans of tuna and of anchovy fillets to add additional flavor to various dishes should also be available. Cans of green and black olives, several bottles of extra virgin olive oil, red wine vinegar and balsamic vinegar. A jar of capers and peppercorns.

Packages of dried porcini mushrooms are a good idea, since they keep for long period of time. I also keep saffron for risotto, soups, and meat dishes.

A wedge of Parmesan cheese and a wedge of pecorino cheese are essential ingredients for Italian cooking, and they should be stored in he refrigerator, tightly wrapped in aluminum foil. They should be grated fresh as needed. Both mozzarella and fontina cheeses are good to have on hand, and they, too, must be kept in the refrigerator. Do not forget to have in the refrigerator unsalted butter, the only butter the Italians use for cooking.

Other refrigerator items include a tube each of anchovy paste, garlic paste, and tomato paste. The tubes are better to use and not wasteful. Pesto sauce in a jar or plastic container for pasta or to add to sauces, soups, or to spread on bread should also be kept in the refrigerator. I usually buy a large whole piece of pancetta (Italian bacon), keep it in the refrigerator and slice it when needed Also I buy a thick chunk of prosciutto and cut it when needed.

Almonds, pine nuts, and walnuts should be kept in the freezer because they will remain fresh longer than if stored in the refrigerator. In my freezer, I also have homemade chicken, beef, and vegetable stocks for risotto, sauces, and soups. My freezer also contains some Italian sausages.

Espresso coffee should be stored in a tight glass jar in the refrigerator or you can buy the espresso beans and grind them fresh as needed.

Basic Ingredients for Italian Cooking

This list of basic ingredients for Italian cooking will help acquaint you with many of the ingredients used in the recipes in this book. It is always a good idea to use only the freshest ingredients available; choose only the finest and prepare them with care.

Beans

In Italy cranberry beans and cannellini beans are grown in the summer and eaten fresh at that time. The rest of the year dried ones are used, particularly in soups, such as minestrone and *pasta e fagioli*. They are also very tasty boiled, then drained and seasoned with olive oil, salt, and pepper. Beans are combined with tuna in a salad and with tomato sauce for a side dish.

Cheeses

Italy produces many wonderful cheeses. Try to buy imported Italian cheeses, as the domestic imitations do not always match the taste and style of the Italian original. Some of the best known Italian cheeses are:

Parmesan
Parmesan cheese comes from the Parma region. It is made from cows' milk and aged for two or three years. It is a cheese used primarily for grating. Always grate Parmesan cheese fresh when needed in a recipe if you want to create a truly wonderful Italian dishes. Store it tightly wrapped in the refrigerator. Parmesan cheese is used in sauces, with pasta, with soup, with meat, salad, and with bread. This cheese is excellent cut in chunks and eaten with a glass of wine.
Pecorino
Pecorino is a cheese made from sheeps' milk. When aged for few months, it is eaten as a snack or as a dessert. When aged longer, it is used for grating. The Italian pecorino that is more familiar in this country for grating is the Romano. It has a sharper flavor than Parmesan cheese. Sometimes the two cheese are used together. Romano cheese is an excellent combination with pesto sauce.

Fontina

Fontina cheese, made from cow's milk, is a soft cheese with a delicate nutty flavor. Great eaten plain with bread or used in chicken or veal dishes.

Gorgonzola

A very delicate blue-veined cheese used in salads or just eaten by itself..

Mozzarella

Mozzarella is made from cows' milk and is the basic pizza cheese, but is also used in many other dishes. In Italy, a genuine mozzarella is made from water buffalo milk and is served fresh, often with tomatoes and basil.

Ricotta

The best Italian ricotta is dry and made from sheeps' milk. Ricotta sold in this country most often is made from whole milk, and is not as perishable as true ricotta. Ricotta is used in many desserts.

Provolone

This is the cheese that you see hanging in Italian stores and in pictures of Italian markets. It is a firm cheese with a smokey flavor.

Mascarpone

This is a rich fresh cheese that is often used in desserts and pastries instead of whipped cream.

Cold Cuts

Prosciutto

Also called Parma ham, prosciutto is one of the most common foods in the Italian diet. It comes raw or cooked. Prosciutto is salted and air dried fresh ham. The seasoning and aging process cures the ham completely. It is cured for many months.

Prosciutto varies in flavor depending on the region of its origin. Some are more salty and some sweet. In some regions it is smoked, which is very unusual. When a recipe calls for prosciutto, it refers to the uncooked ham. Prosciutto should always be cut paper thin,

Bresaola

Bresaola originated in the region of Lombardy. It has now become a favorite appetizer all over Italy. Salted, air dried, and pressed, it may be made from different cuts of beef. You can serve it very simply, sliced like prosciutto with a little lemon juice and oil, or use it in sauces for pasta with butter, cream, and herbs. Bresaola can be compared with the German Bundnerfleisch.

Mortadella

The best mortadella in Italy is made in Bologna. Mortadella is made from finely ground, pure pork, and is flavored with wine. Sometimes pistachio nuts are added, as well as large white cubes of fat.

Salami

Salami is a mixture of lean pork, pork fat, and some beef. Sometimes veal is substituted for beef. It takes weeks or even months to cure salami. There are many different kinds of salami. Each region in Italy has its own version.

<u>Sausages</u>

Sausages come in two versions — mild and spiced. They are basically made with ground pork and pancetta. Some domestic sausages are seasoned with fennel seeds.

<u>Pancetta</u>

This is Italian bacon. It is not smoked, but is cured with salt and spices. However, some pancetta is smoked. It is mostly used for flavoring dishes, particularly pasta sauces.

Olive Oil

Olive oil is an essential ingredient in Italian cuisine. It is used for sautéing, browning, braising, and broiling; in soups, stews, risottos, and pastas. Olive oil is the dressing for salads and the condiment for antipasto dishes. it is also the finishing touch for vegetables.

The very best olive oil is extra virgin oil which is obtained from the first cold pressing of the finest, hand picked olives. Green or green-gold in color, it is aromatic and tastes mellow and nutty, with no bitter aftertaste. The second best grade of olive oil is virgin. It is obtained through continuing pressing of the olives and is aromatic, green in color and flavorful. Pure olive oil is the last grade produced for general use and the kind most imported in this country. The word pure means nothing more than the oil came only from olives. It is pale yellow in color, and has only a slight olive aroma and taste.

Tomato Paste

Tomato Paste is not a substitute for tomatoes, but sometimes one teaspoon or tablespoon of tomato paste adds special zest to a dish. The Italian imported brands are packaged in tubes so that you can use a little at a time.

Herbs, Spices and Other Flavor Enhancers

There is a world of difference in the taste of fresh herbs and dried ones. Fresh herbs can either be grown in a little garden plot or on the kitchen window sill. They can also be purchased at many supermarkets.

Since I have a vegetable garden, I always grow rosemary, sage, oregano, basil, thyme, and mint. I also have Italian and regular parsley. .

The following is a brief description of some of the herbs and spices used in Italian regional cooking:

BAY LEAVES

The bay leaf is a sweet, aromatic herb native of the Mediterranean area. Dried or fresh, whole or chopped, it is used with fish and meats.

BASIL

Basil is more pungent fresh. When dried, it loses much of its smell. However, basil freezes well. To freeze basil, rinse the leaves, pat them dry, then freeze in plastic bags. Chop while they are still frozen and add them to cooked dishes. Also make pesto and freeze it, or place basil in a glass jar, fill the jar with good olive oil and cover tightly. It will keep for months and the basil will retain the color and fresh flavor. Basil is a natural companion of tomatoes.

BLACK PEPPER

Black Pepper should always be freshly ground with a pepper mill. There are five different kinds of peppercorns — white, black, red, green, and rose — and they are used either whole or ground.

GARLIC

The fresher the garlic is, the more subtle the flavor. Garlic is essential to Italian cooking. It is used whole, crushed, minced, slit or chopped in many recipes. Garlic should be stored in a cool, dry place. You may keep peeled garlic in a jar covered with olive oil in the refrigerator. However, do not store it for a long period of time because it will lose some of its strength.

MARJORAM and OREGANO

They are related plants. Marjoram is sweet and has a more delicate flavor than oregano. Marjoram is used more in northern Italy. Oregano is used in pizza, seafood dishes, and spaghetti sauces in southern Italy.

MINT

Mint is the herb of the early Romans. Although used in fruit drinks and with poultry, and fish, mint is primarily used for garnish.

NUTMEG

Nutmeg is used in egg dishes and white sauces and with some vegetables. It is also used as a spice in baking.

PARSLEY

Parsley can be used as a flavoring or garnish. The Italian parsley has a flatter leaf and is more pungent than the curly-leafed variety.

ROSEMARY

This herb thrives in the sea air and heat of the Mediterranean but it also grows well in other climates. It is traditionally used with meat dishes, primarily lamb, poultry, and also some seafood.

SAFFRON

Saffron is a spice used mainly in risotto. It has its own characteristic flavor and turns brilliant yellow when mixed with food. Saffron is also use in fish soups and chicken dishes.

SAGE

Sage is a great flavor enhancer for poultry, veal and roasted potatoes. Sage is also used with wild game, especially the small birds.

THYME

When using fresh thyme, use only the leaves. Whole leaves, fresh or dried, are excellent with seafood, cheese dishes, eggs, meats, soups, and Mediterranean vegetables such as eggplant and zucchini.

In addition to herbs and spices the following also add flavoring to Italian cooking.

LEMON

Lemon has a distinctive perfume and flavor in both its juice and peel. It adds a piquancy to almost any type of food, including meat, chicken, fish, fruit, and vegetables.

MUSHROOMS

Porcini are the most popular wild mushrooms in Italian cooking, but other types are also used. The cultivated mushrooms are primarily eaten raw in a salad. Fresh or dried mushrooms are used as seasonings in sauces, risottos, pastas, omelets, and soups. When dried mushrooms are used in Italian cooking, it is always the porcini because of their special aroma. To reconstitute them, procini mushrooms should be soaked in warm water for half an hour and then rinsed to wash away any dirt that might still cling to them The soaking liquid should be strained through a fine sieve and can be used in soups and sauces.

ONIONS

There are different kinds of onions. Yellow onions are used for frying and sautéing; and for soups and sauces; and in meat, fish, poultry, wild game, and vegetable dishes. The red onions are used raw in green salads, with sliced tomatoes, white beans, raw meat, and tuna, salmon, or chicken salads.

TOMATOES

Although fresh tomatoes are always preferred, canned Italian plum tomatoes are frequently used in cooking. They are firm, fleshy and flavorful.

The indoor market in Florence. Photo collection of the author.

Pasta and Rice

Pasta

Which is better, "fresh pasta or dried pasta"? This is an impossible question to answer, because only you can decide which of the two you prefer. There are many good brands of dried pasta from which to choose on the shelves of the supermarkets. Fresh pasta is usually sold in the dairy case.

Italians prefer dried pasta, as do I. It gives me better control when cooking, and I like the consistency better. I prefer to spend my time making a good sauce instead of making fresh pasta by hand or by machine.

The cooking time for pasta depends on whether it is dried or fresh. In either case it should be cooked *al dente* or "to the tooth." Fresh pasta usually takes 2 to 3 minutes to cook. As soon as it is done, pour a glass of cold water into the pot before you drain it. This will immediately stop the cooking action and prevent the pasta from becoming mushy. Dried pasta will take 8 to 10 minutes to cook for most types. When boiling the pasta, make sure you are using a large pot with plenty of water. Add one teaspoon of salt per quart of water and always bring the water to a high boil before adding the pasta. Drain the pasta after it has finished cooking.

There are different ways of serving pasta. A plain or stuffed pasta served with different sauces or it may be cooked in broth. Pasta cooked in the oven is baked in layers in a sauce, and pasta can be part of a frittata. Pasta is also used to make different kinds of pasta salads.

There are so many different pasta names and shapes that even Italians sometimes get confused, because in different regions they are called by different names. Pasta comes in different forms, sizes, thickness, textures, and colors. It may be long and narrow, short and broad, smooth or ridged, solid or hollow. Different pastas require different sauces. You will find a great variety of regional pasta recipes in this book.

Rice

Italy's prime rice-growing region is the Po Valley where four types of rice are grown, ranging from short to long grain. The best and most exported variety of Italian rice is Arborio. This rice is ideal for risottos because it absorbs a lot of liquid while cooking and swells up without breaking apart.

Rice can be served boiled and mixed with butter and Parmesan cheese or in a salad with tuna, grilled bell pepper, tomatoes, and a few anchovies. It is used in soups and stuffings, as well as for croquettes, fritters, and baked rice molds.

Concerning Raw Eggs

Always check eggs for broken shells and discard any found in that condition. Refrigerate eggs as soon after purchase as possible.

Dishes containing raw eggs should be consumed immediately. Freezing dishes containing raw eggs in a O° F. freezer keeps the bacteria from growing. Items containing raw eggs should be kept at room temperature only as long as it takes to prepare them.

EQUIPMENT FOR ITALIAN COOKING

I do not use many cooking implements, just a few well-made things that I use repeatedly. There are many varieties of cooking equipment on the market and I have listed the most important ones for Italian cooking, some of which might not be considered standard equipment in other kitchens.

THE SAUTÉ PAN

Many of my recipes are made in a sauté pan. It is a pan 10-to 12-inches in diameter, with either flaring or straight sides, flat bottom, and with a closely fitting lid. When buying this pan, make sure that it is of the heaviest, solid construction that you can afford. I frequently cook vegetables, fish, meat, frittatas, potatoes and pasta sauce in a sauté pan. In this pan you can cook either at high heat, or simmering slowly. It can also be used for deep-frying,

STOCK POT

A sturdy stock pot is necessary to make broth or stock or for boiling large quantities of food. It should have two handles because it is heavy when full.

CASSEROLE

Made of heavy material a casserole is very helpful. A round casserole is good for making risotto, stew, or boiling potatoes or pasta. In Italian cooking the word casserole refers to a heavy pot instead of the glass or ceramic dishes that are common in American cooking.

LASAGNA PAN

The perfect lasagna pan is made of heavy metal, the sides of the pan must be at least 3 inches high, otherwise the sauce will spill over the top when cooking. The corners of the pan should be at sharp right angles because lasagna pieces are cut straight when being served.

COLANDER

A colander is necessary for draining pasta. It is a perforated half-sphere that rests, curved side down, on three little feet and has two handles for lifting and shaking off excess water. It drains not only pasta, but any other ingredients cooked in water.

CHEESE GRATER

It is an indispensable gadget. Freshly grated cheese is used in most of the Italian cooking. This gadget is a 2-piece hand-held grater that clamps the cheese against a revolving perforated drum. However, when I need large amount of grated cheese for making lasagna, I use the food processor.

FOOD PROCESSOR

I use the food processor when I need large quantities of ingredients chopped for meat sauces, pesto sauce, to chop pancetta, prosciutto or mortadella, and ingredients for a pasta stuffing or for any other kind of stuffing. I also use it to chop all kinds of herbs and vegetables. Do not chop onions in the food processor, however, because it forces out too much liquid.

SPATULA

A pierced spatula is good for long, flat meat, chicken breast. or fish, when removing it temporarily from the pan.

SLOTTED SPOON

This is practical for removing small, chunky things, such as meatballs, stew, or croquettes.

MEZZALUNA (Half Moon)

This implement is used for hand chopping in Italy. It is a curved knife shaped like a half moon and has two wooden knob-like handles on each end. The rolling back and forth motion of the half moon is less tiringthan using a knife because you do not have to lift it after each stroke. Once you are used to it, it is very fast and you will prefer it as do all Italians. It is also very easy to clean.

ESPRESSO MACHINE

To finish an Italian meal properly, you need to serve espresso coffee. I consider an espresso machine an absolute must as a coffee maker. There are excellent small espresso machines for the home. One is a Moka express which uses steam pressure to force the water to go through the ground coffee into the top of the pot. This is done on top of the stove. You can also buy electric espresso machines that make coffee for two or for four people.

PASTA MACHINE

If you prefer to make your own fresh pasta, then you need either a manual pasta machine or an electric one.

The Italian Regions
Their menus
and
Recipes

Valle d'Aosta

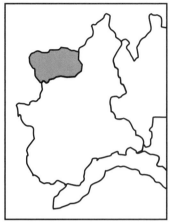

Valle d'Aosta, in the northwest corner of Italy, is a tiny but spectacular region of narrow valleys and towering mountains. It is the smallest of the Italian regions but has the tallest mountain, Monte Bianco (white mountain). The region borders France, Switzerland, and the Piedmont region of Italy. The majority of the people speak a French dialect, but they also speak Italian. Both French and Italian are taught in the schools. The climate of this region is cool in the summer and very cold in the winter.

Roman ruins, medieval castles, and modern ski resorts are scattered throughout the Valle d'Aosta region. Alpine farmhouse are typical in the area. Valle d'Aosta is a favorite Italian area for tourists, who enjoy the mountain scenery, as well as local culinary specialties of soups and numerous game dishes.

Valle d'Aosta's food is rich and hearty, which is typical of Italy's mountain cooking. This type of cuisine is very satisfying after a day of mountain hiking or skiing.

One of the mainstays of Valle d'Aosta's cooking is a variety of soups, which are often very thick. Nearly all of the soups are made with beef, chicken, or veal plus vegetables and herbs. A pot of stock invariable simmers on the back of kitchen stoves in most mountain homes.

Zuppa alla Valdostana is a rich vegetable soup, made with chestnuts, bread, potatoes, nettles, onions, cabbage, rye flour, and cheese. *Seupa* is a very thick soup consisting of layers of black bread, butter, and local fontina cheese. and broth. The soup is made in a clay tureen and baked in the oven. Another soup is called *valpeulleunenze*, which is made with layers of boiled cabbage leaves and a few spoonfuls of gravy from roasted beef.

The local polenta is prepared with roughly-milled corn. It is darker than usual because this yellow cornmeal for making polenta is mixed with buckwheat flour grown in the high altitudes of the region.

Polenta concia is made for special occasions. It is a rich and ancient dish which the mountain people traditionally ate on Sundays. *Polenta concia* consists of layers of polenta, fontina cheese, and melted butter. It is baked and served with truffles.

Since cattle breeding is one of this region's prime agricultural activities, veal and beef are the main meats of Valle d'Aosta's cuisine. *Carbonade* is the classic local meat dish, which is prepared with cubed beef that is dipped in flour, browned in butter, and cooked in red wine. *Cotoletta Valdostana* consists of a veal chop stuffed with prosciutto, fontina, and white truffles, then coated with bread crumbs and fried in butter.

In the hunting season Valle d'Aosta's cuisine is even richer. Wild goat, partridge, hare, dormouse, pheasant, and marmot are served braised or roasted. Game is also marinated in wine, then cooked and served with peppers, or stewed in Barolo wine. Although not as prevalent, wild boar, mountain goat and, especially chamois, can still be found in the local forests.

Mocetta is a cured and smoked prosciutto that is made with the ham of a wild goat. It is very tasty and has been made in the same manner for centuries. *Mocetta* is also made using lean chamois meat that has been marinated in brine with garlic, sage, rosemary, and bay leaves. It is then air dried. These versions of *mocetta* are similar to traditional prosciutto but they are much more flavorful and the meat is leaner.

Production of fontina cheese, a mild but flavorful cheese, is centered in the valleys around Aosta, the region's capital. Cheese is very important in the cooking of Valle d'Aosta. It is used in the preparation of numerous dishes. Tomini are small cheeses made primarily from cows milk. They are usually served with olive oil and lemon juice as part of an antipasto.

There are two traditional desserts in the Valle d'Aosta region. One is *crema cotta*, a cooked cream. It is made by mixing milk, cream, sugar, and gelatin, then barely cooked, and poured in a mold to set. It is served cold.

The town of Aosta with the Alps in the background.
Photo collection of the author.

The other dessert is called *fiandolein*. It consists of *crema Inglese* that is flavored with rum and lemon zest, and then poured over thinly sliced rye bread in a dish. Other desserts usually feature fruit, such as pears in wine and cream, blueberries with fresh creamy cheese, and apples with bread crumbs.

As the higher slopes of the mountains are covered with chestnut trees, chestnuts have become in integral part of Valle d'Aosta desserts. They are typically boiled, roasted, or used in the sweet *monte bianco* dessert. This dessert is made with pureed chestnuts which are molded into the shape of a mountain. A topping of whipped cream gives the dessert its name of white mountain — the famous peak in Valle d'Aosta.

Wines

There is an ancient tradition of wine making in Valle d'Aosta, but the amount that is produced is very small. Most of the wines are reds, with a few dry whites. Grappa is a powerful distilled spirit from the residue of the winegrape crush. It is very popular in Valle d'Aosta and neighboring Piedmont. Usually a small glass of grappa is offered after the dessert to complete a meal and to help digestion.

Una Cena Invernale
A Winter Dinner

Serves 6

Polenta con Fontina
Polenta with Fontina Cheese

Fagiano con Funghi
Pheasant with Mushrooms

Insalata di Sedani Peperoni e Arugula
Celery Salad with Peppers and Arugula

Mele Croccante
Apple Crisp

Caffe
Coffee

A Winter Dinner

It is very cold in the region of Valle d'Aosta in the winter, thus the food is rich and hearty to give a warm feeling. In the hunting season the cuisine is even richer.

This Valle d'Aosta winter meal starts with a rich and ancient dish made with layers of polenta, fontina cheese, and melted butter, which is then baked in the oven.

For the main course pheasant is braised with cognac or brandy and flavored with pancetta, broth, and mushrooms. The flavors of the pheasant blends well with the polenta, making a great combination.

The celery salad with peppers and arugula is a cooling and refreshing interlude before the apple crisp dessert, which ends this winter dinner with a sweet flavor.

Preparations

The polenta can be made the day before since it needs to cool. The morning of the dinner, slice it and assemble it with the fontina cheese and butter. In the evening place the polenta in the oven for about 45 minutes.

Make the pheasant and mushroom dish a day or two ahead and refrigerate it. Reheat the pheasant slowly in the evening of the dinner until completely hot.

In the morning of the dinner prepare all of the ingredients for the salad. Clean, cut, and place them in a plastic bag, and refrigerate until ready to assemble the salad. Make the salad dressing just before your guests arrive. Toss the salad just before serving.

Make the apple crisp dessert either the day before or in the morning of your party. If you prefer, warm up the apple crisp while you are having dinner. Then serve it with a scoop of vanilla ice cream.

Polenta con Fontina
Polenta with Fontina Cheese

Serves 6

8 cups water
2 teaspoons salt
2 cups coarse-grained yellow
   cornmeal
Butter, for greasing pan

1/2 pound fontina cheese, thinly
   sliced
White pepper
6 tablespoons unsalted butter, cut
   into pieces

Bring the water and salt to a boil in a large, heavy, deep saucepan. Gradually whisk in the cornmeal. Stir briskly with a wooden spoon until the mixture boils and thickens about 2 minutes. Cook over low heat, stirring often for about 40 minutes or until the mixture comes away cleanly from the sides of the pot. It should have the consistency of mashed potatoes.

Pour the polenta into a deep dish and leave it to cool. When the polenta is cold, cut it into 1/2 -inch thick slices.

Generously grease a large baking dish with butter. Place a layer of sliced polenta on the bottom of the dish. Then cover the polenta with a layer of fontina cheese. Season with white pepper. Repeat these layers until all of the ingredients are used up, finishing with a layer of polenta on top. Add the pieces of butter on top.

Place the baking dish into a preheated 450° F. until the top is brown. If assembling the polenta when it is cold, bake it in a preheated 375° F. oven, with foil covering the top, for the first half-hour. Then remove the foil, increase the heat to 450° F., and bake for another 10 to 15 minutes, or until the top is brown.

Fagiano con Funghi
Pheasant with Mushrooms

Serves 6

2 pheasants, about 2 pounds each
4 tablespoons olive oil
4 tablespoons unsalted butter
1/2 teaspoon salt
1/2 teaspoon freshly ground black
  pepper
1/2 cup cognac or brandy
2 slices pancetta or unsmoked
  bacon, chopped
1 onion, finely chopped

2 celery stalks, finely chopped
2 garlic cloves, finely chopped
4 sage leaves
2 tablespoons finely chopped
  parsley
Pinch of thyme
2 cups chicken broth
1 pound mushrooms, crimini,
  porcini, or portabello

Rinse the pheasants, pat them dry with paper towels and cut them into serving pieces.

Heat 2 tablespoons of the oil with the butter in a heavy Dutch oven or large saucepan over medium-high heat and sauté the pheasant pieces until golden in color.

Season the pheasants with salt and pepper. Pour the cognac over them and let it evaporate. Then add the chopped pancetta, onion, celery, garlic, and herbs and cook over medium heat until the pancetta starts to brown and the onion and celery are soft. Add the broth and continue cooking, covered, over low heat until the pheasant pieces are tender, about 45 minutes to 1 hour. Cooking time will vary depending on the age and size of the pheasants.

Clean the mushrooms with a damp cloth, remove the stems, and slice the caps. Heat the remaining 2 tablespoons of olive oil in a skillet and sauté the mushrooms over medium-high heat for about 5 to 10 minutes, or until all the water has been absorbed.

Transfer the mushrooms to the pheasant pan, stir gently and cook for a few more minutes for the sauce to absorb the flavor of the mushrooms.

Serve the pheasant pieces with the sauce and with a big helping of the polenta and fontina casserole.

Insalata di Sedani, Peperoni e Arugula
Celery Salad with Peppers and Arugula

Serves 6

2 large bunches celery
2 large bunches arugula
2 yellow peppers
1/2 cup green olives
1/4 cup extra virgin olive oil

1 teaspoon French mustard
2 tablespoons whipping cream
1/2 teaspoon salt
1/2 teaspoon freshly ground black
  pepper

Remove the coarse outer stalks of the celery. Separate each stalk apart and rinse under water. Remove any strings from the celery, then cut the celery into diagonal slices and place them in a salad bowl. Rinse and remove the stems from the arugula, pat dry, and cut into pieces. Wash the peppers and dry them. Cut them in half and remove the seeds. Then cut the peppers into 1/2-inch wide strips and place them in the salad bowl.

Remove the pits from the green olives, cut them coarsely, and place them in the salad bowl.

Mix the olive oil, mustard, cream, and salt and pepper until well blended. Then pour the dressing over the salad, and toss until completely blended. Serve the salad with small slices of baguette bread.

Mele Croccante
Apple Crisp

Serves 6

8 large or 10 medium Granny
    Smith, pippin, or McIntosh
    apples, peeled, cored, and thinly
    sliced
1 1/2 tablespoons lemon juice
1 cup all purpose flour

1 cup sugar
1 1/2 teaspoons cinnamon
1/2 teaspoon salt
1/2 cup (1 stick) unsalted butter,
    cut into pieces

Grease a 10-inch cake pan with butter.

Place a layer of sliced apples in the pan and sprinkle with some lemon juice. Repeat the layers until all of the apples are in the pan. Gently press down on the apples to even them out and smooth the top.

Mix the flour, sugar, cinnamon, and salt in a food processor until well combined. Add the butter and process, using on-and-off pulses until the mixture resembles coarse meal.

Press the crumb mixture evenly over the apples, making sure the edges are well sealed.

Place the cake pan in a preheated 350° F. oven and bake until the top is golden in color and the apples are tender, about 1 hour and 15 minutes. Check the apple crisp after one hour of baking time by inserting a toothpick in the center of the cake. If it comes out clean then it is done, if not continue baking.

Serve the apple crisp warm with a scoop of vanilla ice cream.

Un Pranzo Sontuoso
A Sumptuous Dinner

Serves 6

Gnocchi alla Fontina
Baked Gnocchi with Fontina Cheese

Costolette alla Valdostana
Veal Chops Stuffed with Cheese and Prosciutto

Spinaci Saltati
Sautéed Spinach

Crema Cotta con Salsa di Fragole
Molded Cream with Strawberry Sauce

Caffè
Coffee

A Sumptuous Dinner

This dinner from the Valle D'Aosta region is an elegant and rich meal. The first course of potato gnocchi (dumplings) dressed in a rich, creamy sauce of butter, fontina and parmesan cheeses is a dish of complex and enjoyable flavors.

The veal chops, stuffed with fontina cheese and prosciutto, are dipped in eggs, flour, and bread crumbs and then fried in butter. This is a very artistic presentation — a golden crisp veal chop with a juicy and piquant filling. The sautéed spinach makes a perfect companion for the veal dish.

For dessert I chose a molded, cooked cream, served with a strawberry sauce. This light yet rich dessert ends this sumptuous dinner from Valle D'Aosta.

Preparations

Some of the preparations for this dinner can be made ahead in order to allow you to enjoy your guests.

Make the gnocchi in the morning, place them, separated, on a floured baking sheet. Then cover the gnocchi and set them aside. In the evening before your guests are due to arrive, boil the gnocchi and simmer the butter, cream, nutmeg and fontina cheese until melted. Assemble the gnocchi and sauce in a casserole, but do not bake them. Add the Parmesan cheese just before you are going to place the casserole in the oven.

You can stuff the veal chop with the cheese and prosciutto late in the afternoon, dip in egg, then in flour and in bread crumbs. Cover the chops with plastic wrap and set them aside. The veal chops should be fried just before serving them. They cook them quickly, as their flavor is best when served immediately after cooking.

Boil the spinach early in the day, squeeze it very well, and set it aside. In the evening, sauté the garlic and the chopped anchovies and then add the spinach. Cook for 5 minutes, or you can cook the spinach completely late in the day and reheat it that evening.

The cooked cream and the strawberry sauce can be made the day before, and assembled the evening of the dinner.

Gnocchi alla Fontina
Baked Gnocchi with Fontina

Serves 6

2 pounds baking potatoes of the
   same size, washed
1 1/3 cups all purpose flour plus
   more as needed

1 teaspoon salt
1/4 teaspoon ground white pepper

   Boil the potatoes until tender and peel them while they are hot.
   Pour the flour onto a work area and make a well in the center. When the potatoes are still warm, pass them through a potato ricer into the center of the flour well or mash them and add to the well. Sprinkle with salt and white pepper. Using floured hands incorporate the flour into the potatoes and knead until the mixture is well mixed and smooth. It should be very soft without being sticky.

   Take small handfuls of the dough and knead them into short round logs 1/2-inch thick.. Cut each log into 2-inch pieces. Using your hand, dust each piece with flour and roll it on the concave side of a fork, pressing lightly with your thumb in a quick movement. The pieces should have an indentation on one side and the imprint of the fork's prongs on the other. Place the gnocchi, well separated, on a floured baking sheet.

   Bring a large pot of water to a boil over high heat. Add a batch of gnocchi and 2 tablespoons of salt to the water and stir with a wooden spoon. As soon as the gnocchi rise to the surface, scoop them out with a slotted spoon and place them in a colander. Repeat with the remaining gnocchi and then place them in a oven-proof casserole.

Sauce

4 tablespoons unsalted butter,
   melted, plus butter to grease
   casserole
1/3 cup cream

1/8 teaspoon nutmeg
1/2 cup shredded fontina cheese
1/2 cup freshly grated Parmesan
   cheese

   Simmer the butter, cream, nutmeg, and fontina in a double boiler until the cheese melts. Pour the cheese sauce over the gnocchi and sprinkle with Parmesan cheese. Bake on the top shelf of a preheated 400° F. oven until the cheese melts, about 5 minutes. Serve at once.

Costolette alla Valdostana
Veal Chops Stuffed with Cheese and Prosciutto

Serves 6

6 veal chops or cutlets with bone
6 thin slices fontina cheese
6 thin slices prosciutto
Salt
Freshly ground black pepper

1/2 cup flour
2 eggs, beaten
3/4 cup dry bread crumbs
6 tablespoons unsalted butter
6 sprigs fresh parsley, for garnish

Cut the veal chops in half almost to the bone in order to make a pocket for the filling, or have the butcher cut it for you. Place one slice of cheese and one slice of prosciutto flat in each chop. Close the chop by firmly pressing the top and bottom together, then seal the edges by beating hard with the dull end of a kitchen knife.

Sprinkle the veal chops on both sides with salt and pepper. Then dip the chops first in flour, then in egg, and finally in bread crumbs. Use your hands to pat the crumbs into the meat.

Heat the butter in a large frying pan over medium heat. When the butter foam begins to subside, add the chops and fry them on both sides until golden brown, about 10 to 15 minutes. Drain the chops on paper towels and serve one chop per person garnished with parsley.

Spinaci Saltati
Sautéed Spinach

Serves 6

2 pounds spinach
1 teaspoon salt
4 tablespoons unsalted butter

2 garlic cloves, chopped
3 anchovy fillets, finely chopped
1/4 teaspoon ground black pepper

Wash the spinach thoroughly in several changes of water. Discard the stems and bruised leaves. Put the wet leaves of spinach into a large saucepan with the salt. Cover the saucepan and cook over medium heat for about 10 minutes or until the spinach is tender. Drain well in a colander and cool slightly. Squeeze the spinach to remove as much water as possible.

Heat the butter gently, and add the garlic and chopped anchovies. Sauté over medium heat for 1 minute. Before the garlic changes color, add the spinach. Season with salt, if needed, and pepper and keep turning the spinach over and over to mix in all of the ingredients thoroughly. Cook for 5 minutes, over low heat to blend the flavors.

Crema Cotta con Salsa di Fragole
Molded Cream with Strawberry Sauce

Serves 6

6 (1-cup) ramekins
3/4 cup sugar
1 teaspoon lemon juice
1 tablespoon plus 1 teaspoon pow
    dered plain gelatin

4 tablespoons water
2 cups heavy cream
1/2 cup plus 3 tablespoons milk
1 teaspoon vanilla extract
4 tablespoons white rum

Heat the ramekins in a very low oven. Make the caramel sauce by dissolving 6 tablespoons of the sugar, 3 tablespoons water, and the lemon juice in a small saucepan and bring to a boil, stirring constantly. Then without stirring boil the mixture over high heat until the liquid turns golden brown and caramelizes. Divide the caramel among the ramekins and whirl it around to coat the bottom of each dish.

Place the powdered gelatin in a bowl with 4 tablespoons of warm water and let it to soak for about 5 minutes. Heat the cream, milk, vanilla extract, rum and the remaining sugar in a saucepan over medium heat. Bring to a boil slowly, stirring constantly, then reduce the heat to low and simmer for 1 minute.

Add 2 tablespoons of the cream mixture to the gelatin and stir until the gelatin has dissolved. Then pour the gelatin mixture into the remaining cream and mix thoroughly.

Pour the cream into the ramekins and chill in the refrigerator until set. Unmold the ramekins onto plates and serve with the strawberry sauce.

Strawberry Sauce

3 cups strawberries, washed   1/4 cup sugar

Puree the strawberries and sugar in a blender or food processor and then pass the mixture through a fine metal strainer.

PIEDMONT

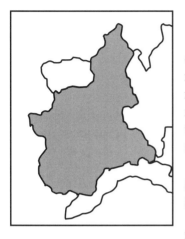

Situated at the foot of the Alps Piedmont is one of the extreme northern regions of Italy. Piedmont is formed by the Alps, is part of the Apennines mountains, and the Po Valley. The climate of this region is very cold in winter and is usually dry in the summer, but very hot. It rains primarily in autumn and spring.

Piedmont is one of the most important rice-growing regions of Italy. Corn and wheat are also grown there.

Vegetables are eaten in abundance in Piedmont. Some of the best Italian vegetables, particularly asparagus, onions, cardoons, celery, beans, and garlic are grown in Piedmont. The region is especially known for its garlic, which is eaten in large quantities. The most famous antipasto of Piedmont is *bagna cauda* (hot garlic and anchovy sauce) served with an assortment of raw and cooked vegetables.

Piedmont is also known for its porcini and white truffles. There is a festival in Alba each October in honor of the truffle harvest.

Dairy products are very important in Piedmont's cuisine. A great variety of cheeses are produced in this region. They include tomini, Gorgonzola, ribiola del becco, the world famous fontina, and ricotta Piedmontese. This ricotta is softer and creamier than the ricotta of other regions. Butter is also an important ingredient in the region's cooking and baking.

A variety of soups are specialties of the region. The Piedmontese people prefer to have soup rather than rice or pasta as a first course. *Grissini*, crisp, thin bread sticks, are a specialty of Turin, the capital of the region. Turin is also known fo its boiled candies (sweet), which were invented there.

Piedmontese cooking is simple but with rich flavors and aromas. This cuisine has an abundance of meat and game dishes, which are cooked for long periods of time in wine and herbs. Some of the beef for these dishes comes from the famous *bovino* cattle, which is raised in Piedmont. In addition to meat the *bovine* are also a source of milk and consequently butter and cheeses. Piedmontese veal, called *sanato*, is the best veal in Italy. *Bollito misto* is the great boiled meat dish of Piedmont that traditionally contains at least five different cuts of meat.

Agnolotti (stuffed squares of pasta with ruffled edges) and *cannelloni* (stuffed pancakes) originated in Piedmont.

There are many Piedmontese recipes for risottos. Risotto al Barolo is prepared with Barolo wine. Other risottos are made with artichokes, pumpkin, truffles, cardoons, and fonduta (a cheese sauce) and the famous risotto with porcini.

Puddings, cakes, chocolates, sweets, *torrone* (Italian nougat), *zabaione* (also spelled *zabaglione*), *crema cotta* (cooked cream) and *baci di dama* (lady's' kisses) are typical desserts of Piedmont. The *baci di dama* consists of two almond cookies held together with melted chocolate.

Wines

There is a great variety of wines in the Piedmont region. It is primarily known for its red wines. Barbera is a strong red wine which goes well with roasts and red meats. Barolo is another excellent wine, particularly with roasts. It has a strong bouquet which improves with four or five years of aging. Barbaresco is similar to Barolo, but a little more delicate and has less alcohol. Dolcetto wine pairs well with any dishes that contain truffles. Freisa wine is a semi-sparkling wine with low alcohol content that goes well with *bagna cauda*. Cortese wine goes well with fish dishes. Grignolino is another good wine, but is often hard to find in the United States

The Piedmont region also has many excellent sparkling wines. Vermouth was invented in Piedmont.

View of Lake Orta in the Piedmont region.
Photo collection of the author.

Pranzo con Buoni Amici
Dinner with Good Friends

Serves 12

Risotto alla Zucca
Butternut Squash Risotto

Brasato al Barolo
Beef Braised in Barolo Wine

Funghi Saltati
Sautéed Mushrooms

Insalata Mista
Mixed Salad

Pere al Vino Rosso
Poached Pears in Red Wine

Caffe
Coffee

Dinner with Good Friends

When I was planning this Piedmontese menu winter had arrived and we were experiencing chilly evenings. The Christmas season was approaching and I wanted to plan a terrific meal for our friends so that we could celebrate the holidays together. With the busy holiday season, I wanted to plan a menu with dishes that could be made ahead of time and reheated the evening of the dinner. This way I could relax by the fireside with my friends while sipping a glass of Piedmont red wine.

I took advantage of the winter squash to make the risotto. It is a colorful, mild and tasty dish. The entree of braised beef served with its sauce is very rich and full of flavor. It is complimented by the sautéed mushrooms.

The mixed salad adds a refreshing touch to this meal. The poached pears for dessert provide a perfect ending.

Preparations

This dinner is a hostess's dream because all of the major preparations can be done ahead.

The risotto of butternut squash can be made in the afternoon up to the point of adding the rice. Simmer the broth later just before adding the rice. You can set the partly cooked squash aside and finish cooking the risotto fifteen minutes before dinner.

The braised beef can be prepared several days ahead and then reheated one hour before dinner.

The mushrooms can be made earlier on the day of the dinner with the cooking process stopped before they are completely cooked. They can be finished just before dinner.

Prepare the various salad greens in the morning and assemble the salad in a large bowl, cover it, and refrigerate. Make the dressing and set it aside.

The poached pears should be made several days ahead as the more the pears soak in the wine, the better they are.

Risotto alla Zucca
Butternut Squash Risotto

Serves 12

8 cups chicken broth
1 1/2 pounds butternut squash
4 tablespoon unsalted butter
3 ounces thickly sliced, lean
   pancetta, cut into small cubes
1 large onion, finely chopped

Salt and pepper
4 cups Arborio rice (Italian rice)
1/4 cup dry white wine
1/2 cup freshly grated Parmesan
   cheese
2 tablespoons chopped fresh parsley

Bring the chicken broth to a simmer in a saucepan. Peel the butternut squash and cut it into 1/4-inch cubes.

Melt 2 tablespoons of the butter in a large saucepan over medium heat and add the pancetta and sauté for a few minutes. Then add the onion and butternut squash and cook gently until the onion and butternut squash are softened. Add the rice and sauté it for a few minutes, stirring constantly. Add the wine and let it evaporate. Then add the simmering broth and mix thoroughly. Bring to a boil, lower the heat, and cook covered for 15 minutes or until the rice is cooked but al dente.

Remove the pan from the heat, stir in the remaining 2 tablespoons of butter and the Parmesan cheese. Sprinkle fresh parsley on top of the rice, mix thoroughly and serve immediately.

Brasato al Barolo
Beef Braised in Barolo Wine

Serves 12

This classic Italian dish originated in the Piedmont region. It is cooked in Barolo wine, whose grapes grow in this region. This dish is traditionally made with chuck or rump roast. I prefer using the rump roast. The dish improves in flavor as it sits, so it is wise to make it a day or two ahead.

Originally this dish used pork fat to provide moisture for the beef. The beef was simply larded with fat and then marinated in wine with vegetables, herbs and spices for at least 2 days. I use pancetta instead of the pork fat and do not marinate the meat.

8 pounds beef rump roast, neatly tied
4 slices pancetta, cut into 1/4-inch strips
4 garlic cloves, finely chopped
4 tablespoons finely chopped fresh parsley
2 tablespoons finely chopped fresh sage
3 tablespoons finely chopped fresh rosemary
1/2 cup all-purpose flour
2 teaspoons paprika
1/4 teaspoon dried marjoram

1/4 teaspoon dried tarragon
1/4 teaspoon dried thyme
1/4 teaspoon nutmeg
1/2 teaspoon salt
1/2 teaspoon freshly ground black pepper
4 tablespoons unsalted butter
6 tablespoons extra virgin olive oil
2 medium onions, quartered
2 medium carrots, cut into thick pieces
3 celery stalks, cut into large pieces
2 bay leaves
1 bottle Barolo wine

Use a small sharp knife to make deep slits all over the rump roast and use the end of a teaspoon to insert a strip of pancetta into each slit, pushing the pancetta deep into the roast.

Combine the garlic, parsley, sage, rosemary on a large platter. Add the flour, paprika, marjoram, tarragon, thyme nutmeg, salt and pepper and mix thoroughly. Dredge the rump roast in the seasoned flour on all sides and shake off any excess. Save the flour.

In a large heavy cast iron pot (casserole) or Dutch oven, melt the butter and olive oil over medium heat. Add the onions and cook gently for about 4 minutes, stirring until softened. Push the onions to the side of the pan, add the roast and cook until browned on the bottom, about 5 minutes. Turn the roast over and add the cut carrots, celery and bay leaves placing them around the roast. Cook the roast until browned on the second side, about 5 minutes. Remove the roast to a platter and keep it warm.

Preheat the oven to 325° F.

Add the remaining seasoned flour to the pot, mix it into the vegetables and cook for 1 minute. Add 1 cup of the wine and boil over high heat, scrapping the bottom of the pan with a wooden spoon, until the wine is reduced by half. Stir in the remaining wine and bring the mixture to a simmer. Return the roast with its juices to the pot and season with additional salt and pepper, if desired. Cover the pot with a tight lid and place it in the preheated oven.

Continue cooking the roast in the oven for about 4 hours, turning the meat every 30 to 45 minutes and adding a little water to the pot if the sauce looks too thick or if the roast begins to stick. The meat is cooked when it can easily be pricked with a fork. Skim the fat from the surface and discard the bay leaves.

Puree the sauce through a food mill, taste, and season, if needed. Carve the meat into 1/2-inch slices. Place some of the pureed sauce in a deep oven-proof casserole, arrange the sliced beef flat in the bottom of the casserole. Add more sauce over it and keep adding beef and sauce until all is used up. Finish with the sauce on top.

Let the roast and sauce cool, then cover and refrigerate for up to 2 days.

When ready to use, bring the casserole to room temperature. Then place it in a preheated 350° F. oven for about 1 hour.

To serve, arrange one or two slices of meat on each individual plate, place some sauce over the beef, and serve with the sautéed mushrooms. This classic dish may also be served with mashed potatoes or oven cooked polenta.

Funghi Saltati
Sautéed Mushrooms

Serves 12

3 pounds fresh mushrooms, white, crimini (brown), shiitake, portabello
4 tablespoons unsalted butter
6 tablespoons extra virgin olive oil

4 garlic cloves, chopped
4 tablespoons chopped parsley
1/2 teaspoon salt
1/2 teaspoon freshly ground black pepper

Rinse and dry the mushrooms and cut them into thick slices.

Heat the butter and oil in a large skillet. Add the sliced mushrooms and sauté over medium-high heat for 5 minutes, or until the mushrooms juice has evaporated.

Add the chopped garlic and parsley and sauté for a few more minutes, until the mushrooms are golden in color. Do not let the garlic brown. Serve immediately.

Insalata Mista
Mixed Salad

Serves 12

1 medium head romaine lettuce
1 small head radicchio
2 large Belgian endive
2 large bunches arugula
3 stalks celery, thinly sliced
1/2 small red onion, chopped

2 large fennel bulbs, cut into thin strips
Salt and freshly ground pepper
1/3 cup extra virgin olive oil
2 tablespoons red wine vinegar
2 tablespoons fresh lemon juice

Rinse all the greens and dry them well. Break the greens into medium-size pieces.

Toss all the salad ingredients together in a large bowl. Season with salt and pepper, to taste, and dress with the oil, vinegar and lemon juice. Taste and adjust the seasonings if needed.

Pere al Vino Rosso
Poached Pears in Red Wine

Serves 12

12 firm pears with stems	*6 whole black peppercorns*
14 tablespoons granulated sugar	*2 whole cinnamon sticks*
1 1/2 bottle of red wine	*4 whole cloves*

Peel the pears, leaving their stems in tact. Do not remove the core. Cut a thin strip off at the base of each pear so that the pear will stand upright.

Choose a saucepan large enough to accommodate all the pears. Add the sugar, red wine, peppercorns, cinnamon, and cloves to the pan and bring to a boil over medium-high heat. Stir thoroughly to melt the sugar and when the mixture is like a thin syrup, gently stand the pears up in the syrup. Cover the pan and simmer over low heat until the pears are tender, about 20 to 25 minutes depending on the size of the pears. Remove the saucepan from the heat. Leave the pears in the wine syrup until completely cold, then turn the pears on their side. Refrigerate the pears, turning them occasionally so that they will absorb some of the wine syrup.

This recipe may be prepared two days ahead and then refrigerated. The pears will be more flavorful because they will have absorbed more syrup.

Half hour before serving the pears, remove them from the wine syrup and boil the syrup in a saucepan over high heat, to reduce and thicken it.

Serve each pear with some of the syrup. If desired, serve with a spoonful of mascarpone cheese or cream.

Una Cena Festiva
A Festive Dinner

Serves 6

Antipasto di Peperoni
Peppers Antipasto

Quaglie alla Piemontese
Quails Piedmont Style

Insalata e Sedano con Arugula
Lettuce and Celery with Arugula

Torta di Frutta e Noci con Zabaglione
Fruit and Nut Cake with Zabaglione Cream

Caffe
Coffee

A Festive Dinner

A festive dinner can celebrate any type of occasion. Italians love celebrations of any type and do not wait for a special holiday or Saint's day to celebrate. Just getting together with friends and enjoying a meal is a reason to be joyous.

This festive Piedmont dinner starts with an antipasto of red bell peppers which have been cooked in milk and olive oil with garlic and anchovies. The result is a very tasty and colorful dish.

The main course consists of braised quail in a Marsala wine sauce served with Italian rice. Fresh sage and basil give this light and simple dish an interesting flavor and a great aroma.

The salad of lettuce with celery and arugula is a light and refreshing interlude before a traditional dessert of Piedmont.

The fruit and nut cake with zabaglione cream is an elegant ending to this festive dinner.

Preparations

This is an easy dinner to prepare, allowing you to spend time with your guests.

The antipasto of red bell peppers may be made a day ahead and reheated before serving.

The quails can be cooked completely in the morning and warmed up slowly before serving.

Prepare the rice that evening because it is very simple and quick to make.

The salad ingredients can be prepared in the afternoon and refrigerated. Mix the salad dressing and keep it at room temperature. Toss the salad with the dressing just before serving.

The fruit and nut cake can be made several days ahead, but the zabaglione cream has to be made at the last minute before serving the dessert.

Antipasto di Peperoni
Peppers Antipasto

Serves 6

These peppers can be served with boiled beef, veal, chicken, or any type of steak. In the Piedmonte region these peppers are traditionally served as a hot antipasto.

5 large yellow bell peppers
1 (2 ounce) can fillets of anchovies,
   drained
2 garlic cloves

4 tablespoons olive oil
2 tablespoons unsalted butter
1/2 cup milk

Cut the peppers in quarters and remove the seeds. Wash the peppers and dry them with paper towels. Remove the bone from each of the anchovies and chop them finely together with the garlic.

Place the oil and butter in a large frying pan over medium heat. Add the chopped anchovies mixture, adding the milk and mixing often. Add the peppers to the frying pan, cover and cook them for 5 minutes. Remove the cover and continue cooking, turning the peppers occasionally so that they will absorb the flavor of the anchovies and the garlic sauce. Cook for about 20 to 30 minutes. The peppers should be soft, but still al dente. Serve 3 of the pepper quarters per person.

Quaglie alla Piemontese
Quails Piedmont Style

Serves 6

12 quails
Salt
Freshly ground black pepper
12 slices pancetta
1 sprig parsley
1 sprig fresh basil
1 sprig fresh sage
Celery leaves from 1 celery stalk
10 tablespoons unsalted butter

1/2 cup dry Marsala wine
3 tablespoons flour
3 cups chicken broth
4 cups water
Salt
2 cups arborio rice
1/3 cup freshly grated Parmesan
   cheese
1 white truffle, thinly sliced, optional

Wash the quails and pat them dry with paper towels inside and out. Sprinkle the cavities and the outside of the birds with salt and pepper. Place one slice of pancetta over each quail breast and secure it with a toothpick or a string. Tie the parsley, basil, sage, and celery leaves together in a little bundle with kitchen string.

Heat 4 tablespoons of the butter in a large skillet over medium heat. When the butter is melted, add the quails, fitting them close together, and add the bundle of herbs. Cover and cook over medium-high heat until the quails are roasted and brown in color, turning the birds often. Add the Marsala wine.

Then heat the chicken broth in a small saucepan to a simmer. Melt 3 tablespoons of the butter in another small saucepan over medium heat. When the butter has melted, add the 3 tablespoons of flour and stir constantly with a wooden spoon until well blended. Add the simmering broth to the flour mixture, stirring constantly, until the sauce starts to boil. Then pour this sauce over the quails. Mix thoroughly and continue cooking, covered, over low heat for about 30 to 40 minutes depending on the size of the quails, turning the birds occasionally.

Bring the water to a boil in a large saucepan. Add 1/2 teaspoon of salt and the rice and mix. When the water boils again, cover the saucepan, reduce the heat to low, and cook for 15 minutes or until the rice is done, but al dente.

When the quails are cooked, remove them from the skillet and keep them warm. Remove any fat from the skillet and discard the bundle of herbs. Strain the sauce through a sieve.

When the rice is done, remove it from the heat. Add the remaining 3 tablespoons of butter and the Parmesan cheese. Mix thoroughly and place the rice on a large platter, smoothing the top to make it even. Place the quails on top of the rice and then pour the strained sauce over the birds. Sprinkle the sliced truffles over the top.

Serve two quails and spoonfuls of rice for each person.

Insalata e Sedano con Arugula
Lettuce and Celery with Arugula

Serves 6

1 large Romaine lettuce
2 to 3 large celery stalks
1 cup chopped arugula
5 tablespoons extra virgin olive oil

Juice of 1 large lemon
1/2 teaspoon salt
1/4 teaspoon freshly ground black
  pepper

Wash the lettuce, spin dry and tear it into bite-size pieces. Wash the celery stalks, pull off any coarse strings, and cut the celery into small pieces. Rinse the arugula, remove some of the stems, spin dry, and chop coarsely. Mix the lettuce, celery and arugula in a salad bowl.

Combine the olive oil, lemon juice, salt, and pepper in a small bowl. Pour the dressing over the salad, toss thoroughly, and serve on individual plates.

Torta di Frutta e Noci con Zabaglione
Fruit and Nut Cake with Zabaglione Cream

Serves 6 or more

1 egg
2 egg yolks
1 cup granulated sugar
8 tablespoons (1 stick) butter,
  melted and cooled to lukewarm
1 1/2 teaspoon grated lemon peel
1 1/2 teaspoons grated orange peel
1 teaspoon anise seeds
1 teaspoon anise extract
1 tablespoon Grand Marnier
  liqueur

1/4 cup pine nuts
1/4 cup dark raisins
1/4 cup light raisins
1/4 cup mixed candied fruit, coarsely
  chopped
3 cups all-purpose flour, sifted
2 teaspoons baking powder
1/2 teaspoon salt
1 cup milk

Beat the egg, egg yolks, and sugar together until thick and pale yellow. Beat in the melted butter, then add the lemon peel, orange peel, anise seeds, anise extract, Grand Marnier, pine nuts, dark and light raisins, and candied fruit.

Sift together the flour, baking powder, and salt. Mix half of the flour mixture into the batter. Then stir in half the milk, add the remaining flour, and mix well. Add the remaining milk, and mix thoroughly.

Pour the batter into a greased and floured large Bundt pan or 10-inch tube pan. Bake in a preheated 350° F. oven for 50 to 60 minutes, or until a cake tester inserted in the center of the cake comes out clean. Cool the cake on a wire rack and then remove it from the pan. Serve wedges of the cake with hot Zabaglione Cream.

Zabaglione Cream

8 egg yolks
1/2 cup sugar

Grated peel of 1/2 lemon
3/4 cup Marsala

Beat the egg yolks and sugar in the top of a double boiler with a wire whisk until thick. Add the lemon peel and beat in the Marsala. Place over simmering water and beat vigorously until hot, foamy, and fluffy, about 5 to 6 minutes. Spoon the hot zabaglione cream over a thick slice of the cake. Serve immediately while it is hot.

Liguria

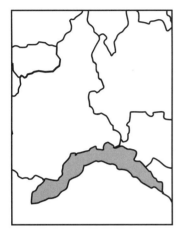

It was in Liguria that pesto was created. An unusually fragrant basil, which is the basis of pesto, grows in this region. A mild olive oil, made from the olive trees that grow on the hillsides and mountains of Liguria is also a key ingredient in Ligurian pesto. Garlic and pine nuts, other key ingredients of pesto, grow in abundance in Liguria. In this region pesto is still made in the traditional way — pounded by hand in a mortar.

Liguria, one of Italy's smallest region, is in a crescent shape, extending from the Emilia-Romagna region on the east to France on the west. A range of mountains divides this region from Piedmont in the north. In many places the mountains drop almost vertically to the sea. Fishing villages are built on top of cliffs and in the tiny bays.

The Ligurian region is one of the most populated regions in Italy and is one of the most prosperous and industrious. Technology and service industries have made this region rich. Traditionally, however, the men of Liguria were men of the sea. These seamen were not fishermen because fish along the coast were of poor quality. They were involved in foreign trade, bringing goods to Genoa and other European ports. Genoa, capitol of this Liguria, made its wealth by being the port where spices of the East were trans-shipped to other markets of Europe. Christopher Columbus is one of the most famous native sons of Liguria.

The temperate climate of Liguria, moderated by sea breezes, has made it possible to grow a wide variety of vegetables and aromatic herbs. Many popular herbs, as well as salad greens, grow wild in the region. The mountains to the north help protect the region from severe winter weather. It is very rare that there is snow in the mountains.

The gastronomy of Liguria is characterized by scented herbs, olives, and some seafood. Olives for extra virgin olive oil, fragrant basil, rosemary, and thyme grow on the hills of Liguria. *Borragine* (borage) is a strong wild herb that also grows on the hillsides in the spring and is a prime ingredient in the Ligurian ravioli.

Borage gives this large, triangular ravioli, called *pansoti*, a distinctive taste. Walnuts are used in the sauce to flavor *pansoti*. The pasta dough is made with one egg to each one and three-quarter cups of flour, in addition to water and dry white wine. The dough then is stuffed with chopped wild herbs, prescinsena, Parmesan cheese, egg, and a little garlic. Prescinsena, a cow's milk curd cheese made in Liguria, is a main ingredient in many traditional dishes. It is also used in the dough of focaccia and bread, the stuffing of ravioli, and in making walnut sauce.

Focaccia is a simple bread, but in Liguria focaccia is extra special. It is a bread-dough seasoned with extra virgin olive oil and salt, then covered with sliced onion or stuffed with fresh local cheese.

On the Riviera of Ponente, part of the coastline of Liguria, there is a famous pizza invented by Admiral Andrea Doria, which is called pizza all'Andrea, or *pissaladeira* in dialect. It is simply a focaccia bread enriched with anchovies, tomatoes, black olives, garlic, olive oil, salt and pepper.

Another specialty of Liguria is *torta pasqualina*, a torte with a salty taste. It is made at Easter time and takes a great deal of patience, skill, and time to prepare. The dough is made with flour and water to which a little olive oil is added. It is similar to Middle Eastern filo pastry, thin and transparent. Traditionally this torta is made with 33 layers of this pasta-like dough (Christ's age at the time of crucifixion). However, today it is made with only 18 layers, each brushed with olive oil. The torte is stuffed with ricotta, or with cooked vegetables and whole eggs.

A typical Ligurian dish, *cappun magru*, is an antipasto made with different fish, dry biscuits soaked in vinegar and a variety of vegetables. At one time Genoese men were at sea for months at a time and when they returned their wives prepared this dish to welcome them home. The men craved for fresh vegetables as their food at sea was mostly dry biscuits, dried beans, and some fish that they caught.

Meat, particularly beef, is not prevalent in Ligurian cuisine because the strip of land that is Liguria is too narrow for pasture land. For the same reason butter is not used in cooking. In the hills chicken is prepared by grilling or barbecuing. Rabbit is one of the main meats and is cooked with olives and pine nuts or fried. In mushroom season, mushrooms are cooked in alternate layers with potatoes.

The Genoese have created many delicious dishes, such as anchovies marinated in olive oil and lemon juice. *Buridda*, a fish stew, is made with angler, cuttlefish, or squid and sometimes pieces of soaked *stoccafisso* (dried cod). All of these ingredients are stewed in layers with onions, tomatoes, dried wild mushrooms, pine nuts, and salted anchovies. Then the stew is covered with olive oil and dry white wine.

Ciuppin, a fish soup, is made with fish of all kinds from the local catch. The soup is often pureed and strained to eliminate all of the bones from less desirable fish. A specialty of La Spezia, an important port on the east coast of Liguria, is *scabeccio*, pickled fried mullet seasoned with rosemary and sage.

There are many mollusks in the Liguria region and the best are found in the Gulf of La Spezia, where there are a large number of mussel farms. Also found there are *datteri di mare*, known as sea dates because their shape is like a date. They cling to the rocks and must be pried away. There are also *tartufi di mare*, which are very small clams.

The dish *lattuga ripiena*, which is lettuce cooked in beef broth, is usually served at Easter. The lettuce leaves are stuffed with brains, sweetbreads, mushrooms, garlic, parsley, and bread crumbs. Then the leaves are rolled up, tied with strings, and braised in the broth.

Another local specialty of Liguria, which is often found in the city's finest restaurants, is *cima alla genovese*. It is a breast or shoulder of veal that is stuffed with brains, sweetbreads, peas, herbs, garlic, pistachio nuts, and grated cheese. It is boiled for two hours, then cooled before slicing.

Many different ravioli are made in Liguria. *Ravioli magri* have a vegetable filling. *Ravioli dolci* are little sweet egg dough envelopes stuffed with ricotta, candied peel, and chocolate. *Ravioli alla Genovese* contain veal, brains, sweetbreads, eggs, bread crumbs, Swiss chard, borage, and grated Parmesan cheese. There is also a delicate ravioli made with ricotta and Parmesan cheese. The ravioli are usually served with a sauce made of mushrooms or with just butter and grated cheese.

The Ligurians make a form of polenta, called *farinata*. It is made with a chickpea paste that is cooked with oil in a wood burning oven. Minestrone enriched with a spoonful of pesto can be found in any town, city, or village in the Liguria region.

There are also a variety of local pasta. *Trenette* is similar to tagliatelle. The dough for this pasta is made by replacing some of the eggs with water. This makes a softer, less tasty pasta but makes the dough easier to handle than

Bocca 'Dasso, Genova. Photo courtesy of Mario Cavallaro

dough that is made only with eggs. Another local pasta is *trofie* which is a twisted pasta, that is tapered at the end. There is a local variety of large ribbon pasta, lasagna. These pastas are always served with pesto, and occasionally garnished with beans.

Ligurian cuisine includes a variety of sweet breads. There is a sweet focaccia, called *focaccia castelnovese*. It is made with pine nuts and usually eaten at Christmas and Easter. *Pandolce Genovese* is a bread flavored with candied peel, seedless raisins, pine nuts, pistachio nuts, and marsala.

Candied fruit, raisins and pine nuts are all local products and are used in most Ligurian desserts. Ring-shaped pastries called, *canastrelli*, can be found in all the bakeries. When fruit is in season, a favorite dessert is *pesche ripiene al forno*. This dessert consists of peaches stuffed with crumbled macaroons and baked.

Wines

The most famous wines of Liguria are produced in the district of Spezia around the five villages known as Cinque Terre, five lands. The wines are made from Albarola, Bosco, and Vermentino grapes. These wines are all white, dry and delicate, and pair well with the local seafood.

Other wines of Liguria are: Sciacchettra Bianco, a white wine with a slightly bitter bouquet, Sciacchettra Rosso, a red dessert wine. A famous wine is Rossese di Dolceaqua, a red wine enjoyed by Napoleon; Vermentino; Ligasolio; and Polcevera.

Pranzo al Fresco
Dinner al Fresco

Serves 6

Crostini con Salsa di Pomodori Secchi
Crostini with Sun-dried Tomato Sauce

Trenette al Pesto
Trenette with Pesto Sauce

Fricassea d'Agnello con Carciofi
Lamb with Artichokes

Condiggion
Summer Vegetable Salad

Torta Paradiso
Paradise Cake

Caffe
Coffee

Dinner al Fresco

This menu consists of typical dishes from the Liguria region.

The crostini with the sun-dried tomato sauce is made with black olives, capers, garlic, hot pepper flakes, oregano, olive oil, and ricotta. The combination of flavors results in an excellent taste.

The trenette pasta is combined with green beans and potatoes and topped with a traditional Genovese pesto sauce for a very unique dish.

The entree is a lamb fricassee. It is prepared with baby artichokes and flavored with strips of prosciutto, onion, garlic, and marjoram. The mildness of the boiled potatoes is a good contrast to the many wonderful flavors of the lamb fricassee.

The crunchy summer vegetable salad is a refreshing interlude before the dessert.

Paradise cake, an old traditional favorite, is a very light and delicate dessert. It is a perfect ending for this informal meal.

Preparations

Several items on this menu may be prepared ahead.

The sun-dried tomato sauce for the crostini can be made a day ahead and then refrigerated. Toast the slices of bread that evening and spread the tomato sauce on them just before your guests are to arrive.

The pesto sauce can be made days ahead, covered, and placed in the refrigerator. That evening bring it to room temperature while you are cooking the pasta with the potatoes and string beans.

The entree of lamb with artichokes has to be made that evening. However, a few items can be prepared ahead. Clean and slice the artichokes early in the afternoon and keep them soaking in water with the lemon juice until ready to cook. Cut the prosciutto into strips and keep them, in the refrigerator. Thirty minutes before your guests are to arrive, slowly boil the potatoes. When cooked, drain them, and set them aside.

Just before you are going to serve dinner, peel the potatoes, slice them and keep them warm by covering them with foil. Then cook the lamb tenderloins with the prosciutto strips and herbs. Cook the lamb slices until browned, then remove them and keep them warm. Cook the artichokes, then add the lamb slices back and turn off the heat. Finish cooking the dish just before you are going to serve it. Then add the egg yolks and assemble the lamb with the potato slices.

The vegetable salad should be made in the morning so that all of the flavors will meld together.

Make the paradise cake the day before, cover, and set it aside. Sprinkle the confectioner's sugar over it before serving.

Crostini con Salsa di Pomodori Secchi
Crostini with Sun-dried Tomato Sauce

Serves 6

3 ounces sun-dried tomatoes
2 ounces pitted black olives
1 tablespoon capers, drained
1 sprig parsley
1 garlic clove
1/4 teaspoon hot pepper flakes

1/4 teaspoon dried oregano
3 tablespoons extra virgin olive oil
Pinch of salt
2 ounces fresh ricotta
1 loaf country bread, sliced

Place the dried tomatoes in a saucepan, add enough water to cover them, and boil, over medium-high heat, for 1 minute. Remove saucepan from the heat and let the tomatoes cool off in the pan for about 1 hour. Drain the tomatoes, squeeze them to remove excess liquid, and then place them in a food processor. Add the pitted olives, capers, parsley, garlic, pepper flakes, oregano, 1 tablespoon of the olive oil and a pinch of salt. Process until all the ingredients are blended. Then add the ricotta, mix well and add the remaining 2 tablespoons of olive oil. Continue mixing until it is a smooth sauce.

Toast the slices of bread in the oven until golden in color.

Smoothly spread some of the tomato sauce on each slice of the toasted bread and serve as an antipasto. The crostini may also be served with a glass of wine for cocktails.

Trenette al Pesto
Trenette with Pesto Sauce

Serves 6

Pesto is a sauce of Persian origin, but now is associated primarily with Italy, especially the Liguria region. The traditional sauce is made with fresh basil, garlic, olive oil, pecorino and Parmesan cheeses. Sometimes walnuts or pine nuts are added, depending on the local tradition.

To make the best pesto crush the basil, along with the other ingredients, in a large mortar instead of using a metal blade for chopping. To make this recipe more delicate, butter or cream may be added.

Pesto sauce is used to dress potato gnocchi. One tablespoon of pesto is typically added to minestrone and other soups. Pesto is also delicious served on crostini as an antipasto. Trenette are always dressed with pesto.

Trenette is pasta the size and shape of a ribbon. It originated in Liguria and was traditionally made at home. This pasta resembles tagliatelle. Dried trenette are now available. The same shape may also be called tagliatelle, linguine, *bavette* (long ribbon-like pasta, like spaghetti), or fettuccine.

Pesto Sauce Genovese

2 large garlic cloves, crushed
1/2 cup pine nuts
1/2 teaspoon salt
2 cups, packed full of basil leaves
3 tablespoons freshly grated
  pecorino cheese (Romano)

3 tablespoons freshly grated
  Parmesan cheese
2/3 cup extra virgin olive oil
1/2 teaspoon freshly ground black
  pepper

Pound the garlic and pine nuts in a large mortar with a little salt. Add the basil leaves, a few at a time, grinding the leaves against the sides of the bowl, or use a food processor and grind everything together.

Then add the pecorino and Parmesan cheeses gradually and mix very well. Little by little beat in the olive oil until the oil is blended with the ingredients.

Pesto can be prepared days ahead. When doing so, cover it with plastic wrap and refrigerate. Bring it to room temperature before using. This quantity of pesto is enough for a pound and a half of pasta.

2 medium potatoes, peeled and cut
  into 1/2-inch cubes
1/4 pound green beans, trimmed and
  cut into 3-inch pieces
Salt

1 pound trenette, fettuccine,
  tagliatelle, or linguine
Pesto alla Genovese
Additional pecorino and Parmesan
  cheese

Place the cubed potatoes and green beans in a large saucepan with sufficient salted water to boil the potatoes and beans and later the pasta. Bring to a boil and cook over medium heat until both are almost done. Then add the trenette and cook the 3 together until the pasta is cooked, but still firm to the bite. Drain, reserving one ladle of the cooking water.

Place the noodles, potatoes, and green beans in a large heated dish.

Dilute the pesto with a little of the cooking water. Then add the pesto to the noodle mixture and toss it thoroughly to coat the pasta and vegetables. Sprinkle with black pepper. Serve while the pasta is hot, accompanied by a bowl of additional grated cheese.

Fricassea d'Agnello con Carciofi
Lamb with Artichokes

Serves 6

5 medium potatoes
2 1/2 pounds lamb tenderloin (fillet)
12 small or 4 medium young
   artichokes
Juice of 1 lemon
1/4 cup olive oil
1 onion, finely chopped
1 garlic clove, finely chopped
2 ounces prosciutto with fat, cut
   into small strips

2 fresh marjoram leaves or
   1/4 teaspoon dry marjoram
1 teaspoon salt
1 teaspoon freshly ground black
   pepper
1 cup dry white wine
3 egg yolks
Juice of 1 lemon

Boil the potatoes slowly in salted water until tender, about 20 to 30 minutes, depending on the size of the potatoes. When cooked, remove them from the water and set aside. Cut the lamb tenderloin into 1 inch thick slices and set them aside. Wash the artichokes, remove the tough outer leaves, trim off the tops and cut them into quarters. If they have chokes, remove them with a sharp knife. Place the quartered artichokes in a bowl of cold water with the juice of 1 lemon.

Heat the olive oil in a large saucepan over medium-high heat. Add the chopped onion, garlic, prosciutto strips, marjoram and parsley and sauté until these ingredients begin to brown. Add the lamb slices and brown them on each side, about 5 minutes. Season with salt and pepper. Add the wine and let it evaporate over high heat, then remove the lamb slices and keep them warm.

Add the artichokes, cover, and cook until they are tender about 4 to 5 minutes. Return the lamb slices to the pan, mix the meat with the artichokes and cook for a few minutes, then remove the pan from the heat.

Beat the egg yolks with the juice of 1 lemon in a small bowl and pour it over the lamb, mixing constantly until the sauce has thickened and is well blended.

Peel the potatoes and slice them, not too thin or they will brake apart.

Arrange about 4 slices of potatoes on each plate and place 2 to 3 slices of lamb with some artichokes and some sauce over the potatoes.

Condiggion
Summer Vegetable Salad

Serves 6

3 yellow or red peppers, rinsed
1 cucumber, cut into 1/4-inch slices
3 ripe tomatoes, cut into wedges,
   seeds removed
1 small red onion, thinly sliced
5 black or green olives, pitted,
   cut in half
3 anchovy fillets packed in oil,
   drained and cut into small pieces

2 tablespoons capers, drained
2 tablespoons chopped fresh basil
   leaves
1/4 teaspoon dry oregano, crumbled
1 teaspoon salt
1 teaspoon freshly ground black
   pepper
3 hard boiled eggs, quartered
1/2 cup extra virgin olive oil

Cut the peppers in half, then remove the ribs and seeds and cut the peppers into strips.

Place the peppers in a large salad bowl and add the sliced cucumber, tomato wedges, red onion, olives, anchovies, capers, basil, and oregano and season with salt and pepper. Toss thoroughly, then add the quartered eggs and pour the olive oil over the vegetables and mix again until blended. Make this salad in the morning if planning to serve it in the evening. It needs to absorb all of the flavors.

Torta Paradiso
Paradise Cake

Serves 8 to 10

Paradise Cake is a specialty of a well-known Ligurian bakery in Liguria. The bakery has kept the secret of this cake for almost one hundred years. This recipe is an imitation that now is being used in Ligurian families.

1 1/4 cups sifted all purpose flour	*3 large eggs, separated*
1/4 teaspoon baking soda	*2/3 cup sour cream*
8 tablespoons (1 stick) unsalted	*1 teaspoon vanilla extract*
butter, softened	*2 teaspoons lemon zest*
1 1/2 cups sugar	*Confectioner's sugar*

Butter and flour a 9 x 5-inch loaf pan. Sift together the flour and baking soda and set aside.

In a bowl cream, the butter and sugar until fluffy, about 3 minutes. Add the egg yolks and beat well. Add 1/3 of the flour and beat to incorporate. Then add 1/2 of the sour cream and beat again. Continue adding flour and sour cream alternately and beating until blended. Stir in the vanilla and lemon zest.

In a separate bowl, beat the egg whites until very stiff, the fold them into the batter with an over and under motion, using a wooden spoon.

Pour the batter into the prepared pan. Bake the cake in a preheated 325° F. oven for 1 hour and 20 minutes or until the cake is golden and a cake tester inserted in the center comes out clean. Let the cake cool in the pan, then remove it and place it on a serving plate. Before serving, sprinkle confectioner's sugar over the cake.

Primavera in Liguria
Spring Time in Liguria

Serves 4

Crostini di Mare
Seafood Crostini

Risotto del Campagnolo
Rice with Sausage, Artichokes and Peas

Coniglio alla Sanremese
Rabbit San Remo Style

Zucchine a Funghetto
Zucchini with Garlic and Oregano

Pizza di Noci e Canditi
Walnut and Candied Peel Pie

Caffe
Coffee

Spring Time in Liguria

A great abundance of vegetables are grown in the Liguria region. They are harvested from late spring into fall. starting from spring time on. This menu features some of the vegetables of Liguria.

The meal with starts with seafood crostini prepared with mussels, clams, shrimp, and olives. All of these ingredients are used in typical dishes of Liguria.

The risotto is prepared with spring vegetables, such as artichokes and baby peas. They are cooked with porcini mushrooms and sausages for a spring-like dish.

The entree is rabbit San Remo style. It is a very colorful and elegant preparation, as well as being delicious. The rabbit is served with sliced zucchini sautéed with garlic, parsley, and oregano.

The meal ends with a walnut and candied peel pie, which has a mild chocolate flavor. If desired, top the pie with fresh fruit for a typical spring dessert of Liguria.

Preparations

This is a very simple menu with many of the items prepared ahead.

The seafood for the crostini can be made the day before or the morning of the dinner and refrigerated. The night of the dinner, toast the sliced bread and place some of the seafood mixture on each slice.

You may prepare the risotto in the early afternoon up to the point of adding the rice, then finish cooking it that evening.

The rabbit should be made at least a day ahead, so that it can absorb the flavors of the sauce. Refrigerate the rabbit after is made and reheat it slowly, covered, in the evening of the dinner.

The zucchini with the garlic and oregano can be cooked ahead, but make sure that the zucchini are al dente. Reheat and finish cooking the zucchini that evening, or you can place the olive oil, zucchini, parsley and garlic in the sauté pan and set it aside until almost time to serve it. It will only take 5 to 10 minutes to cook the vegetable that evening.

The dessert can be made the day before or in the morning of the dinner.

If using fresh fruit, clean and slice the fruit in the morning. Place it in a bowl and sprinkle with sugar, stir, and refrigerate until needed.

Crostini di Mare
Seafood Crostini

Serves 4 to 6

1/2 pound mussels
1/2 pound clams
1/2 pound medium shrimp
10 green olives, pits removed
2 tablespoons capers, drained
2 tablespoons chopped fresh parsley

1 tablespoon extra virgin olive oil
Juice of 1/2 lemon
1/2 teaspoon salt
1/2 teaspoon freshly ground black
  pepper
12 slices baguette bread

Remove the mussels' beards. Scrub the mussels and clams with a brush and rinse them under cold running water. Place 1 cup of water in a large saucepan over high heat, add the cleaned mussels and clams. Cover and steam them, shaking the pan from time to time, for about 5 to 7 minutes. Discard any unopened mussels and clams. Remove them from their shells when cooled and place them in a bowl.

Add 4 cups of water to the same saucepan in which the mussels were cooked and bring to a boil over high heat. Add the shrimp and boil for 2 to 3 minutes, depending on size of the shrimp. Drain and peel the shrimp after they have cool.

Chop all of the cooked seafood together with the olives, capers and parsley until the mixture is in small pieces, but not in a paste. Place the chopped seafood mixture in a bowl and season with olive oil, lemon juice, salt, and pepper. Mix thoroughly until well blended.

Toast the slices of bread in the oven until golden in color. Spread some of the seafood mixture on each slice of toasted bread. Serve the crostini cool or place them in a preheated 350° F. oven for 5 minutes and serve them warm.

Risotto del Campagnolo
Rice with Sausage, Artichokes, and Peas

Serves 4

3 medium artichokes
Juice of 1 lemon
1 1/2 ounces dry porcini mushrooms
1 tablespoon olive oil
4 Italian pork sausages, crumbled
4 tablespoons unsalted butter
1 onion, finely chopped
1 garlic clove, finely chopped
2 tablespoons fresh chopped parsley

3/4 cup frozen baby peas, thawed
1/4 teaspoon salt
1/4 teaspoon black pepper
1/2 cup dry white wine
1 1/2 cups Arborio Italian rice
2 cups broth, chicken or beef
1/2 cup freshly grated Parmesan
  cheese

Cut and trim the artichokes, cut off and trim the stems, then cut them in half lengthwise. Using a paring knife, tear off the artichokes outer leaves, leaving only the tender inner leaves. Cut across the top of the artichoke with scissors. Trim off any tough parts, cut each base into quarters lengthwise and cut out the choke. Place the quartered artichokes in water with the lemon juice.

Soak the dry porcini in a small bowl with 1 cup of warm water for 15 minutes, then drain, rinse, and chop the mushrooms into small pieces. Reserve the soaking water, since it will be used later in the risotto.

Heat the oil in a large saucepan over medium heat and add the crumbled sausages. Brown the sausage meat for about 5 to 7 minutes, stirring occasionally. Remove the cooked meat with a slotted spoon and set aside.

Add 2 tablespoons of the butter to the saucepan over medium heat. When the butter starts to foam, add the chopped onion, garlic, and parsley, and sauté until the onion is transparent, about 4 minutes. Add the artichokes, stir, and sauté for about 5 minutes, stirring constantly.

Then add the chopped mushrooms and peas and mix ,and then sauté for a few minutes. Season with salt and pepper, mix ,and add the cooked crumbled sausage meat and mix again.

Add the wine, stir, and let the wine evaporate over high heat for a few minutes. While the wine is evaporating place the broth with the mushroom water in a saucepan and bring it to a low simmer.

Add the rice to the saucepan and stir to coat it with the pan juices. Add the hot broth, stir, and when the broth is boiling, cover the saucepan. Reduce the heat to low and cook slowly for about 15 minutes. The rice is done when it is cooked through but still al dente.

Remove the saucepan from the heat, stir in the remaining 2 tablespoons of butter and the Parmesan cheese, and mix thoroughly. Serve at once.

Coniglio alla Sanremese
Rabbit San Remo Style

Serves 4

1 rabbit, 3 pounds or more	1/2 teaspoon salt
1/2 cup extra virgin olive oil	1/2 teaspoon freshly ground black
2 garlic cloves, cut in half	pepper
1 bay leaf	1 cup red wine
1 small sprig thyme or 1/4 teaspoon	6 walnut halves, chopped
dry thyme	3 tablespoons pine nuts
1 rosemary sprig	2/3 cup broth
1 onion, finely chopped	12 black olives
1 celery stalk, finely chopped	

Cut the rabbit into 8 serving pieces, rinse, and pat dry with paper towels.

Heat the olive oil in a large saucepan over medium-high heat. Add the rabbit pieces, garlic, bay leaf, sprig of thyme, and rosemary, and sauté until the pieces of rabbit are golden brown all over, about 5 to 8 minutes. Discard the garlic and remove the herbs. Also remove the rabbit pieces and keep them warm.

Add the chopped onion and celery to the same saucepan and sauté until the onion is translucent. Add the sautéed rabbit pieces and season with salt and pepper. Then add the wine and cook, over medium heat, until the wine has evaporated. Add the chopped walnuts, pine nuts, and pour in some broth. Cook for about 1 hour, adding broth as needed.

When the rabbit is done, add the black or green olives and cook for another five minutes.

Serve two pieces of rabbit with some olives, walnuts, pine nuts and sauce for each person.

Zucchine a Funghetto
Zucchini with Garlic and Oregano

Serves 4

4 medium zucchini, about 1 pound
4 tablespoons extra virgin olive oil
1 garlic clove, finely chopped

1 tablespoon finely chopped parsley
Pinch of oregano
Salt

Wash the zucchini under cold running water until the skin is smooth. Cut off and discard both ends of the zucchini. Cut it into round thin slices.

Place the olive oil in a large sauté pan over medium heat. Add the sliced zucchini, chopped garlic and parsley and sauté, stirring often. Sprinkle the zucchini with a pinch of oregano, and season with salt and continue cooking until the zucchini are cooked, but al dente, about 5 to 10 minutes.

Pizza di Noci e Canditi
Ligurian Walnut and Candied Peel Pie

Serves 6 to 8

1 2/3 cups shelled walnuts
5 eggs, separated
2/3 cup sugar
5 squares bitter chocolate, grated

Grated rind of 1/2 lemon
1/3 cup diced mixed candied peel
Butter and fine dry bread crumbs,
  for pan

Grind the walnuts to a powder. Beat the egg yolks with the sugar until fluffy. Beat the egg whites until stiff peaks form.

Mix the beaten egg yolks with the powdered walnuts, chocolate, grated rind, and the candied peel, Then gently fold in the beaten egg whites.

Pour the walnut mixture into a pie pan or tart pan that has been buttered and sprinkled with bread crumbs. Place the pie pan in a pre-heated 375° F. oven and bake for about 1 hour. When done the pie should be about 1/2-inch thick, just like a pizza. Turn the walnut pie out and then leave it to cool on a cake rack.

Serve sugared sliced fresh fruit of your choice with this pie. For example, 1 basket of fresh fruit, strawberries or raspberries, mixed with 2 tablespoons of sugar.

Lombardy

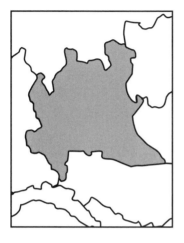

Lombardy, the richest region of Italy, has always known material wealth. Through the centuries Lombardy has been the most advanced in agriculture. Its people have always been hard working. By draining the marshes and irrigating the fields, the people of Lombardy have made the region very productive.

Lombardy is situated in the center of northern Italy, bordering Switzerland to the north with the Piedmont region on the west, and Veneto on the east. It is named for the Lombards, a tribe that once lived in this region. Milan, one of the three most important cities in Italy, is the capital and cultural center of the region.

The people of Lombardy both grow and consume the most rice of any region in Italy. Before rice picking was mechanized, it was done by women called *mondine*, who spent their days wading in the marshy rice fields. To keep their long skirts from getting wet they stuffed them into their drawers.

The rice grown in Lombardy is short-grain, of which there are many varieties. The round Originario and Padano rice are used in soups and for stuffing vegetables. Rice is cooked in broth, in the well-known vegetable soup called *minestrone alla Milanese*.

Carnaroli and the famous Arborio rice, which retain their firmness and bite, are primarily used in risottos. In Lombardy risotto is made with every imaginable ingredient, such as meat, fish, vegetables, and herbs. The risotto of Lombardy is generally dry, not liquid like that of neighboring Veneto. The most famous risotto, known as *risotto alla milanese*, is made with saffron. It is also called *risotto giallo*, yellow risotto. Other risottos are made with sausages, mushrooms, pumpkin, cabbage, or with bone marrow and saffron.

Risotto alla certosina, a meatless risotto, was invented in Pavia in southern Lombardy by monks. In olden days the monks were not allowed to eat meat so they invented many rice dishes with freshwater fish, frogs, and crayfish. The monks farmed these in pits near the abbeys.

Butter has been used in Lombardy since Roman times. In olden times the Romans used butter to grease their bodies before sporting competitions and battles. Today, however, butter is preferred as a cooking fat in Lombardy.

Polenta has traditionally been the food of the poor people. Originally they made it with wheat, barley, oats, millets, and/or buckwheat. Food historians say that cornmeal polenta came into being in Lombardy in the beginning of the eighteenth century when corn started to be grown there.

Today polenta is typically made with cornmeal, water and/or milk. Occasionally other grains, such as buckwheat and black flour (*fraina*) are added. It is served as a mush, or cooled and then sliced and fried or grilled. Polenta is served with butter, cheese, tomatoes, and/or pork fat. It can be served with beans, vegetables, sausages, or stews made with pork, veal, or game. Bergamo has its own specialty called *polenta e osei*, which is a mound of polenta topped with small roasted birds that have been cooked on skewers.

Polenta has traditionally been very important in the mountain cooking of Lombardy. It is now very fashionable all over Italy. Polenta is now also part of an elegant antipasto. It is served with gorgonzola cheese melted on top or it is grilled and served with sautéed mushrooms.

Although the people of Lombardy rarely ate pasta before 1950, there are two traditional pasta recipes of the region — *ravioli di zucca*, a pumpkin ravioli from Mantua and *pizzoccheri* from Valtellina. The latter are tagliatelle made with buckwheat flour, eggs, and milk. The tagliatelle are cooked with cabbage and potatoes and dressed with a butter, sage, garlic, and taleggio or fontina cheese sauce.

Lombardy is the prime livestock and milk producing region in Italy. Cream is used in making many Milanese dishes including soups and puddings. The use of cream in Lombardy cooking is due to the strong link between Milanese and French cooking. Over the centuries Lombardy nobility frequented France and took their chefs along to learn the nuances of French cooking.

The milk produced in Lombardy is used to make all types of cheese, some of which are considered to be the best cheeses in the world. Four of the famous cheeses are: stracchino, robiola, taleggio, and tartufelle. All of these cheeses are aged in caves.

Stracchino cheese is made from cows milk while it is fresh and still warm with some milk from the previous evening added. Taleggio is a soft, slightly salted cheese with a reddish crust. Robiola cheese also is made with fresh milk that is warm, mixed with cream from the night before. Grana Lodigiana is a goat cheese, and Quartirolo cheese is soft with a fresh creamy taste.

The world famous Gorgonzola cheese is made in the town of Gorgonzola, not far from Milan. Gorgonzola, a blue-veined cheese, is made with cow's milk in small shapes of ten by twelve inches weighing around four and a half pounds. It is ready in forty-five to fifty days. This cheese is very delicious, especially when spread on grilled polenta.

Two other cheeses made in Lombardy are mascarpone and bel paese. Mascarpone is a very delicate cream cheese. It can be eaten plain and is also used to make desserts. Bel paese, a soft and mild cheese, is used as a spread on sliced bread and it is also eaten with fresh fruit.

Meat is prevalent in the cooking of Lombardy including veal, chicken, pork, rabbit, and lamb. Organ meats, such as brains, heart, calf's liver, kidney, and sweetbreads are popular. They are boiled, used in stews, and for making *fritti misti* (mixed fry).

In Lombardy meat is typically braised or stewed rather than grilled or roasted. Much of the meat is marinated first in wine and vegetables, then cooked slowly for 3 to 4 hours. *Bolliti misti* (boiled meats) are frequently served with *frutta di mostarda*, fruits preserved in mustard-flavored syrup.

The Lombardy region has many meat specialties. *Busecca* is a favorite Milanese dish of tripe. It is served as a thick stew, usually over polenta. *Ossobuco*, probably the most famous dish of Lombardy, consists of floured veal shanks, cooked with wine and tomato. They are generally served with a *gremolata*. *Gremolata* is made with finely chopped garlic, lemon rind, and parsley to give additional flavor to the veal. *Cassoeula* is another popular Milanese dish, which is made with pork, sausage, savoy cabbage and is served with polenta.

Another specialty of Milan, *costoletta alla Milanese*, is a crisp juicy veal cutlet breaded and fried. *Vitello tonnato*, leg of veal slowly boiled and served cold with a tuna, capers, and mayonnaise sauce is another very popular dish particularly for summer.

Cremona, a town in southeastern Lombardy, besides being the birthplace of Stradivarius the great violin maker, is known for its *salumi* and sausages. Two well-known are *culatello* and *fiocchetto*, which are salted and spiced lean hams in sausage casings that take one year to mature. *Salamella di Cremona*

Bellagio on Lake Como in Lombardy. Photo courtesy of Tom Vano.

is a coarsely cut, pure pork *salumi* and *varzi* is pork flavored with salt, pepper, garlic, and wine.

In Brianza in the foothills of the Alps, the local cuisine is known for its sausages, *salumi*, and guinea hen cooked in clay. The well-known Luganega sausages are fried or grilled and served with rice. They are also used in soups. Another famous meat product is *bresaola*, which is spiced beef that is air dried.

Lombardy is not known for its cultivation of vegetables but potatoes, cabbages, turnips, beans, asparagus, peppers, and yellow pumpkin are grown in the region. In the hills there are many apple, pear, apricot, and peach orchards. Strawberries and raspberries are also grown. In the mountains orchards of chestnut trees spot the landscape. White truffles and many kinds of wild mushrooms, including porcini, ovoli, chanterelles and prataioli are found in the woods.

Fish from the lakes are plentiful. They include eel, trout, sturgeon, perch, carp, and whitefish, which are prepared by grilling or poaching.

The Milanese claim that they invented *panettone*, a buttery yeast cake containing seedless raisins and candied peel. This is a cake that is typically served in every Italian home at Christmas and which is exported all over the world. *Colomba*, a dessert made at Easter time, is made in the shape of a dove to commemorate the doves that were present at the battle of Legnano in 1176, in which the Milanese were victorious.

Another dessert is a *lodigiana* cake made with almonds, flour, eggs, lemon rind, and vanilla. Other desserts are *busecchina*, which are stewed chestnuts served with cream, and *laciaditt* which are apple fritters that are served with sugar.

The Milanese love wine with their meals. They still drink their usual aperitif at midday. It is a bitter, served with olives and very crisp potato chips.

Wines

Lombardy has a number of fine wines. The best come from the hills. These wines are Cortese, Clastidio, Frecciarossa, Barbera, Sangue di Giuda (the blood of Judas), and Buttafuoco. In the Valtellina, a valley between Lake Como and Lake Garda, Nebbiolo grapes are used with other native grapes to make good, hearty, everyday reds. Sasella and Valgella, full-bodied, slightly tannic and aromatic reds are served with roasts and game.

Other good wines are: Grumello, Inferno, Riviera del Garda, Botticino, Chiaretto, Tocai di San Martino, the delicate white Lugana, and the popular Franciacorta reds, whites and champagne.

Autunno in Lombardia
Autumn In Lombardy

Serves 6

Bresaola della Valtellina
Bresaola from Valtellina

Risotto con Luganeghe
Risotto with Sausages

Costolette alla Milanese
Breaded Veal Chops Milanese Style

Bietole al Burro
Swiss Chard with Butter

Funghi Fritti
Fried Mushrooms

Laciaditt Specialita Milanese
Apple Fritters, Specialty of Milan

Caffe
Coffee

Autumn In Lombardy

In planning this menu I took advantage of the many ingredients that are grown and produced in Lombardy, some of which are available only in the autumn season.

The antipasto of bresaola, or air-dried beef, served with arugula and slivers of Parmesan cheese starts this elegant menu. If bresaola is not available prosciutto may be substituted.

The rice, which grows in Lombardy, is cooked with pork sausages and onion in a broth. Before serving this risotto, butter and Parmesan cheese are added, as is traditional with many risottos.

The entree of breaded veal chops is the classic Milanese dish. The Swiss chard cooked with butter and the fried mushrooms are an excellent accompaniment of contrasting flavors to the veal dish.

Golden, juicy, sweet apple fritters end this elegant autumn dinner from the Lombardy region.

Preparation

Several items on this menu can be prepared ahead.

Prepare the arugula for the antipasto by removing the stems, then rinsing it under cold running water. Drain the arugula well, then chop it and refrigerate. Prepare the Parmesan cheese by cutting it into slivers and place them in the refrigerator. Make the dressing for the arugula and refrigerate. All of this can be done in the morning. In the evening, before you are going to serve the antipasto, assemble the bresaola with the arugula and dressing.

The risotto can be made up to the point of adding the rice. Simmer the broth just before adding the rice. Finish cooking the risotto while you are eating the antipasto of bresaola.

The veal chops can be breaded early in the afternoon and refrigerated. Bring them to room temperature one hour before you are going to fry them.

You can cook the Swiss chard in butter late in the afternoon and then reheat it briefly just before serving. Also clean the mushrooms, cut them in slices, if needed, then dip them in the beaten eggs, then in the bread crumbs, but do not fry them. Set the mushrooms aside until you are going to fry them. It will not take too long to cook them, because mushrooms cook fast.

One hour before your guests are to arrive, make the batter for the apple fritters. Peel, core, and cut the apples into thin slices and grate the lemon rind, and then place the apples and lemon rind into the batter and mix. Cover the apples with plastic wrap and set aside. When you have finished your dinner, serve coffee to your guests and then fry the apples and serve them with granulated sugar. The apple fritters should be served hot and, if you like, with a scoop of your favorite ice cream.

Bresaola della Valtellina
Bresaola from Valtellina

Serves 6

Bresaola is a specialty of Valtellina, an alpine valley in Lombardy. It is a raw fillet of beef, which is cured in salt and air dried, and is ready to be eaten within 2 to 3 months.

Bresaola is always served as an antipasto on special occasions and for important dinners. It can be served plain with just a little olive oil, a few drops of lemon juice, and freshly ground black pepper. Bresaola is also served with arugula, baby artichokes, mushrooms, or red radicchio. Its taste is delicate, but with a little more bite then the prosciutto di Parma. Bresaola needs to be served and eaten within a few hours after being sliced; if not it will turn dark in color and become leathery.

24 very thin slices bresaola
1 bunch arugula, stems removed
*   and chopped*
1/2 cup slivered fresh Parmesan
*   cheese*

6 tablespoon extra virgin olive oil
Juice of 1 lemon
1/4 teaspoon salt
1/4 teaspoon freshly ground black
*   pepper*

Arrange four slices of bresaola, slightly overlapping, on each individual plate. Sprinkle some chopped arugula and a few slivers of Parmesan cheese over the bresaola.

Make the dressing by mixing the olive oil and lemon juice in a small bowl and season with the salt and pepper. Pour the dressing over the arugula and serve with slices of baguette bread.

Note If bresaola is unavailable in your area, a good quality prosciutto may be substituted in this recipe.

Risotto con Luganeghe
Risotto with Sausages

Serves 6

4 cups meat broth
6 tablespoons unsalted butter
1 medium onion, finely chopped
4 Italian pork sausages, skinned and
   crumbled in pieces

2 cups arborio rice
1/2 cup freshly grated Parmesan
cheese

Bring the broth barely to a simmer in a saucepan.

Heat 3 tablespoon of the butter in a saucepan. Add the chopped onion and the crumbled sausages and sauté over medium heat until the onion and sausages are golden in color. (You can stop the cooking at this point and continue later.)

Pour in the rice, stirring to coat the rice grains with the cooking liquid. Add the simmering broth and bring the mixture back to a boil. Reduce the heat to low and cook, covered, for 15 minutes until the rice is cooked through but still firm to the bite.

Remove the rice from the heat, stir in the remaining 3 table-spoons of butter and the grated cheese. Mix thoroughly and serve on individual plates or from a warm platter.

Costolette alla Milanese
Breaded Veal Chops Milanese Style

Serves 6

6 (3/4-inch thick) veal loin chops
   with the bone, each weighing
   about 6 ounces
2 large eggs, beaten
1/2 teaspoon salt

2 cups bread crumbs
5 tablespoons unsalted butter
Salt and freshly ground black
   pepper
1 lemon, cut into 6 wedges

Place the meat part of the veal chop between two sheet of parchment paper and pound them lightly.

Dip the veal chops into the beaten eggs letting excess egg fall off the veal, then coat them with the bread crumbs. Press the crumbs into the chops with the palms of your hands.

In a large heavy skillet, heat the butter over medium heat. As soon as the butter foams, place the veal chops into the skillet and cook them for about 3 to 4 minutes on each side, or until the chops are golden brown and crispy. Season the chops with some salt and pepper and serve one veal chop per person with a lemon wedge.

Bietole al Burro
Swiss Chard with Butter

Serves 6

1 1/2 to 2 pounds Swiss chard with
   stalks
4 tablespoons unsalted butter
1 cup broth

1/2 teaspoon salt
1/2 teaspoon freshly ground black
   pepper

Discard any blemish leaves of the Swiss chard. Wash and then cut the chard, including the stalks, into 1/2-inch thick slices.

Heat the butter in a large saucepan over medium heat. When the butter starts to foam, add the chard. Mix well, increase the heat to high and add the broth. Cover the saucepan, reduce heat to medium-high and cook the chard for about 5 to 7 minutes, depending if the chard is tender or tough. Season the chard with salt and pepper, stir again and serve hot with the breaded veal chops.

Funghi Fritti
Fried Mushrooms

Serves 6

2 pounds mixed wild mushrooms
4 eggs
Salt and ground black pepper

2 cups bread crumbs
1/2 to 1 cup olive oil, for frying
2 lemons, cut in quarters

If the mushrooms are big, cut them into slices and leave the small ones whole. Remove the stems and wipe the mushrooms clean with a damp cloth.

Beat the eggs with salt and pepper in a shallow bowl and place the bread crumbs on a piece of aluminum foil.

Pour some oil into a large deep skillet and heat over medium-high heat. Dip the mushrooms in the beaten eggs and let the excess run off, then roll them in the bread crumbs. Place the mushrooms gently in the hot oil and sauté them in batches until they are cooked, light gold in color and crispy all over. Serve the mushrooms garnished with lemon wedges.

Laciaditt Specialita Milanese
Apple Fritters, Specialty of Milan

Serves 6

2 cups all purpose flour
Pinch of salt
1 egg
1 1/4 cups milk
1 1/4 cups water

3 large green apples, peeled and
*   thinly sliced*
Grated rind of 1 lemon
3/4 to 1 cup oil, for frying
Granulated sugar

Place the flour in a large bowl with the salt. Add the whole egg, and stir it into the flour until well mixed. Combine the milk and water and slowly add it to the flour mixture, beating constantly, until the batter is smooth. Let the batter sit for 1 hour.

Add the sliced apples and the lemon rind to the batter and mix gently.

Heat a large deep pan with the olive oil over medium-high heat. When hot, using a small ladle, add few slices of apple with the batter to the oil and fry the apple slices until pale golden in color turning them once. When cooked, remove them with a slotted spoon, drain them on paper towels, and then sprinkle each fritter with sugar before serving them hot.

Cena Fredda alla Milanese
Cold Dinner Milan Style

Serves 6

Insalata di Funghi con Prosciutto
Mushroom Salad with Prosciutto

Minestrone all Milanese
Vegetable Soup Milanese Style

Vitello Tonnato
Cold Veal with Tuna Sauce

Asparagi con Limone
Asparagus with Lemon

Patate in Insalata
Potato Salad

Crema al Mascarpone con Frutta
Cream Cheese with Fruit

Caffè
Coffee

Cold Dinner Milan Style

Since Milan, the principal city of Lombardy, is very hot and humid in the summer months, particularly in August, most of the inhabitants leave the city for cooler environs.

Realizing that our summers can also be very hot, I have put together a menu with several dishes that can be served cool and made ahead of time.

I have chosen to start this summer dinner with an antipasto of mushrooms with prosciutto, a typical dish of Lombardy as mushrooms are in abundance there.

The vegetable soup with rice provides a light and refreshing first course to this dinner. It is served at room temperature or may be warmed, if you desire. This light minestrone is flavored with pancetta.

The entree of veal marinated in a tuna sauce is one of the most famous dishes of Milan. It is a cool and refreshing dish for warm days. Fresh asparagus and potato slices are served with the veal.

A very smooth cream cheese mousse served with fresh fruits ends this cold Milan-style dinner.

Preparations

Almost all of the preparations for this meal must be done well ahead.

Clean and slice the mushrooms and celery on the afternoon of the dinner, place them in a plastic bag, and refrigerate. Assemble the mushrooms and celery in the evening and dress them with the lemon vinaigrette and serve them with the prosciutto slices.

Make the vegetable soup a few days ahead. You may even freeze it, then thaw it, and leave it at room temperature. The soup may also be made ahead, refrigerated and then brought to room temperature. You may serve the vegetable soup either at room temperature or slightly heated. Before serving the soup, stir in the chopped basil.

The vitello tonnato has to be made at least a day ahead for the veal to absorb the tuna sauce.

In the afternoon cook the asparagus al dente and either keep it at room temperature or store it in the refrigerator until half an hour before serving. Then remove it and bring to room temperature. Make the lemon dressing and pour it over the asparagus just before serving. The potato salad can also be made in the afternoon up to the point of adding the oil. Add it when ready to serve.

Make the cream cheese dessert the day before, scoop the mixture into individual glasses, and refrigerate, Also prepare the fresh fruit and refrigerate it. Assemble the dessert just before serving and accompany it with some cookies.

Insalata di Funghi con Prosciutto
Mushroom Salad with Prosciutto

Serves 6

12 *cremini or white mushrooms*
1 *celery stalk, thinly sliced*
Juice of 1 lemon
1/4 *teaspoon salt*
1/4 *teaspoon freshly ground pepper*

6 *to 8 tablespoons extra virgin olive oil*
18 *slices of prosciutto (raw ham), thinly sliced*
24 *slivers fresh Parmesan cheese*
6 *fresh sprigs basil, for garnish*

Wipe the mushrooms with a damp cloth to remove any dirt. Slice them as thin as you can and place them in a salad bowl. Add the sliced celery and sprinkle with the lemon juice, salt and pepper and olive oil. Mix thoroughly until well blended.

Place 3 slices of prosciutto on each plate, slightly overlapping them. Add some of the mushrooms salad in the center of the plate over the prosciutto slices and add 4 slivers of cheese for each plate. Garnish the plate with a fresh basil sprig.

Minestrone alla Milanese
Vegetable Soup Milanese Style

Serves 6 to 8

1/2 pound borlotti or dried white
beans or 2 1/2 cups canned beans,
   drained
4 tablespoons unsalted butter
1/4 pound pancetta or unsmoked
   bacon, chopped into small pieces
2 large onions, finely chopped
2 garlic cloves, finely chopped
3 sprigs parsley, finely chopped
2 carrots, cubed
3 celery stalks, cubed

3 large boiling potatoes, cubed
4 large ripe tomatoes, peeled and
   chopped or 6 ounces canned
   plum tomatoes
1 small savoy cabbage, shredded
2 cups fresh or frozen peas
2 medium zucchini, thinly sliced
1 cup Arborio rice
2 tablespoons chopped fresh basil
2/3 cup freshly grated Parmesan
   cheese

Soak the beans overnight in cold water and drain.

Melt the butter in a large saucepan over medium heat. Add the chopped pancetta and onion and sauté until the onion is soft. Add the garlic and parsley and stir for 2 minutes. Then add the carrots and celery and sauté for 2 more minutes, stirring often. Add the potatoes, tomatoes and the soaked beans. (If using the canned beans, add them at the end.) Cover with lots of water (about 10 cups) bring to a boil, cover the saucepan and simmer over low heat for about 1 and 1/2 hours. Add salt when the beans have begun to soften. Add the shredded cabbage, canned beans, if using them, the peas and zucchini and simmer for 15 more minutes. Add the rice and continue cooking for another 20 minutes or until the rice is tender but not overcooked.

Before serving the soup, either hot or at room temperature, stir in the chopped basil. Pass the grated cheese at the table.

Vitello Tonnato
Cold Veal in Tuna Sauce

Serves 6

This dish is a specialty of Milan and the Piedmont region. Vitello tonnato is a typical summer dish because it has a cool and fresh taste. This dish can also be served as an antipasto or as a main course for a light lunch.

2 1/2 to 3 pounds veal roast, from
    top round or shoulder or thigh
1 carrot, chopped
2 celery stalks, chopped
1 onion, sliced

2 bay leaves
2 cups water
2 cups dry white wine
1 teaspoon salt

Have your butcher tie the veal roast, loosely with strings.

Place the carrot, celery, onion, and bay leaves in a large saucepan. Add the water, wine, and salt and bring to a boil over medium-high heat. Add the veal roast and bring back to a boil. Cover the pan and reduce heat to low and simmer for about 1 and 1/2 to 2 hours, turning the meat over several times. The meat is cooked and tender when a fork can easily be inserted into the veal. Remove the pan from the heat and let the veal cool in the broth. Make the sauce.

Tuna Fish Sauce

1 (7 ounce) can tuna fish in oil,
    drained
4 anchovy fillets
3 tablespoons capers, drained
Juice of 1 lemon

1/2 cup olive oil
1 1/4 cups mayonnaise
Gherkins (pickles), for garnish
2 tablespoons capers, drained, for
    garnish

Place the drained tuna, anchovy fillets, capers, lemon juice and olive oil in a food processor and process until the mixture is a fine paste. If the sauce is too thick, add a few tablespoons of the veal broth and mix thoroughly again.

In a small bowl combine the tuna fish mixture with the mayonnaise and mix until well blended. Refrigerate the sauce, covered, until ready to use.

Remove the cold veal from its broth and remove the strings. Cut the veal into thin slices and set them aside.

Place some tuna fish sauce on a serving platter and spread it over the bottom of the platter. Arrange the veal slices, slightly overlapping, on top of the sauce. Cover the veal with the remaining sauce. Cover the platter with plastic wrap and refrigerate overnight. When ready to serve, garnish with a few gherkin pickles and the capers sprinkled on top of the veal slices.

Asparagi con Limone
Asparagus with Lemon

Serves 6

2 1/2 pounds asparagus
Juice of 1 lemon
1/4 teaspoon salt

1/4 teaspoon freshly ground black
   pepper
1/3 cup extra virgin olive oil

Trim the asparagus of any leaves below the tip and cut off the tough ends. Rinse the asparagus in cold water, divide them into two bunches with string or rubber bands.

Place the asparagus upright in an asparagus cooker or stock pot. Add 3 inches of cold, lightly salted water. Bring to a boil, cover, and cook over high heat for 4 to 6 minutes, depending on the thickness of the asparagus. Remove the strings and place the asparagus on a platter lined with paper towels to drain. Then put them in the refrigerator to cool.

Combine the lemon juice and salt and pepper in a small bowl and whisk in the oil until blended

To serve, bring the asparagus to room temperature, remove the paper towels underneath the asparagus and pour the dressing over it.

Serve few asparagus with the vitello tonnato.

Patate in Insalata
Potato Salad

Serves 6

2 pounds boiling potatoes (all the
    same size)
4 tablespoons red-wine vinegar

1 teaspoon ground black pepper
1/2 cup extra virgin olive oil
2 tablespoons chopped fresh parsley

Place the unpeeled potatoes in a large saucepan and cover them with cold water by 2 inches. Bring to a boil over medium heat and cook the potatoes until tender, but not soft, about 35 minutes. Drain the potatoes and peel them as soon as they can be handled. Cut the potatoes into slices about 1/4-inch-thick and place them on a large serving platter. Immediately sprinkle the vinegar over the potato slices and set aside.

When ready to serve, season the potatoes with salt and pepper and pour the olive oil over them. Sprinkle the parsley on top and serve warm or at room temperature with the vitello tonnato.

Crema al Mascarpone con Frutta
Cream Cheese with Fruit

Serves 6

1 pound mascarpone cheese, at room
    temperature
1/2 cup granulated sugar
4 egg, separated
1/2 cup rum or brandy

3 baskets of raspberries, blueberries,
    any fruit in season, rinsed
4 tablespoons sugar
Juice of half a lemon
Plain cookies

Mix the cheese and the 1/2 cup of sugar together in a large bowl. Add the egg yolks, one at a time, beating constantly, then add the rum or brandy. Beat the egg whites in another bowl until soft peaks form. Then fold the egg whites into the cheese mixture until well blended. Scoop the mixture into individual glasses and refrigerate for a least two hours.

Place the fruit into a bowl, add the 4 tablespoons of sugar and lemon juice and refrigerate.

When ready to serve, place 1 or 2 spoonfuls of fruit on top of the mascarpone mixture and serve with cookies.

Trentino-Alto Adige

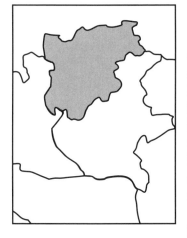

Trentino-Alto Adige is a spectacular region of mountains, the Alps and Dolomites, plus rivers and beautiful valleys. On the north this region borders Switzerland and Austria. It also borders the regions of Veneto to the southeast and Lombardy to the west. Alto Adige takes its name from the river Adige, which runs through the region. It is the second longest river in Italy after the Po. This region has cool temperatures in the summer months and in the winter it is generally very cold.

Trentino-Alto Adige is one region, having been unified for administrative reasons after World War I. While unified administratively, from a culinary standpoint, the two areas are entirely different. The cooking of Trentino is similar to the cooking of the Veneto region. The cooking of Alto Adige, which is the northern part of the region, is very similar to Austrian cuisine.

The peoples of these two administrative units are also different from each other. The people of Alto Adige in the north speak German and those in Trentino, in the south, speak Italian. To complicate the language even more, in a few of the mountains areas, the Dolomites in particular, the people speak Ladino. This is a language derived from Latin, but different from Italian.

Trentino-Alto Adige has many turreted houses, old castles, and convents. Many of the latter two have become hotels and restaurants for tourists who come to enjoy the mountains.

The cooking in Alto Adige is Tyrolean and based on the pig and its *speck* (bacon), in particular. *Speck*, salted and smoked pork, is made from local pigs and is typically served either for breakfast, as an appetizer, or as an afternoon snack. It is also used in cooking.

The pigs are killed in the winter and hams are made at this time. The hams are boned, then covered with a mixture of salt, saltpeter, pepper, bay leaves, and juniper berries. They are then left to rest for 3 weeks in order to let the liquid of the pork run out. Then the meat is hung in the fireplace and smoked with fruit wood and juniper for a few hours a day and allowed to cool off after each smoking. This procedure continues for 3 months, after which the hams are left to age in a well-ventilated attic for about 6 months.

Polenta is the staple food of Trentino. It is made with cornmeal, buckwheat flour, or wheat flour mixed with buckwheat and potato flour. When it is made with buckwheat flour it is called black polenta, because the buckwheat flour gives the polenta a darker color.

Polenta is served with tomato sauce, or fried and eaten with *salumi*, cheeses, or fish. It is also eaten with mushrooms which are found in the Dolomites. The harvest of wild mushrooms in the mountains of the region includes porcini, *chiodini*, chantarelles, *russole*, plus many other mushrooms that are special to specific areas. In Trento there is a weekly mushroom market which lasts from summer through autumn.

One of the typical Austrian-Tyrolean dishes of Alto Adige is *knōdel*, which are bread dumplings usually cooked in soups or stews. They are also steamed and served with roasts and boiled meats. Another Austrian-inspired dish is *gulash*. It consists of pieces of beef cooked with onions, chili pepper, tomatoes, sage, rosemary, broth, and paprika. Trout from the lakes and streams of the area form part of the cuisine. Local game is cooked in wine and vinegar.

The main vegetables of the region are cabbage and potatoes. White cabbage is frequently made into sauerkraut. Red cabbage is cooked in red wine with onions and bacon.

Applesauce, bilberry jam and sour cream are some of the basics of Alto Adige cooking. Many kinds of sausage and *salumi* are typical of this region. Apples grow in large quantities and are used in many recipes for salads, risottos, puddings, vegetables, and desserts.

There is only one traditional pasta dish in Trentino-Alto Adige, It is *ravioli alla pusterese*. The dough is made with rye and wheat flours and is stuffed with either spinach and ricotta, or sauerkraut. If stuffed with sauerkraut, the ravioli are sautéed in butter, otherwise they are boiled in water.

Bread is a very important part of the food of Trentino-Alto Adige. It is made with rye, barley, or wheat flour. Some of the bread is dark. Bread is typically made in round loaves. Some are very hard and can only be eaten after soaking in soups. Soft light bread is eaten with *speck* and the local vezzena cheese. Most of the cheeses are made from cow's milk and the best known is vezzena cheese. It is made in the mountains and is used as a table cheese when fresh or is grated when aged.

Many of the desserts are from Austrian recipes. *Kastanientorte* (chestnut torte) is a dessert made with puree of chestnuts mixed with butter, flour, sugar, and eggs.

As in Austria, strudel is a well-known dessert. The strudel is made with seasonal fruit and egg custard, flavored with poppy seeds, raisins, and pine nuts. *Krapfen*, doughnuts, are filled with jam and poppy seeds or with cream. Other desserts are plum tarts, prune dumplings, chestnut cake, puddings, stuffed pancakes, and pastries filled with nuts and marzipan.

Zelten is a dessert made with rye flour and filled with dried figs, golden raisins, dates, pine nuts, and walnuts.

Wines

Alto Adige is the great wine-producing area of Italy and many of the wines are exported. The region is known for its great whites. The red wines that are produced in the alpine vineyards are mainly sent to Switzerland, Germany, and Austria. Merlot and Cabernet are the best known reds and the whites are Pinot Bianco, Pinot Grigio, Riesling, Traminer, and Chardonnay

The very popular wine Lago di Caldaro is made from the local Schiava grape. It is a light soft wine with the flavor of strawberries and almonds. Santa Maddalena wine has a delicate fragrance with a little hint of violets and almonds.

In Alto Adige, the people learned to make dry white wines from the French. From the Germans they learned how to make dry, light and delicate wines that are just sweet enough to have a perfumy and fruity taste.

Trentino wines are light with a good flavor. There are also some good Cabernets, Merlots, and Pinot Neri.

Some of Italy's best white Pinot Bianco, Chardonnay and sparkling wines are made in Trentino.

Cortina d'Ampezzo, Trentino-Alto Adige.
Photo courtesy of Grayce Roessler.

Polenta con Cervo Salvatico
Polenta with Venison

Serves 6

Polenta con Funghi
Polenta with Mushrooms

Grigliata di Cervo
Grilled Venison

Salsa di Cren
Horseradish Sauce

Insalata di Cavolo e Mele
Cabbage and Apple Salad

Torta di Mele e Mandorle
Apple and Almond Cake

Caffè
Coffee

Polenta with Venison

Polenta is a staple in Trentino-Alto Adige and is served in many ways. For this venison dinner from Trentino-Alto Adige I chose polenta served with mushrooms stewed in tomato sauce, since a great variety of mushrooms are found in the Dolomite area.

For the main course venison chops or steaks are marinated for a day and then grilled or barbecued. They are served with the strained cooked marinade sauce, which gives the meat a wonderful flavor. There is also a horseradish sauce for the venison.

The green cabbage with the cubed apples is a refreshing salad for your palate, especially after partaking of the horseradish.

The apple and almond cake dessert has a piquant flavor of apples and lemon juice. Almonds add a little crunch to the cake.

Preparations

Prepare the mushroom sauce for the polenta early in the morning and set it aside. Reheat just before serving the polenta.

The polenta has to be made the evening of the dinner . You can use either regular cornmeal or a packaged instant polenta mix.

Marinate the venison chops or steaks the day before and refrigerate. Bring to room temperature before grilling. Strain and heat the marinate while the steaks are cooking.

Make the horseradish sauce the day before and refrigerate.

In the morning prepare the cabbage for the salad by cleaning, rinsing, drying, and chopping it. Chop the onion. Peel, core and cube the apples and sprinkle them with some lemon juice. Also refrigerate the onion and apples. Early in the afternoon make the dressing and set it aside. Assemble the cabbage, onion, and apples in the evening and toss with the dressing before serving it.

Make the dessert a day ahead or on the morning of the dinner.

Polenta con Funghi
Polenta with Mushrooms

Serves 6 or more

Polenta

6 cups water
1 1/2 teaspoons salt
2 cups cornmeal or 1 package
    instant polenta imported from
    Italy

6 tablespoons (3/4 stick) unsalted
    butter, cut into pieces
1/2 cup freshly grated Parmesan
    cheese

Bring the water to a boil in a large saucepan and add salt. Gradually add the cornmeal in a thin stream and stir constantly with a wooden spoon until the mixture boils and thickens, about 2 minutes.

Reduce the heat to low and continue cooking the mixture over low heat until thick, stirring occasionally, about 30 minutes. The polenta is cooked when it comes away cleanly from the sides of the pot. It you are using the instant polenta it will take 5 to 6 minutes to cook.

When the polenta is cooked, add the pieces of butter and the Parmesan cheese.

Sauce

1 pound fresh crimini mushrooms
2 ounces dried porcini mushrooms
3 tablespoons extra virgin olive oil
2 tablespoons unsalted butter
1 medium onion, finely chopped
3 cups canned peeled tomatoes,
    chopped

1/2 teaspoon salt
1/2 teaspoon freshly ground black
    pepper
8 fresh basil leaves, coarsely
    chopped

Clean and slice the fresh mushrooms. Soak the dried mushrooms in a bowl with warm water to cover the mushrooms for 20 minutes. Drain the porcini, reserving the soaking water, and rinse them under running water. Cut the porcini into pieces. Strain the mushroom water through a fine sieve and set it aside.

Heat the oil and butter in a large sauté pan, add the onion and sauté over medium heat until the onion is soft. Add the fresh mushrooms and the porcini. Cook together over medium-high heat for about

5 minutes, stirring to coat the mushrooms with the pan juices. Add the tomatoes and continue cooking, uncovered, over low heat for 20 minutes, stirring often so that the water evaporates. Add salt and pepper and the basil. Stir thoroughly and serve.

The sauce is finished when all of the mushrooms are soft but still a little firm to the bite.

Serve the sauce hot over the cooked polenta.

Grigliata di Cervo
Grilled Venison

Serves 6

6 venison chops or steaks
1 1/2 cups red wine
2 tablespoons olive oil
1 onion, chopped coarsely
4 garlic cloves, sliced
1 teaspoon cinnamon

Grated rind of 1 lemon
1 bay leaf
10 juniper berries, crushed
1 teaspoon salt
1/2 teaspoon freshly ground black
   pepper

Place the venison chops or steaks in a glass bowl. Place all of the remaining ingredients in another bowl and mix thoroughly. Pour this mixture over the venison chops, lifting the chops so that the liquid flows underneath them. Place the chops, covered, in the refrigerator for one day, turning the meat a few times.

Cook the meat under the broiler or on the grill. Place the meat on a grill and barbecue it. Cook the meat for about 10 minutes, 5 minutes on each side, or until it is cooked. Pour the marinade into a saucepan and cook over medium-high heat until it starts to boil, then reduce it to a sauce. Strain the sauce and serve it with the meat, the polenta, and mushrooms. Serve some horseradish sauce on the side of the plate .

If venison is not available, substitute a 2-pound piece of pork cut into 6 large steaks and marinated them the same as the venison.

Salsa di Cren
Horseradish Sauce

Serves 6

This strong flavored sauce of Alto Adige is usually served with all kinds of boiled or roasted meats. In the Trentino area, the horseradish sauce is called ravanada. The sharpness of the sauce can be made to your taste. Serve some of this sauce with the grilled venison steaks.

1 piece(1 1/2-inch) horseradish root
Pinch of salt
2 tablespoonss sugar

1/2 cup whipping cream
2 tablespoons bread crumbs
5 tablespoons white wine vinegar

Finely grate the horseradish. Place the grated horseradish, sugar, whipping cream, and bread crumbs in a small bowl. Mix together thoroughly. Add the viengar and mix again.

Instead of whipping cream, half of a grated raw apple and half of a cooked and whipped apple may be substituted.

Insalata di Cavolo e Mele
Cabbage and Apple Salad

Serves 6

1 large green cabbage
1 small white onion
2 apples, such as golden delicious
1 tablespoon caraway seeds
3 juniper berries

4 tablespoons extra virgin olive oil
2 tablespoons apple-cider vinegar
2 tablespoons lemon juice
1 teaspoon salt

Remove the outside blemished leaves of cabbage, then cut and remove the hard inner core. Rinse the cabbage in cold water, pat dry cut it into thin strips. Finely chop the onion and set it aside. Peel and core the apples and cut them into small cubes.

Place the cut cabbage, onion and apples into a large salad bowl. Add the caraway seeds and juniper berries. In a small bowl combine the olive oil, vinegar, lemon juice and salt and using a fork mix thoroughly until well blended.

Pour the dressing over the salad and toss until well mixed.

Torta di Mele e Mandorle
Apple and Almond Cake

Serves 6 to 8

1 cup blanched hazelnuts or
    almonds, or a mixture of both
6 Granny Smith apples
4 eggs, separated
1 cup sugar

Juice of 1 large lemon
1 cup all purpose flour
2 tablespoons butter, melted
Butter for greasing pan
Sugar for sprinkling on top of cake

Chop the hazelnuts or almonds, or both, and place them in a dry frying pan. Toast the nuts over medium heat, shaking the pan so that the nuts will brown all over. Peel, core, and slice the apples and set them aside.

Beat the egg yolks with the sugar in a large bowl. Add the lemon juice and gradually add the flour, beating constantly. Beat the egg whites in another bowl until stiff and then fold them in the egg-flour mixture. Then fold in the toasted nuts and mix gently.

Butter a 10-inch spring form pan and dust with flour. Pour half of the cake batter in the pan, then arrange a layer of apples on top and then pour the remaining cake batter over them. Arrange the rest of the apple slices in circles on top. Brush with the melted butter over the apple slices and then sprinkle them with sugar. Bake in a preheated 350° F. oven for 1 hour and 25 minutes or until a toothpick pushed into the cake comes out clean. Place the cake under the broiler for 1 minute to give the top a caramelized look. Let the cake cool.

Slice the cake into large wedges and serve it with whipped cream.

Festa di Ottobre
Oktoberfest

Serves 6

Knödel alla Tirolese in Brodo
Bread Dumplings in Broth

Crauti e Salsicce
Sausages and Sauerkraut

Patate coi Ravanei
Potatoes with Turnip

Strudel di Mele
Apple Strudel

Birra
Beer

Oktoberfest

German is spoken in Alto Adige in the north and the cooking of Alto Adige has an Austrian and mid-European influence.

Since all of the dishes that I have chosen for this menu are of German/Austrian origin, I decided to call it Oktoberfest and serve plenty of beer.

Traditional bread dumplings start this celebration. A light broth is served with the delicate dumplings for a first course.

Pork sausages with sauerkraut and apples are the main course. The flavor of the sausages are enhanced by being steamed in the sauerkraut. They are served with a mixture of seasoned potatoes and turnips, a most unusual and flavorful combination.

To end this Oktoberfest there is an apple strudel for dessert, which is made with   apples and pine nuts. This unique strudel is flavored with cinnamon and lemon zest.

Preparations

If you are planning to serve homemade broth with the dumplings, make it several days ahead, refrigerate, and reheat in the evening of your party.

Make the dumplings in the morning and boil them in water. Then drain the dumplings and set them aside. In the evening bring the broth to a boil, add the cooked dumplings and let them sit in the broth for about 5 to 10 minutes before serving the soup.

Early in the afternoon, cook the sausages, remove them; then cook the sauerkraut for 1/2 hour and finally put the sausages back into the skillet and turn off the heat. Finish cooking the sausages and sauerkraut the last 30 minutes while your guests are having drinks.

Late in the afternoon prepare the potatoes, boil and peel them and keep them covered. Grate the turnip and cover it. Prepare the dressing by mixing the olive oil, vinegar, salt, and pepper. Just before you are going to serve the main course, toss the potatoes and turnip with the dressing and serve the mixture on a lettuce leaf, sprinkled with some chopped chives.

The dessert can be prepared completely ahead and reheated for a few minutes in the evening. However, you can also make the dessert in the afternoon up to the point of baking. Refrigerate it until time to bake. Then bake the strudel for 45 minutes after your guests have arrived and it will still be warm at the time of serving dessert.

Knödel alla Tirolese in Brodo
Bread Dumplings in Broth

Serves 6

In Italy stale bread is never thrown away. It is used in many different ways. These bread dumplings are a Tyrolean specialty. When making them, try to use peasant-style bread, if available. Bread dumplings are typically served in a broth, dressed with melted butter and sage leaves, or with the juices of a roast.

Speck (similar to bacon) is a traditional pork product of Alto Adige. It is put into dumplings or served with sauerkraut and other cuts of pork.

8 ounces stale bread, crusts removed, then sliced	2 extra large eggs, beaten
4 tablespoons unsalted butter	1 teaspoon salt
1 onion, coarsely grated	1/4 teaspoon ground black pepper
2/3 cup chopped speck (smoked prosciutto), lean bacon, or smoked ham	1/2 cup milk
	1/2 teaspoon baking powder
	1/4 cup flour
	7 to 8 cups meat broth
4 tablespoons chopped fresh parsley	2 tablespoons chopped fresh chives

Break the bread into small pieces and set aside.

Place the butter in a skillet over medium heat and when the butter starts to foam add the onion, speck, bacon, or ham, and the parsley and sauté until the onion is soft. Then add the pieces of broken bread and mix well for a few minutes. Then let the mixture cool.

In a bowl mix together the eggs, salt and pepper, and milk. Mix the baking powder and flour and slowly sift into the egg mixture,

When the bread mixture has cooled slightly, add it to the egg mixture. Then mix all of the ingredients together thoroughly, cover, and let the mixture sit for about 1/2 hour.

Bring the broth to a boil in a large pot. Shape the bread mixture into dumplings the size of a tablespoon and then dip them into the boiling broth, making sure that they do not touch as they cook.

Cover the pot and simmer gently over low heat for 5 minutes, until they rise to the top. Ladle 2 to 3 dumplings and broth into each individual soup bowl and sprinkle some chopped chives on top.

The dumplings can also be boiled in salted water for later use. It is good to test cook one dumpling for stability at the beginning so that if it falls apart a little more flour can be added to the mixture.

Crauti e Salsicce
Sausages and Sauerkraut

Serves 6

Sauerkraut, cabbage preserved with salt and vinegar, at one time was the only vegetable consumed by the peasants in the mountains during the long winter months. Each family used to prepare sauerkraut at the end of autumn and kept it *conz dei crauti*, in a wooden vat.

2 tablespoons olive oil
6 fresh pork sausages
2 pounds canned sauerkraut
2 large Granny Smith apples,
  grated

1/4 teaspoon cloves (4)
2 cups broth to cover sauerkraut
1/2 teaspoon salt
1/2 teaspoon freshly ground black
  pepper

Place the oil in a large skillet over medium heat. Prick the sausages with a fork and add them to the skillet. Sauté the sausages until golden brown on all sides, turning them often. When cooked remove them and set aside.

Rinse the sauerkraut under running water and drain well. Place the sauerkraut in the skillet in which the sausages have been cooked.

Add the grated apples and cloves to the sauerkraut and cover with the broth. Cook, covered, over low heat for about 1 hour, adding more broth, if needed. The last 30 minutes of cooking add the cooked sausages to the sauerkraut. Season with salt and pepper and mix thoroughly.

Serve a sausage with some sauerkraut per person.

Patate coi Ravanei
Potatoes with Turnip

Serves 6

4 medium potatoes
1 small turnip
4 tablespoons extra virgin olive oil
1 tablespoon apple-cider vinegar
1 teaspoon salt

1 teaspoon freshly ground black
  pepper
6 lettuce leaves
2 tablespoons fresh chopped chives

Boil the potatoes in sufficient salted water to cover until tender and cooked. Then peel the potatoes, let them cool, and cut them into small cubes.

Peel the turnip and rinse it under cold water and pat dry with a paper towel. Grate the turnip and place it and the cubed potatoes in a salad bowl.

Mix the olive oil, vinegar, salt, and pepper in a small bowl until well blended and pour over the potatoes and mix. Arrange one leaf of lettuce per person on a dinner plate. Place a scoop of the potatoes over the lettuce leaf and sprinkle with some chopped chives. Add the sausage and sauerkraut and serve.

Strudel di Mele
Apple Strudel

Serves 9 to 18

1 tablespoon extra virgin olive oil
1 egg
1/3 cup warm water
1/4 teaspoon salt
1 1/2 cups sifted flour
1/3 cup unsalted, melted butter
6 tablespoons fine dry bread crumbs
8 cups peeled, cored, and thinly
    sliced tart apples

2 tablespoons honey
2 tablespoons sugar
1/2 teaspoon cinnamon
1/4 cup finely chopped pine nuts
1/4 cup raisins
Grated rind of 1 lemon
Confectioner's sugar or whipped
cream, optional

In a bowl, beat together the olive oil, egg, water, and salt. Add the flour while continue to beat the mixture, until a firm dough that pulls away from the bowl is formed. Knead the dough several times until smooth and elastic.

Cover and let stand for 30 minutes. Then cut the dough into 2 equal parts with a sharp knife. (You can freeze 1 part of the dough and make only 1 strudel. If doing so, cut the filling ingredients in half.)

Roll our each piece of dough on a floured cloth to a 12-18-inch rectangle. Brush each with melted butter. Then sprinkle evenly with bread crumbs. Spread 4 cups of the apples lengthwise down the center of each piece of dough. Sprinkle each piece with 1 tablespoon of honey, 1 tablespoon of sugar, 1/4 teaspoon cinnamon, 2 tablespoons pine nuts, 2 tablespoons raisins and half of the grated lemon peel.

Fold the dough over the apples on one side, the fold over the other side. Slide the dough rolls onto a greased baking sheet. Brush with melted butter and bake in a preheated 400° F. oven for 45 minutes.

Cut each roll into 2-inch slices. Serve warm or cold, sprinkle with confectioner's sugar or topped with whipped cream.

Friuli-Venezia Giulia

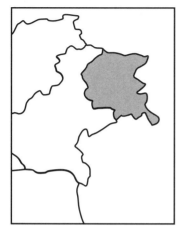

Friuli-Venezia Giulia is the eastern-most region of northern Italy. Its territory lies between the Alps and the Adriatic sea. The region borders with Austria and Yugoslavia to the north and the east, and with Veneto to the west. Most of the population is centered on the Friuli plain where the soil is very fertile.

As its double name implies Friuli-Venezia Giulia is a region formed by two separate areas. The two names have a Latin origin derived from the word Gens Julia — the family of Julius Caesar. The name Friuli comes from Forum Julii, an old Roman name. The name Venezia Giulia is recent in honor of the Venetian people.

Much of the region is mountainous, with the area bordeing Yugoslavia being very rocky. The mountainous areas provide lots of wild game. There are trout in the streams. Sheeps and goats are raised on small farms.

The cooking of Friuli-Venezia Giulia has been influenced by its neighbors, Austria and Yugoslavia. Toward the north and the Alps, the food is simple and hearty. It is based on meat, game, and cheese, as befits cold weather cuisine. In the south and along the Adriatic coast, the cooking is more delicate and based on seafood. The people of Friuli-Venezia Giulia use ingredients from the Po Valley and the Alps, but the use of spices and cream are an Austria influence. There is also a Slavic influence to the cuisine, such as *gulash*.

The cooking of Friuli is based on polenta, soup, and beans. Corn is the main crop of the region, followed by beans, turnips, and other vegetables and fruit. There are also many vineyards planted in the valleys and on the hillsides. Fruits that are grown in this region are apples, peaches, and cherries. Recently kiwi has been added to the array of fruits. They are used to garnish many traditional dishes.

The Friuliani have a way with vegetables and herbs. The asparagus of Aquilea and of Sant Andrea near Gorizia are famous. Equally well-known is the dwarf chicory, which has a delicate but bitter taste.

In the mountains the heart of cooking is polenta. It is white in color from the white corn that grows on the Friuli plain. The people cook the polenta thick and pour it onto a wooden board, then they cut a cross on it with a ladle and eat it with hot salami sprinkled with vinegar. Polenta is typically served daily in the winter with roasted birds, pork, game, fish, and with *frico*, a grated cheese cooked in a pan until it is crisp. Venison is served on special occasions and is frequently cooked in wine and served with polenta.

Thick soups are a mainstay of Friuli-Venezia Giulia cuisine, just as pasta is in other parts of Italy. Although many of these soups are made with dried beans they are further thickened with barley. *Cialzon*, local ravioli, are served in soup. Classic *jota* is a vegetable soup made with sauerkraut and cumin. Other soups are made with root vegetables and rice.

Pork is the basis of many dishes. In Friuli-Venezia Giulia almost every family raises pigs for their own use. The pigs are small, brown ones. A traditional dish is white turnips served with sausages or pork meat. There is even a soup with pasta, beans, and pork rind. Pork roasts are cooked on a spit with herbs that permeate the air. The well-known local prosciutto of San Daniele in the northern mountainous area has a sweet taste.

Milk is often used to cook pork and *bollito misto* (boiled meats) are eaten with *brovada*. The latter is a relish of turnips fermented for 30 days in marc (the residue of grapes left after pressing out the juice for wine). This relish is the most typical food of the area. When used with bean soup, it is called *fasui e broade*, beans and *brovade*.

Bigoli is a pasta of Venetian origin. It is a thick spaghetti which is made by pressing pasta dough through a small tool called a *bigolaro*. The dough is made with flour, butter, and eggs. *Bigoli* pasta is frequently served with anchovy sauce or with a sauce made with onion and mashed duck giblets.

Another traditional dish is *cialzons*, a half-moon shaped ravioli stuffed with different ingredients, such as candied citron, spices, herbs, golden raisins, spinach or even grated chocolate. *Cialzons* are served with ricotta and local cheese. The local cheese is Montasio, a table cheese when it is fresh, and grated when aged.

Trieste, street in medieval section.
Photo collection of the author.

Gnocchi, part of the heritage of Austria, are very popular in Friuli-Venezia Giulia. They can be made small or large, round, square, or oval. They are usually made with potatoes mixed with smoked ricotta, pumpkin, or with eggplant and stuffed with prunes or ham.

Friuli has good local seafood and fish along the coast. *Risotto alla marinara* is a specialty in that area. The bigger fish are cooked on the grill or fried.

Other specialties of Friuli-Venezia Giulia are *gulash* with sauerkraut and sausages with sauerkraut. At Easter people eat ham baked in bread with a horseradish sauce. Throughout Venezia Giulia there is a variety of sweet and sour flavors.

The sweets are very hardy. They are mostly made with dried or fresh fruit and spices, especially cinnamon. Apples are a favorite pastry filling. *Gubana* is a filled sweet bread that is rolled like a jelly roll. *Pinza* is another sweet bread that is made with dried figs. *Millefeuille* is a pastry filled with nuts, spices, and a little liqueur. Another favorite dessert, *castagnole*, is a chestnut-shaped sweet *gnocchi*. These are found throughout Friuli. *Zelten* is a rich Christmas cake, similar to a fruitcake, but lighter. Strudel filled with savory or sweet ingredients, is prevalent all over the region.

Wines

A large variety of grapes are grown in the foothills of Friuli-Venezia Giulia. Wines produced in this region are: Aquilea, Grave from Friuli, Carso, Collio Goriziano, Isonzo Colli, Orientali from Friuli and Latisana. Pinot Grigio is the region's most famous wine.

Un Pranzo d'Anatra
A Duck Dinner

Serves 6

Bigoli con Salsa d'Anatra
Spaghetti with Duck Sauce

Anatra Arrostita
Roasted Duck

Verze e Patate
Savoy Cabbage and Potatoes

Torta di Castagne
Chestnut Torte

Caffè
Coffee

A Duck Dinner

The mountainous region of Friuli-Venezia Guilia has an abundance of wild game, including duck, and there are numerous recipes for preparing and cooking game.

Since wild duck is not readily available in our markets or is liked by everyone, I decided to use domestic duck in this dinner of typical dishes of Friuli-Venezia Guilia.

For the first course a duck sauce is served with spaghetti. It is cooked with porcini mushrooms, pancetta, onion, herbs, wine, and tomato paste, then diluted with broth.

The roasted ducks for the entree are seasoned with sage, rosemary, and bay leaves, then roasted and sprinkled with brandy. This wonderful duck dish is accompanied by sautéed cabbage and potatoes with butter and garlic.

A traditional fall dessert ends this duck dinner. The chestnut torte is usually prepared for meals in the fall when chestnuts are ripe and hunting season is in full swing.

Preparations

The duck sauce for the spaghetti can be made one or two days ahead and refrigerated. Bring it to a simmer while you are boiling the spaghetti on the evening of the duck dinner.

The ducks for the entree need to cooked that evening. Season the ducks and place the herbs inside the cavity. Then put the two ducks in a roasting pan, ready to be cooked.

While you and your guests are having drinks, roast the ducks. Carve them when cooked and serve them hot.

Early in the afternoon prepare the cabbage and potatoes in a large saucepan with water and set them aside. Boil the cabbage and potatoes in the early evening, drain, and then cook them in oil and butter and garlic. Reheat the vegetables at dinner time.

The chestnut torte can be made either the day before or on the morning of the dinner.

Bigoli con Salsa d'Anatra
Spaghetti with Duck Sauce

Serves 6

 Bigoli, Venetian in origin, are thick spaghetti which are made by pressing pasta dough through a small tool called a *bigolaro*. The dough is made with whole wheat flour, butter, and eggs. Bigoli are the only traditional pasta made with whole wheat flour. Most people outside of Italy use commercially made pasta.

1/2 cup dried porcini mushrooms
2 cups hot water
1/4 cup olive oil
1 (5 to 6 pound) domestic duck, skinned, meat cut into 1-inch pieces, save the bones
2 large onions, chopped
1/3 cup chopped pancetta or bacon
1/2 pound chicken livers, coarsely chopped
2 bay leaves

1 large sprig fresh rosemary
3 garlic cloves
1 cup dry white wine
4 tablespoons tomato paste
3 cups broth
1 teaspoon salt
1/2 teaspoon ground pepper
1 pound regular spaghetti
1/2 cup freshly grated Parmesan cheese

 Soak the porcini in a medium bowl with two cups of hot water and let them soak for 30 minutes. Drain the porcini and save the liquid for later. Chop the porcini and set them aside.

 Heat the olive oil in a large Dutch oven over medium heat. Add the duck pieces and the bones and sauté for about 8 minutes or until golden in color. Drain off all but 1 tablespoon of the duck fat.

 Add the chopped onion and pancetta and sauté until the onion and pancetta are golden in color, about 5 minutes. Add the chopped chicken livers and the porcini and continue to sauté for 2 more minutes, stirring often. Then add the bay leaves, rosemary and garlic cloves and sauté for 5 more minutes. Add the wine and cook until almost all of the liquid has evaporated, stirring often, about 4 minutes.

 Mix in the tomato paste, slowly pour in the broth and reserved mushroom liquid, leaving any sediment in bowl . Bring to a boil. Reduce heat to low and simmer until the duck meat is tender, about 1 hour.

 Remove the bones, bay leaves, rosemary sprig and garlic cloves from the sauce. Skim off any fat from the surface and simmer the sauce until it thickens, about 10 minutes. Season with salt and pepper and mix thoroughly.

Cook pasta in a large pot of boiling salted water until tender but al dente. Drain the pasta thoroughly, pour it back into the same pot and pour 1/2 cup of the duck sauce over the pasta. Toss the pasta and spoon remaining duck sauce over it. Sprinkle with Parmesan cheese, toss again, and serve.

The duck sauce can be made one to two days ahead and refrigerated. Bring to a simmer before using.

Anatra Arrostita
Roasted Duck

Serves 6

2 domestic ducks, 4 to 5 pounds each	2 small onions, cut in halves
1 tablespoon salt	4 bay leaves, coarsely broken
2 teaspoons freshly ground black pepper	2 sprigs sage, plus 1 sprig, chopped
Juice of 2 lemons	2 sprigs, rosemary, plus 1 sprig, chopped
	8 tablespoons brandy

Remove the duck gizzard, liver and excess fat and keep for another use.

Sprinkle the ducks inside and out with salt and pepper and lemon juice. Place the onions inside the cavity and 1 bay leaf, 1 sprig sage, 1 sprig rosemary for each duck. Sprinkle the remainder of the bay leaves, the chopped sage and rosemary over the outside of the ducks.

Place the 2 ducks in a roasting pan and place it in a preheated 400° F. oven, with the breasts side down, for about 30 minutes. Turn the birds over, prick the skins all over with a fork to let the melting fat escape. Bake for another 30 minutes longer. Remove the pan from the oven, pour off all the fat. Pour the brandy over the ducks, return the ducks to the oven, and roast until the ducks are done.

If less done duck meat is desired, roast the ducks for less time.

To serve, carve each duck into 6 parts. Remove the onion, bay leaves, rosemary and sage sprigs. Serve 2 pieces of duck per person, one light and one dark meat.

Verze e Patate
Savoy Cabbage and Potatoes

Serves 6

*1 large Savoy cabbage, about 2
    pounds
3 medium potatoes
1/4 cup olive oil
2 tablespoons unsalted butter*

*3 garlic cloves, crushed
1 teaspoon salt
1 teaspoon freshly ground black
    pepper*

Remove outside damaged leaves, core the cabbage and cut the leaves into thin strips.

Peel and cut the potatoes into quarters. Bring about 4 quarts of water to a boil in a large saucepan, add the potatoes first, and cook them for about 10 minutes. Add the cabbage and cook both vegetables until they are tender, about 10 to 15 minutes longer. Drain the vegetables thoroughly.

Heat the oil and butter in a large skillet over medium heat and brown the garlic. Then add the cabbage and potatoes and season with salt and pepper. Use a fork to mash the vegetables coarsely, but leave lots of lumps.

Continue sautéing until all of the liquid of the vegetables has evaporated, for a few minutes.

Discard the garlic cloves, add more seasoning, if needed, and then serve the vegetables with the roasted duck.

Torta di Castagne
Chestnut Torte

Serves 6 or more

*1 pound fresh chestnuts, or 2 cups
    canned unsweetened chestnut
    puree*
1 1/4 cups milk
5 eggs, separated
1 cup sugar

*8 tablespoons (1 stick) butter,
    softened*
*1 cup blanched almonds, finely
    chopped*
Grated rind of 1 lemon
4 ounces dark chocolate, grated
2 tablespoons cognac

Grease and lightly flour a 10-inch cake pan. If using fresh chestnuts, cut them in half vertically and put them under the broiler. Let them brown on both sides, them peel them while still hot.

In a small saucepan bring the milk to a boil over medium heat. Add the peeled chestnuts and simmer them for about 15 minutes, or until they are soft. Drain the chestnuts and puree them in the bowl of a food processor. Use the canned chestnut puree as is.

Beat the egg yolks with the sugar. Add the butter, chestnuts, almonds, grated lemon rind, chocolate, and cognac. Then beat until a smooth and light mixture is formed.

Beat the egg whites until stiff and gently fold them into the chestnut mixture. Carefully pour the batter into the prepared pan and bake in a preheated 350° F. oven for about 50 to 60 minutes or until a cake tester inserted in the center comes out clean.

Cool the torte on a wire rack, then remove it from the pan. Cut into wedges and serve.

Una Cena Robusta
A Hardy Meal

Serves 6

Minestra di Fagioli
Bean Soup

Gulasch (Gulyas) Triestino
Goulash Trieste Style

Patate alla Triestina
Potatoes Trieste style

Insalata di Arugula
Arugula Salad

Torta di Mele
Apple Pie

Caffè
Coffee

A Hardy Meal

This is a typical winter meal of Friuli-Venezia Giulia. Its dishes are tasty and give a warm feeling.

A bean soup, flavored with pancetta and vegetables starts this hardy meal. Small pasta is added to the soup as a balance to the pasta.

The entree of goulash consists of beef sautéed with prosciutto and onions. The meat is then slowly cooked with hot peppers, sage, rosemary, and a bay leaf, and tomatoes. This very tender and delicious meat is accompanied by crisp, browned potato slices.

The arugula and fennel salad is a refreshing and tangy interlude after the tasty and rich sauce of the goulash.

Flavorful golden delicious apples are used in a pie for the dessert that ends this hardy meal.

Preparations

If possible make the bean soup and the goulash at least a day ahead so that the flavors can meld. When making the bean soup, do not add the pasta until just before it is ready to be served. It should be added when you reheat the soup in the evening of the dinner and cooked at that time.

You can prepare the potatoes in the early afternoon by boiling and slicing them. Also sauté the onion and then add it to the potatoes, mash them with a fork and stop the cooking. Finish cooking the potatoes just before dinner.

Wash, dry, and break the arugula into pieces in the morning and slice the fennel bulbs into wedges. Place them both in a plastic bag and refrigerate. Make the dressing for the salad and toss it with the salad ingredients just before serving.

The pie may be made a day ahead and reheated, if desired. A scoop of ice cream is optional.

Minestra di Fagioli
Bean Soup

Serves 6

1 1/2 cups dry borlotti beans (cran
  berry beans)
1/4 cup olive oil
1 onion, finely chopped
1/4 cup pancetta, chopped in small
  cubes
1 celery stalk, finely chopped
1 carrot, finely chopped
1 garlic clove, finely chopped
1 tablespoon chopped parsley

2 sage leaves, finely chopped
Salt
3 cups broth
3/4 cup pasta, such as little shells or
  small macaroni
6 tablespoons extra virgin olive oil,
  for garnish
Freshly ground black pepper
Grated Parmesan cheese, optional

Soak the dry borlotti beans overnight. Drain and place them in a large saucepan with a little water and bring to a boil. As soon as it boils, drain the beans and discard the water.

Place the beans back in the large saucepan with enough water to cover the beans and bring to a boil. Cover the saucepan and boil on low heat for about 1 hour, or until the beans are tender, but still with a little firmness.

Place the olive oil in a large pan, add the onion, pancetta, celery, carrot, garlic, parsley, and sage and sauté over medium heat until the onion is limp and the pancetta starts to color, about 10 minutes.

Then add the sautéed mixture and the broth to the bean broth. Also add salt, mix, and bring to a boil. Add the pasta and cook for another 10 minutes, stirring occasionally.

Serve the soup warm with one tablespoon extra virgin olive oil in each bowl and sprinkle with ground pepper.

Place a bowl of grated Parmesan cheese on the table for those who want to use it.

Gulasch (Gulyas) Triestino
Goulash Trieste Style

Serves 6

3 ounces fat from prosciutto (raw
  ham) cut into small cubes or
  3 ounces of pancetta
1 tablespoon unsalted butter
2 large onions, thinly sliced
3 pounds lean beef, cut into large
  cubes
1 teaspoon salt
1 hot chili pepper, finely chopped or
  1/2 teaspoon hot pepper flakes

1 pound canned peeled tomatoes,
  chopped
2 tablespoons tomato paste
1/2 tablespoon dried rosemary
1/2 tablespoon dried sage
1 bay leaf
1 cup broth
1 tablespoon paprika

Melt the prosciutto fat with the butter in a large skillet or Dutch oven, over medium-high heat. When the fat starts to become crisp, add the onions. Sauté the onions until translucent and limp, then add the cubed beef. Season with salt and add the chopped chili. Continue cooking, over high heat, stirring until the meat has browned.

Add the chopped tomatoes, tomato paste, rosemary, sage and bay leaf. Add the broth and paprika. Mix thoroughly and bring back to a boil. When boiling, cover, and reduce the heat to low and simmer for about 1 and 1/2 hours or until the meat is tender. Add more broth, if the goulash starts to get too dry.

Serve the goulash with the sauce.

Patate alla Triestina
Potatoes Trieste Style

Serves 6

2 pounds potatoes
2 tablespoons unsalted butter
3 tablespoons olive oil
1 onion, thinly sliced

1 teaspoon salt
1/2 teaspoon freshly ground black
  pepper
1/2 cup broth

Boil the potatoes in salted water in a saucepan until tender, then drain. Peel and cut the potatoes into slices.

Heat the butter and oil in a large non stick frying pan, over medium heat. Add the sliced onion and sauté the onion slices until they are soft and golden, then add the boiled potatoes. Season them with salt and pepper and add the broth. Mix thoroughly and then using a fork crush the potatoes. They should be lumpy, not smooth like mashed potato. Cook the potatoes over medium heat until they are crisp and brown underneath. Turn the potato out onto a plate, put another plate on top and turn over. Then slide the potatoes back into the pan to brown the other side or put the pan under a hot broiler for a few minutes until brown. Serve the potatoes with the goulash.

Insalata di Arugula
Arugula Salad

Serves 6

In Friuli-Venezia Giulia people use wild salad leaves found on their land, such as arugula. In this country we do not have wild arugula, only the cultivated kind.

3 large bunches arugula
2 large fennel bulbs
1/4 cup extra virgin olive oil
Juice of 1 large lemon

1/2 teaspoon salt
1/4 teaspoon freshly ground black
  pepper

Wash and dry the arugula, remove the tough stems and break the leaves into pieces. Remove the outside leaves of the fennel and cut off the stalks and feathery tops. Cut the fennel bulb lengthwise into quarters, then slice them into very fine lengthwise slices.

Place the sliced fennel and arugula in a large bowl. Combine the olive oil, lemon juice, salt and pepper in a small bowl. Pour the dressing over the salad, toss thoroughly, and serve.

Torta di Mele
Apple Pie

Serves 6 to 8

Dough

1 1/2 cups flour

1 1/2 teaspoons sugar

1 teaspoon salt

1/2 cup olive oil

2 tablespoons milk

1 tablespoon rum

Make the pastry by mixing together the flour, sugar and salt. Add the olive oil and milk and mix together until there is a crumb texture. Using your hands work the mass into a soft dough, adding more milk if necessary. Wrap the pastry in plastic wrap and let it sit while preparing the filling.

Filling

6 cups sliced, peeled Golden
 Delicious apples (8-9 apples)

1/2 cup sugar

1/2 cup raisins

1/2 teaspoon flour

1 teaspoon nutmeg

2 teaspoons cinnamon

Juice of a small lemon

1 cup almonds or walnuts, coarsely
 ground

In a large bowl mix all of the ingredients for the filling together. Pat the pastry dough into the bottom and up the sides of a 9-inch pie plate. Place the apple filling into the pastry-lined pie plate.

Topping

1/2 cup flour

5 tablespoons butter, melted

1/2 cup sugar

Combine the flour, melted butter and sugar until there is a crumb mixture and sprinkle the crumbs over the top of the apples.

Place the pie dish on a cookie sheet in a preheated 350° F. oven for about 1 and 1/2 hours, or until it is a golden color. Remove and place the pie dish on a wire rack to cool. The pie will firm as it cools.

Serve the pie warm or at room temperature. Cut into wedges and serve with a scoop of ice cream.

Veneto

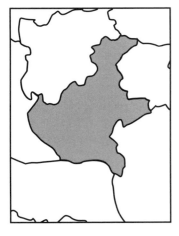

The early settlers of Venice reached the area after fleeing northern invaders. Their cooking was rustic as it was based on the game they hunted on the lagoon's islands. They also fished from the seas surrounding them and much of the early cooking of Veneto was based on seafood.

By the eleventh century Venice, the capital of the Veneto region, was regarded as the fashion leader in food and table manners. Many of the spices of the Far East came to Europe by the way of Venice. The men of the region were seafaring merchants who brought new foods and spices back to their homes. Salt and pepper first came to Europe through Venice as did saffron and tarragon, which were brought by the returning crusaders. Marco Polo brought back ginger from China.

The people of Venice were the first to use a fork (originally called *piron*) in the eleventh century. Historians say that the first napkins were used on the tables of Venice. Exquisite hand-blown glass made on the island of Murano in the Venice lagoon enriched the tables of the early Venetians.

Today the Veneto region, located in the northeastern part of Italy, is one of the most populated in Italy encompassing not only Venice but also the historical cities of Verona, Vicenza, and Padova.

The Veneto region is surrounded by the regions of northeastern Italy. A small area of Veneto's border touches Austria. Much of the Veneto region is covered by water including rivers, streams, lakes, canals, and lagoons. The two main rivers are the Po and l'Adige.

The best dishes of the Veneto region are based on seafood. Antipasto is made with large and small shrimp, squid, crab, cuttlefish, baby octopus, and shellfish. Much of the seafood is served simply with olive oil, chopped parsley, and lemon juice. *Granzeola* is a typical antipasto of poached crab seasoned with olive oil, lemon juice, salt, and pepper. Shellfish soup is simply prepared with olive oil, white wine, and garlic. *Scampi* are dipped in a batter and fried. Scallops are cooked with parsley, garlic, and white wine. Eel is cooked with Marsala wine. *Moleche* are tiny soft-shelled crabs of Murano, which are harvested in the spring and autumn when they molt. These tiny crabs are dipped live in egg batter with garlic and parsley and then fried.

Venetians who lived far from the sea where fresh fish was not available adopted *stoccafisso*, a dried salted cod. *Stoccafisso*, called *baccala* in Veneto, has to be soaked for many hours in cold water until the salt is gone, with the water being changed often. Then the salted cod is cooked with oil, onions, garlic, parsley, anchovy fillets, milk, and Parmesan cheese. This dish is called salt cod Vicenza style. Another variation of salt cod is called cream of salt cod. Presoaked cod is boiled, mashed to a paste, and seasoned with olive oil, garlic, parsley, and pepper. This is served with polenta.

Since Venice was Europe's point of contact with the Near and Far East, the Venetians absorbed culinary ideas from the Arabs. One dish of Arab origin is *pesce in saor*. This is sweet and sour fish made with pine nuts and raisins. It has become a typical dish of the region.

More than forty different delicious risottos are made in Venice. Rice is typically combined with eel, cuttlefish, scallops, quail, tripe, asparagus, spinach, artichokes, cabbage, peas, zucchini, raisins, fennel, pork sausage, mutton, chicken, veal, and mushrooms.

There are only two traditional pasta dishes of Venice. One is called *pasta e fasoi* (pasta and beans), which is a very thick soup. The other pasta is *bigoli*, a thick spaghetti made with flour, butter and eggs — frequently duck eggs. The sauce used to dress bigoli is typically made with anchovies. A sauce made with onion and duck giblets is also frequently served with bigoli.

The Venetians are not meat-lovers. They prefer to eat poultry — ducks, turkeys, chickens, geese, and guinea hens — all are cooked in many ways. Goose is flavored with celery. Ducks are stuffed with pork and sausage meat, garlic, parsley, Parmesan cheese, and salt and pepper. Duck is also cooked in a spicy sauce with anchovies, pork, sausage, and bacon and seasoned with sage, rosemary, lemon, salt, and pepper.

Guinea hen is served with *peverada*, a sauce made with vinegar, lemon juice, anchovies, chicken livers, bread crumbs, grana cheese (similar to Parmesan cheese), peppercorns, lemon peel, and ginger.

Wild duck is marinated in wine vinegar with thyme and marjoram for twelve hours, then cooked with bacon, onion, anchovies, capers, and white wine. This is a typical and traditional dish of the valleys of Veneto.

Another traditional dish is called *paeta al malgaragno*. It is turkey cooked with pomegranate juice and is served with a sauce of pomegranate juice including the seeds.

Fegato alla Veneziana, liver Venetian style, is cooked with onion, vinegar, parsley, salt, and pepper. Another variation is a sweet and sour liver dish in which the liver is dipped in flour, then egg, then bread crumbs, and then fried. The sauce for this liver is made with butter, lemon juice, and sugar.

Polenta is very popular in the Veneto region. It was once eaten for breakfast, lunch, and dinner and as an accompaniment to the main course. The Venetians first started making polenta when corn came to Venice from America.

They liked the taste and mass of the corn-based porridge better than the one based on wheat, which they had been making previously. Polenta became so popular that it was sold by street vendors in Venice, similar to the pasta merchants in Naples. Today there are two kinds of corn-based polenta sold in Veneto, one made with white cornmeal and the other with yellow.

The Venetians like polenta soft and creamy and they use a coarse grind of cornmeal. In some areas of Veneto, however, they make the polenta firm, place the polenta on a board, then slice it and serve it either fried or grilled. Now polenta is typically served with meat, fish, game or stews., although sometimes it is cooked with milk and water and served merely with butter and cheese.

Cows and pigs are raised in the hills and mountains in the northern part of the Veneto region. Hams and sausages are made there. The Venetian hams are lean and tasty. Luganega sausages are grilled, fried or stewed in broth.

The most famous Venetian cheeses are the hard and strong-flavored such as Asiago and Vezzena. The latter is a table cheese when fresh and a grating cheese when aged from six to eighteen months. Smoked ricotta is also made in the Veneto region.

Island of S. Giorgio Maggiore, Venice.
Photo sourtesy of Frank Spadarella.

Veneto is very rich in vegetables many of which are sold throughout Italy. Treviso is famous for its radicchio rosso. The well-known asparagus of Bassano del Grappa is a white asparagus that is generally served with a beaten-egg sauce.

Some of the vegetable dishes commonly prepared in Veneto are: artichoke hearts simmered in broth with olive oil and lemon; green beans flavored with anchovies; pumpkins deep-fried or baked with garlic, vinegar, and basil; green and yellow peppers cooked with olive oil, garlic, tomatoes, parsley, salt, and pepper; and cabbage cooked slowly with white wine and rosemary.

The most successful pudding, *tiramisu*, was created in the town of Treviso. It is now made all over Italy as well as abroad. *Tiramisu* means "pick me up." It was created more than thirty years ago in Treviso by the owner of a restaurant called, El Toula. *Tiramisu* is a dessert made in layers with *savoiardi* (lady fingers) soaked in liqueur and coffee, and layered with mascarpone and egg cream.

Other sweets of the Veneto region are very simple cookies or sweet focaccie. They are usually served with a glass of sweet wine. *Torta sabbiosa*, a light sponge cake made with potato-flour and perfumed with vanilla and anise-flavored alcohol, is one of the most popular cakes.

Crema fritta, fried cream, is also a traditional dessert. *Frittelle*, carnival fritters, are made with pine nuts, raisins, and candied fruit peel. They are also made with apples and wine. Puddings made with milk are very popular. A bread pudding called *torta nicolotta*, originally made by the fishermen, is made with bread flour, raisins, fennel seeds, and milk.

Wines

The best wines from the Veneto region are Valpolicella, Bardolino and Soave. All of Veneto's wines are produced in the hills around Verona.

Soave is an ideal white wine to serve with hors d'oeuvres and fish. Bardolino is a red, light-bodied wine typically served as an aperitif with a simple antipasto. It is also served with poultry, pigeon, rabbit, or white meat.

Tocai Rosso, Breganze-Cabernet and Venegazzu, made from a blend of Bordeaux grapes, are the most admired of the Veneto wines. Amarone is a dry red Recioto, and is the only one in Veneto that is slow-aged. When aged, it is bitter but with flavors of cherry. The name amarone means bitter. This wine pairs well with red meat, game, or rich sauces.

Prosecco can be sparkling, dry or semi-sweet. It is a favorite of Venetians.

Festa di Mare Veneziana
Venetian Seafood Feast

Serves 6

Antipasto di Cape Sante
Scallops Antipasto

Crema di Scampi
Cream of Shrimp Soup

Sfogi in Saor-Sogliole in Sapore
Sole in Sweet-and-Sour Sauce

Asparagi in Salsa
Asparagus with Sauce

Radicchio con Arugula
Radicchio and Arugula Salad

Semifreddo di Cioccolato
Frozen Chocolate Mousse

Caffè
Coffee

Venetian Seafood Feast

This is a perfect menu for seafood lovers. In planning this menu I used the seafood and fish prevalent to the Veneto region and the traditional recipes of that region.

An antipasto of scallops cooked with wine, lemon, parsley and garlic starts this great meal.

This is followed by a cream of shrimp soup as the first course. The soup has the delicate pink color of shrimp and is very tasty and creamy but without any actual cream — a most unusual dish.

The entree is fillet of sole. It is a very unusual dish with an Arab flavor. The fillets are floured, then fried, then placed in a sauce to marinate. The sauce is made with onions, vinegar, wine, raisins, pine nuts, and bay leaves and seasoned with salt and pepper. The asparagus that accompanies the fish is dressed with a sauce of olive oil, lemon juice, and mashed hard-boiled eggs.

The salad of radicchio and arugula is a refreshing interlude. A smooth, frozen chocolate mousse ends this Venetian seafood feast.

Preparations

The antipasto of scallops should be cooked in the evening while your guests are having drinks, and just before you are going to serve it. This will take only about 5 to 6 minutes to prepare. However, in the morning prepare the chopped garlic and parsley and refrigerate. Measure the bread crumbs and keep them in a container, so that everything is ready for you.

Make the cream of shrimp in the morning up to the point of adding the shrimp. Refrigerate the soup and reheat it to a boil in the evening. Then just before you are going to serve the soup, add the cut shrimp and cook them for two minutes. Also prepare the bread cubes ahead of time. Then place them on a baking sheet and toast them in the oven in the evening.

Make the fillets of sole completely with the sauce one or two days ahead and refrigerate. Bring to room temperature before serving them.

You can cook the asparagus and either keep it at room temperature, or store it in the refrigerator until half an hour before serving so that it warms up. Make the sauce ahead of time and either serve it hot or cold. Pour the sauce over the asparagus immediately after they are cooked if serving them hot. If serving the asparagus cold, add the sauce just before serving them.

Clean and cut the salad ingredients early in the day and refrigerate them. Also make the dressing early in the day.

Prepare the chocolate mousse the day before, or on the morning of the dinner, and freeze it. Remove the mousse from the freezer one hour before serving and turn the mold upside down on a serving platter. Cut it into pieces and serve.

Antipasto di Cape Sante
Scallops Antipasto

Serves 6

9 large scallops, cut in half, or 18
   small ones
1/2 cup fine dry bread crumbs
3 tablespoons olive oil
3 tablespoons unsalted butter
1 garlic clove, finely chopped

3 tablespoons fresh chopped parsley
1/2 teaspoon salt
1/2 teaspoon freshly ground black
   pepper
1/2 cup dry white wine
Juice of 1 lemon

Coat the scallops with the bread crumbs pressing the scallops into the crumbs so that the crumbs will adhere.

Heat the olive oil and butter in a large skillet over medium heat and sauté the chopped garlic and parsley for a few minutes. Add the scallops and sauté gently for a few more minutes turning them over carefully. Season with salt and pepper and add the wine and the lemon juice and continue cooking for several minutes or until the scallops become translucent and the wine has evaporated.

Serve 3 pieces of scallops per person.

Crema di Scampi
Cream of Shrimp

Serves 6

18 medium size shrimps, with heads, if possible	1 1/2 cups tomato sauce
3 tablespoons butter	1/2 cup brandy
3 tablespoons flour	1/4 teaspoon hot chili pepper
6 cups shrimp broth	4 slices country bread
	Olive oil

Wash the shrimp and remove the heads. Peel the shrimp, season them with salt and set them aside.

Shrimp Broth

6 cups water	2 sprigs parsley
1 cup dry white wine	Tops of fennel
Heads and shells of shrimp	1 garlic clove
1 carrot, cut in half	1 vegetable bouillon cube
Celery leaves	Salt

Prepare the broth by bringing the water and wine to a boil in a large saucepan. Add the heads and shells of the shrimp, carrot, celery leaves, fennel tops, garlic, bouillon cube, and season with salt. Boil, covered, over low heat for about 45 minutes, then strain the broth through a colander.

Melt the butter in a large saucepan over medium heat, add the flour and stir constantly until the flour is well mixed into the butter. Remove the saucepan from the heat, add half of the broth all at once and mix constantly with a whisk until completely incorporated. Place the saucepan back on the heat and cook the soup, mixing often, for 15 minutes. After 10 minutes of cooking, add the tomato sauce, the brandy and chili pepper. Mix thoroughly and continue cooking. After the soup has cooked, add some more shrimp broth until the soup has the right consistency, not too thick, and not too thin for a cream.

Cut the peeled shrimp in 2 or 3 pieces, add them to the cream soup and gently boil them for few minutes.

In the meantime, brush the slices of bread with some olive oil and then cut them into small cubes. Toast the cubed bread in a hot skillet, without adding any oil, until golden in color, or toast them in a baking sheet in the oven.

Serve the cream of shrimp soup in individual soup bowls. Place the toasted bread cubes in a serving bowl and pass them around.

Sfogi in Saor-Sogliole in Sapore
Sole in Sweet-and-Sour Sauce

Serves 6

Saor is dialect for *sapore*, which means flavor. Marinating in vinegar was an old Italian way of preserving fish before refrigeration. This sweet and sour recipe is an Arab one. Traditionally this dish is served on the night of the Feast of the Holy Redeemer, the third Sunday in July. It is a day of great celebration, ending in the evening with fireworks.

6 fillets of sole, sand dabs, or other delicate fish
1 teaspoon salt
1/2 cup flour
1/3 to 1/2 cup olive oil
1 onion, sliced
1/2 cup white wine vinegar

1 cup dry white wine
4 tablespoons golden raisins
4 tablespoons pine nuts
2 bay leaves
1/2 teaspoon each salt and white pepper

Season the fillets of sole with salt and dredge them in the flour, shaking off the excess. Heat the olive oil in a large skillet over medium heat. When the oil is hot, but not smoking, add the fillets and sauté them until golden brown on both sides about 3 to 5 minutes per side, depending on thickness of the fillets. Drain the fillets on paper towels.

In the same frying skillet and same oil, add the sliced onion and sauté until the onion is soft but not brown. Add the vinegar, wine, raisins, pine nuts and bay leaves. Season with salt and pepper and simmer the sauce over low heat for 10 minutes.

Arrange the fried fillets of sole in a large glass dish and pour the onion and vinegar mixture over them.

Leave the sole to marinate, covered, for several hours before serving it cold. It is best marinated for at least 1 to 2 days to absorb the flavors. Always serve this dish at room temperature.

Asparagi in Salsa
Asparagus with Sauce

Serves 6

2 pounds asparagus
3 eggs, hard boiled
2 tablespoons lemon juice
1/2 cup extra virgin olive oil

1/4 teaspoon salt
1/4 teaspoon freshly ground black
  pepper

Trim the asparagus of any leaves below the tip and cut off the tough ends. Wash the asparagus under cold water and tie them in bundles with string or rubber bands

Place the asparagus upright in an asparagus cooker or stock pot. Add about 3 inches of cold salted water.

Bring to a boil, cover and cook over high heat for 4 to 6 minutes, depending on the thickness of the asparagus. Use a pointed knife to pierce the stalks, and if it penetrates, the asparagus is done. Do not overcook them.

Carefully lift out the asparagus , remove the strings, and place them on a heated platter.

Break up the hard boiled eggs with a fork, mash them and place them in a small bowl. Add the lemon juice and olive oil and season with salt and pepper. Combine the mixture until completely blended like a sauce.

The asparagus can be served hot or cold. It serving them hot, pour the sauce over the asparagus immediately after they are cooked. If serving cold, pour the sauce over the asparagus just before serving.

Radicchio con Arugula
Radicchio and Arugula Salad

Serves 6

There are two kinds of red radicchio: radicchio rosso di Treviso and radicchio variegato di Castelfranco. The radicchio di Treviso has long crisp leaves with a sweet flavor. Radicchio di Castelfranco has round leaves with a slightly more bitter taste. Both radicchio are grown in the Veneto region and are in season from November to March.

A new red radicchio was developed near Chioggia, south of Venice. This radicchio grows all year round and is the one most used in the United States. It is round-cabbage-like with red leaves, and is crisp and pretty. Sadly it does not have the delicate flavor of the two original radicchio varieties.

The three types of radicchio are used in salads, grilled as a vegetable and cooked in risotto al radicchio, a traditional dish made with radicchio di Treviso.

3 heads radicchio
1 large bunch arugula, stems
   removed
5 tablespoons extra virgin olive oil

1 tablespoon vinegar
1/2 teaspoon salt
1/2 teaspoon freshly ground black
   pepper

Rinse and dry the radicchio and arugula. Cut the radicchio into 1/2-inch wide strips and remove the hard core in the middle. Cut the arugula leaves coarsely. Place the radicchio and arugula in a large salad bowl.

Make the dressing by mixing together the olive oil and vinegar and season with salt an pepper. Pour the dressing over the salad just before serving.

Semifreddo di Cioccolato
Frozen Chocolate Mousse

Serves 6

8 ounces bitter or dark chocolate
3 tablespoons milk
6 eggs, separated

2 tablespoons grated orange zest
1 1/4 cups heavy cream

Melt the chocolate with the milk over boiling water in the top of a double boiler over medium heat. Remove from heat. Beat in the egg yolks, one at a time, and then add the grated orange zest.

Whip the cream in a small bowl and then fold it into the chocolate. Whip the egg whites in another bowl until stiff and then fold them gently into the chocolate mixture.

Pour the mixture into a mold lined with plastic wrap so that the frozen mousse can be easily removed. Place the mold into the freezer for several hours until the mixture hardens. Remove the mold from the freezer 1 hour before serving and turn the mold upside down onto a serving platter. Remove the plastic wrap, cut the mold into pieces, and serve.

Un Pranzo Festivo
A Holiday Dinner

Serves 8

Carpaccio Originale di Cipriani
Original Carpaccio from Cipriani

Risotto con Cavolo
Risotto with Cabbage

Paeta Arosta al Malgaragno
Roasted Turkey with Pomegranates

Patate alla Veneziana
Potatoes Venetian Style

Finocchi Gratinati
Fennel au Gratin

Tiramisu
Tiramisu

Caffe
Coffee

A Holiday Dinner

Holidays in Italy are celebrated in grand style, with family and friends enjoying a large meal together. Holiday meals can last 3 to 4 hours with everyone enjoying the food and camaraderie. For this holiday dinner I chose festive recipes from the Veneto region.

I start the meal with beef carpaccio, a recipe from Venice invented by Arrigo Cipriani, a famous restaurateur. This appetizer consists of thinly sliced raw beef served with a sauce of mayonnaise, mustard, cognac, Worcestershire sauce, and Tabasco sauce.

For the first course I am suggesting a risotto made with cabbage. It is one of the many different risottos made in the Veneto region.

The main course is roasted turkey made with pomegranates. This is a traditional Venetian recipe. Sautéed potatoes with onion and crispy fennel accompany the turkey to make a delicious meal.

World-famous Tiramisu dessert is a very light dessert and ends this festive holiday dinner.

Preparations

Prepare the meat for the carpaccio appetizer on the morning of the party. Freeze the meat slightly and then slice it and store the slices in the refrigerator until just before time to assemble it with the sauce. Make the sauce completely for the carpaccio and refrigerate it. Assemble the meat slices in the evening and pour some of the sauce over the meat just before serving.

Make part of the cabbage risotto in early afternoon. Sauté the pancetta, onion, and cabbage and set this aside until just before dinner. Then add the rice and broth and finish cooking the risotto.

Cook the turkey in the afternoon, gauging the time, so that it will be ready when your guests arrive.

You can also prepare the potatoes and fennel in the afternoon. Peel and cut the potatoes and place the pieces in cold water. Thinly slice the onion and set aside wrapped in plastic. Clean, boil and cut the fennel into quarters and place them in a buttered oven proof casserole. Season the fennel quarters with salt and pepper and sprinkle the bread crumbs over them. That evening sauté the potatoes and sliced onions. Place the casserole with the fennel in the oven about 20 minutes before dinner until the top is brown and crispy.

You can make the Tiramisu dessert the day before the party and place it in the refrigerator.

Carpaccio Originale di Cipriani
Original Carpaccio from Cipriani

Serves 8

The name Carpaccio was given to this dish by Arrigo Cipriani of Harry's Bar in Venice in 1961. He named it after the famous painter Carpaccio because there was an exhibition of his paintings in Venice at the time. It was also so named because the colors of the dish reminded him of the reds and whites in the Carpaccio paintings.

Carpaccio is very thinly sliced fillet of beef, dressed with small amounts of mayonnaise to which has been added a touch of mustard, a drop of brandy or cognac, and Tabasco, plus some cream to make the sauce have a fluid consistency. Sometimes a teaspoon of thick tomato sauce is added.

1 1/4 pounds very lean raw beef
1 cup mayonnaise
4 tablespoons whipping cream
1/2 teaspoon dry mustard

1 tablespoon cognac or brandy
1 tablespoon Worcestershire sauce
1/2 teaspoon Tabasco sauce
Salt

Make certain to buy very lean and very tender meat. Fillet is the best. Slice the meat as thin as possible. In order to do this freeze the meat slightly, not hard as a rock, and use an electric knife to slice it.

Place the mayonnaise in a medium bowl, add the whipping cream, mustard, cognac, Worcestershire sauce and Tabasco sauce and beat with a wire whisk until all of the ingredients are completely mixed. Let the sauce rest for 15 minutes to let all of the ingredients blend. Add salt, if needed.

Place the meat slices on individual plates, 4 slices per person. Pour some of the sauce over the meat, but do not cover it completely. Some of the red meat should be visible.

Risotto con Cavolo
Risotto with Cabbage

Serves 8

1 pound cabbage
5 tablespoons unsalted butter
1 tablespoon olive oil
3 ounces pancetta or bacon, finely
 chopped
1/2 medium onion, finely chopped
6 cups beef or chicken broth

1/2 cup dry white wine
3 cups Italian Arborio rice
2/3 cup freshly grated Parmesan
 cheese
Salt and freshly ground black
 pepper, to taste

Wash the cabbage leaves in cold water, drain, and pat them dry with paper towels. Cut the leaves into thin strips about 1/4-inch wide.

Place 3 tablespoons of the butter and the olive oil in a heavy-bottomed saucepan over medium heat. When the butter starts to foam, add the pancetta and chopped onion and sauté for about 5 minutes. While the pancetta and onion are cooking, place the broth in a saucepan and bring it to a low simmer. When the onion is limp, add the cabbage and cook, stirring occasionally, until the cabbage is tender and limp. Add the wine, stir, and let the wine evaporate for a few minutes.

Add the rice to the saucepan and stir to coat it with the pan juices. Add the hot broth, stir, and when the broth is boiling, cover the saucepan. Reduce the heat to low and cook slowly for about 17 minutes. The rice is done when it is cooked through but still al dente.

Remove the saucepan from the heat, stir in the remaining 2 tablespoons of butter and the Parmesan cheese, and mix thoroughly. Season with salt and pepper, stir, and serve at once.

Paeta Arosta al Malgaragno
Roasted Turkey with Pomegranates

Serves 8

The pomegranate juice will darken the turkey sauce and give the meat a pleasing, slightly bitter taste.

1 turkey, about 12 to 13 pounds
4 ripe large pomegranates
Salt
4 tablespoons butter, slightly
  softened
4 to 6 slices bacon

4 tablespoons olive oil
1 slice bacon, finely chopped
1 onion, finely chopped
1/2 teaspoon freshly ground black
  pepper

Remove the giblets and neck from the turkey and save the neck for later use in making broth. Rinse the turkey inside and out with cold running water.

Roll the pomegranates on a hard surface to help get the juice out of the seeds. Make a small hole in the pomegranates and the juice will pour out into a bowl. Continue squeezing 2 pomegranates until the seeds inside comes loose. Another way to remove seeds is to put water into a large bowl and brake up the pomegranate under the water, then drain the seeds.

Rub the turkey inside and out with salt and butter. Tie the turkey legs together and sew up the loose skin at the neck. Place the bacon slices over the breasts of the turkey and secure them firmly with skewers.

Place the turkey into a large oven proof pan and bake in a moderate oven of 325° F. for about 2 and 1/2 to 3 hours, depending on the size of the bird. Baste the turkey often with a brush using the turkey juice that has fallen into the pan.

After the turkey has been roasting for 1 and 1/2 hours, baste it often with the juice of 2 pomegranates and continue roasting until the turkey is tender. Check the turkey leg by pulling it gently. If the meat looks white and the juices run clear the turkey is done.

While the turkey is cooking, chop the giblets. Place them into a small skillet with the olive oil over medium heat. Add the chopped bacon and onion and sauté all together until slightly browned. Add the remaining juice and seeds from the remaining 2 pomegranates and mix thoroughly. Season with salt and pepper, stir and continue cooking over low heat, until the giblets are tender.

When the turkey is cooked, cut off the legs, thighs, wings and cut the breast into slices. Place the turkey pieces and sliced meat into a large oven proof casserole.

Skim the fat off from the turkey drippings and add the drippings to the giblet sauce and mix together. Then spoon some of the giblet sauce over the sliced turkey meat.

Place the casserole in a hot oven of 400° F. for about 10 minutes, just enough time for the turkey meat to absorb some flavor from the sauce.

Serve the turkey with a bowl of the remaining giblets sauce.

The turkey may also be cooked on a spit over an open fire in the same manner. Cook the turkey, make the giblet sauce and add the sauce over the turkey after you have carved it into pieces and slices.

Serve the turkey with the sautéed potatoes and fennel au gratin.

Patate alla Veneziana
Potatoes Venetian Style

Serves 8

5 large potatoes	1 teaspoon salt
4 tablespoons butter	1 teaspoon freshly ground black
4 tablespoons olive oil	pepper
1 large onion, thinly sliced	3 tablespoons fresh chopped parsley

Peel the potatoes, wash them and cut them into pieces. Place the butter and olive oil in a large casserole over medium heat. Add the sliced onion and sauté until the onion is limp, then add the potato pieces and mix well. Sauté them, mixing often until the potatoes are golden brown in color and tender. Season with salt and pepper and sprinkle the chopped parsley over the potatoes. Mix thoroughly and serve with the turkey.

Finocchi Gratinati
Fennel au Gratin

Serves 8

4 large fennel bulbs
6 tablespoons unsalted butter, cut
   into pieces
1 teaspoon salt

1/2 teaspoon freshly ground black
   pepper
1/2 cup dry bread crumbs

    Remove the outside leaves of the fennel bulbs and cut off the stalks and feathery tops. Cut the fennel bulbs in half lengthwise. Boil the fennel in salted water for about 15 minutes, drain well, then cool.

    Butter an oven proof casserole, cut the fennel into quarters and place them in the buttered casserole slightly overlapping. Add the butter pieces, season with salt and pepper and then sprinkle with the bread crumbs.

    Bake in a preheated 400° F. oven for about 15 to 20 minutes or until the top is brown and crispy. Serve the fennel with the turkey.

Tiramisu
Tiramisu

Serves 8

An original recipe from Venice.

6 eggs, separated
6 tablespoons sugar
1 pound fresh Mascarpone cheese,
  room temperature*
2 cups expresso coffee, cooled**
3/4 cup Marsala wine

1 teaspoon vanilla extract
17 ounces ladyfinger cookies
1/2 cup semisweet chocolate,
  finely grated
1/4 cup semisweet chocolate
  shavings

In a large bowl whisk together the egg yolks and sugar until the mixture is very creamy and pale yellow in color. Add the mascarpone cheese and blend together until smooth.

In a medium size mixing bowl, beat the egg whites until stiff peaks form. Gently fold the egg whites into the mascarpone mixture until well blended and smooth.

Place the expresso coffee in a deep bowl, add the Marsala wine, and the vanilla and mix.

Dip one ladyfinger cookie briefly into the expresso mixture, turning to coat it on both sides. Arrange the cookies in a single layer in the bottom of a 10x15-inch glass dish. Pour half of the mascarpone cheese mixture over the ladyfingers, and spread it evenly. Sift 1/4 of the grated chocolate over the top. Repeat the process with the remaining lady fingers and mascarpone mixture. Sift remaining 1/4 cup chocolate over top. Then sprinkle with the chocolate shavings.

Refrigerate the tiramisu for at least 4 hours prior to serving. It is best if prepared one day ahead. Cut into squares and serve.

* Mascarpone is an Italian cream cheese. It, along with the ladyfinger cookies can be found in Italian markets or in large supermarkets. If mascarpone is not available, blend 1 pound cream cheese at room temperature with 1/2 cup whipping cream.

** 2 cups hot water with 8 tablespoons instant expresso powder.

Emilia-Romagna

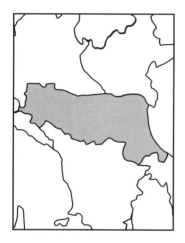

Emilia-Romagna is known in the world of gastronomy for its Parmesan cheese and its prosciutto. The region's cooking is some of the finest in Italy. Although the foods of Emilia are more prominent, the people of Romagna have always enjoyed the plain and simple foods of the countryside and the fruits of the sea.

This regions was traditionally two separate entities which were united for administrative purposes. The combined region stretches from the Adriatic coast through the Po Valley with the Appennines to the southwest. The capital of this region is Bologna and its principal cities are Modena, Parma, and Ravenna.

Emilia-Romagna's rich soil and favorable climate makes it one of the prime agricultural areas in Italy. This region produces wheat, sugar beets, and a myriad of fruits and vegetables. Peaches, plums, cherries, apricots, pears, and strawberries are also cultivated in the Po Valley. Vegetables grown in this region include onions, potatoes, tomatoes, asparagus, zucchini, and mushrooms.

Grapes are grown for eating, wine-making, and to make *aceto balsamico* (balsamic vinegar) the regional treasure. This world-famous vinegar has been made since the eleventh century from unfermented must. It is aged in wooden casks for a number of years.

Milk is imported for drinking. The local milk is used to make cheese such as mozzarella, ricotta, and the most important cheese of Italy —the Parmigiano-Reggiano -- commonly known as, Parmesan cheese.

The cooking of these two regions is different, but it shares a common factor — all of the food is very robust and flavorful. Emilia-Romagna's cooking is some of the finest in Italy. The three basic cooking fats used in the region are butter, lard, and oil, with butter and lard being prevalent because both are produced locally. Butter, cream, cheese, and lard are used in cooking during the winter months when it is very cold. In the warm days of summer, meats are simply grilled or roasted. This also applies to poultry and seafood.

Two of Emilia's delicacies are prosciutto and *culatello*, which is similar to prosciutto, but more spicy . This pear-shaped ham is made by hand by a small number of families. They have passed down the secrets of making *culatello* from one generation to the next. The finest *culatelli* are made by peasants using a very old process of hand massaging the hams during the months when they are maturing. This procedure makes the meat more tender and allows the spices and salt to penetrate.

The Emiliani produce a variety of *salumi* with every province having its own specialties. The towns of Bologna, Reggio, Ferrara, and Modena are known for very unique sausages. In the Bologna area mortadella, a large round sausage made with finely ground pork, pistachios, and wine, is the most famous, and in Reggio it is *fiorettino* and *zucco*. The famous *salama da sugo* is a specialty of Ferrara. It is made with fat and lean pork, calf's and pig's livers and pig's tongue. This melon-shaped sausage is flavored with red wine and spices and is cured for six to seven months. *Cappello da prete* is made in Modena as is *zampone*.

Zampone, the famous sausage of Modena, is shaped like a pig's foot. This sausage was invented four hundred years ago when the town was under siege and the townspeople had no casings for sausage. The problem was solved by using a boned pig's foot to encase the sausage meat.

This pig's-foot shaped sausage is a must for Christmas dinner as Emiliani believe it will bring a prosperous New Year. It is boiled and served with *lenticchie*, lentils. In Emilia-Romagno, *zampone* is always included in a *bollito misto*, a boiled dinner, which might also include beef, turkey, or chicken, veal and sometime a cured pork sausage, *cotechino*. This boiled dinner is served with *salsa verde*, which is a cold green sauce made from pickled cornichons, onion, parsley, and herbs.

Most of these sausages are made of pork and seasoned with garlic, pepper, salt, and spices. Piacenza, in the northwest corner of the region, produces two other famous pork products coppa (cured pork shoulder) and pancetta. Like bacon, pancetta is made from the pork belly.

Three provinces within Emilia-Romagna, Parma, Reggio and Piacenza, claim to have invented Parmesan cheese. However, to keep everyone happy, except the people of Piacenza, it was decided to sell the cheese under the name of Parmigiano-Reggiano.

For centuries there has been a standard procedure in producing Parmesan cheese. Cow's milk from both the morning and evening milking is used to make this cheese. Whey from a previous batch of cheese is added to help the fermentation. The cheese is curdled with calf's rennet, then shaped, and salted and aged for at least twenty-five days. Many of the Parmesan cheeses are aged for a longer period of time, usually a year or more. Parmesan is used to flavor pasta dishes, as well as meat and fish dishes.

As Romagna is a coastal province fish cookery is prevalent with dishes of mackerel, sardines, anchovy, sea bass, and sole. Much of the seafood is used in fish soups. One of the regional specialties is *seppie in umido coi piselli*, which is stuffed cuttlefish cooked with green peas. *Brodetto di Rimini* is a fish soup flavored with onions, tomato, wine vinegar, and olive oil.

Eels of the Comacchio Lagoon, at the mouth of the Po River, are famous all over Italy because of their delicate taste. Some of the best known eel dishes are: *anguilla marinata*, which is eel cooked in wine vinegar with sage, garlic, raisins, and pine nuts; and *anguilla in gratella*, which is eel skewered between bay leaves and grilled. People near the lagoon are fond of their *zuppa di anguilla di Comacchio*, a tomato-based soup with eels that is poured over crisp-toasted bread called *bruschetta*.

Meat is an integral part of the cuisine of Emilia-Romagna. Pork is the basis for many dishes. It is often braised in milk to a creamy tenderness or roasted as a pork loin with a porcini sauce. Pork is also the basis of pancetta, which can be cured or smoked, and is used to flavor many dishes. One of the favorite pork dishes of the region is *trippa piacentina*, which is tripe simmered with white beans, carrots, celery, sage, garlic, tomatoes, and white wine.

There are also many dishes of veal, usually in the form of scaloppini or *costoletta* (chops). Game, such as pheasant, guinea hen, wild boar, and hare are abundant in the fall.

Chicken and turkey are usually cooked in the traditional manner of grilling, roasting, or simmering in a sauce. They are also frequently used as stuffings for pasta. They also provide the basis of *galantina*, which consists of the boned fowl stuffed with a mixture of ground meats, wrapped in a cloth, placed in a pan, covered with water, and simmered with vegetables for about 2 hours. When cold it is sliced and served with diced jelly or aspic made from the stock.

Emilia-Romagna is known for its great variety of homemade pasta, usually made with flour and eggs. Large quantities of pasta are usually consumed daily by the typical family. Every day the local *sfogliatrice* (women who make hand rolled and shaped pasta) cut the dough into different pastas, such as linguine, fettuccine, tagliatelle, lasagna, farfalle and *garganelli*. The latter is a nutmeg-flavored pasta that is a specialty of Romagna. *Garganelli* are small

Historic city center, Bologna. Photo collection of the author.

groved pasta squares which hold sauces well. The pasta makers also produce stuffed pasta such as tortellini, *anolini*, and ravioli.

Stuffed pasta is prevalent throughout the region, using cheese, poultry, meat, fish, shellfish and / or vegetables as stuffings. Every city has its own pasta shape and filling with its own name. For instance, *anolini*, half-moon shaped pasta with ruffled edges, is stuffed with very fine ground pork and vegetables. *Tortelli all piacentina* are stuffed with creamy ricotta and mascarpone cheese.

Bologna has its own traditional pasta dishes. The city is known for its pasta with Sauce Bolognese, a tomato-based meat sauce (*ragu*). Bologna also has a myriad of tortellini dishes. These include tortellini stuffed with mortadella and seasoned with nutmeg (the favorite seasoning of Bologna); tortellini with ragu bolognese (meat sauce), and *tortellini in brodo*, which is tortellini served with chicken broth. The latter is a traditional first course for holidays — Christmas, New Year, Easter, and Ferragoasto (August 15).

Other pastas include, *Cappellacci*, a rounded shaped, stuffed pasta which is made with *zucca* (pumpkin). *Pasticcio* is a pasta pie made with ragu, porcini, and *balsamella* (bechamel) sauce. This sauce is made with butter, flour, milk and nutmeg for flavoring. *Lasagna di magro* is a traditional lasagna made with fish and shrimp instead of pork.

Emilia-Romagna is well known for a variety of desserts. Ferrara, an ancient city in the northeast of this region, is renowned for its baked goods and its bread has the reputation of being some of the best in Italy. One of the famous Ferrara pastries is *ciambella*, which is a traditional ring-shaped Easter cake similar to a yellow sponge cake that is usually served as dessert, but is also traditionally served for breakfast on Easter morning. *Pampepato* is a chocolate Christmas cake flavored with honey, spices, and almonds.

Bologna claims the origin of *Zuppa Inglese*. It is a dessert similar to English Trifle, hence the name. This dessert has two layers of custard, one vanilla and the other chocolate. Ricotta fritters originated in Modena. Vignolia cherries, the best in Italy, are used to make the famous *amarene*, which are cherries preserved in alcohol and served with tortes and ice cream.

Wines

The wines of Emilia-Romagna are among the finest in Italy. One of the best is Lambrusco which pairs well spicy foods. Sangiovese , which is sold in the United States, is deep red in color with a strong aroma and is served with red meat, wild game, and pastas. The Albana wine is an ideal partner for fish. Its grapes are grown along the coast of Romagna.

Other wines include, Trebbiano, Maliasia di Maiatico, Fortanella, Scandiano, and Sauvignon. Barbarossa di Bertinoro is a light robust red and Pagadebit is a medium body wine with spice and floral tones. Trebbiano di Romagna is a white dry wine which is served with local fish dishes.

Un Pranzo per l'Anniversario
An Anniversary Dinner

Serves 6

Antipasto di Prosciutto e Frutta
Prosciutto and Fruit Antipasto

Bomba di Riso coi Piccioni
Rice Mold with Squabs

Asparagi alla Parmigiana
Asparagus Parma Style

Ciambella Bolognese
Bolognese Cake

Caffe
Coffee

An Anniversary Dinner

Recently we were approaching our anniversary and my husband wanted for us to go out to celebrate. I was tempted because I would not have to cook and I could relax and enjoy an evening out.

His intentions were good, but we have had such marginal meals out or, as we are eating, he would say that I could have made it so much better. Consequently we finally decided to have our anniversary dinner at home. I invited two other couples to help us celebrate and planned a menu that did not need much cooking that evening.

The anniversary dinner started with a very simple but traditional Italian appetizer of prosciutto and fruit. I used pears instead of melon because this dinner was in the winter.

Since my husband and I love squab, I decided to use them for the entree. The rice mold with the squab makes an elegant presentation. Included in the rice mold are vegetables cooked with pork. This combination gives the rice a unique flavor and also some color. The steamed asparagus with Parmesan cheese complement the squab.

To make the dessert more elegant for this special occasion, I served each person, a large slice of cake, topped with whipping cream, and a glass of Italian champagne.

Preparations

For a dinner party, I usually set my dinner table in the morning. For this anniversary dinner I used my lovely Italian dishes, crystal glasses, and had a special flower arrangement for the center of the table.

The antipasto dish has to be assembled in the evening, but you can rinse the raspberries and pears, cut the lime and rinse the basil in the morning. Do not peel or cut the pears. Refrigerate the fruit and basil.

In the middle of the afternoon roast the squabs. While the squabs are roasting, boil the rice, sauté the vegetables and pork, assemble all the ingredients and place them in the mold. Do not place the mold in the oven. In the evening after your guests have arrived, place the mold in the oven and finish cooking.

Prepare the asparagus in the morning by cleaning and tying the stalks together. Then place them in a stock pot with the water and set them aside. Steam the asparagus that evening and then add the cheese and melt the butter.

Make the dessert the day before and serve it at room temperature with whipped cream and a glass of Italian champagne. Salute!

Antipasto di Prosciutto e Frutta
Prosciutto and Fruit Antipasto

Serves 6

Pears are a suitable fruit with prosciutto because of their slight acidity. Other slightly acidic fruits may also be used. Cantaloupe or fresh figs are usually served with prosciutto as an antipasto in the summer in Italy.

12 thin slices prosciutto
3 pears, peeled and thinly sliced
1 basket raspberries, rinsed, pat dry

2 limes, sliced thin
6 fresh basil sprigs

Arrange 2 slices of prosciutto per person on a plate and lay them flat but slightly overlapping. Place 4 slices of pears in the middle of the plate. Add 3 slices of lime next to the pears and place 6 raspberries on the prosciutto. Garnish with a basil sprig and serve with slices of coarse Italian bread.

Bomba di Riso coi Piccioni
Rice Mold with Squabs

Serves 6

6 squabs, cleaned
2 teaspoons salt
2 teaspoons fresh grated black pepper
2 tablespoons fresh chopped sage
2 tablespoons fresh chopped rosemary
2 tablespoons chopped garlic
12 slices pancetta
1 cup dry white wine
4 cups beef or chicken broth

2 cups arborio Italian rice
2 tablespoons olive oil
2 tablespoons unsalted butter
1 celery stalk, finely chopped
1 small carrot, finely chopped
1 medium onion, finely chopped
1/2 pound pork loin, cut into small cubes
2 eggs, beaten
1/2 cup freshly grated Parmesan cheese

Rinse the squab under cold water and pat them dry with paper towels. Mix 1 teaspoon each of salt and pepper and season the outside and inside of the squabs. Mix the chopped sage, rosemary and garlic together and place some of this mixture inside each squab. Wrap two slices of pancetta around each bird and secure with toothpicks. Then sprinkle the remainder of the herbs over the squabs.

Place the squabs in an oven proof casserole or baker in a preheated 400° F. oven and roast them for about 40 minutes to 1 hour depending on the size of the squabs. Add the white wine during the last 20 minutes of cooking. Remove the squabs from the oven, set them aside and cover loosely with foil. Reserve the pan juices.

Bring the beef broth to a boil in a medium saucepan over medium-high heat. Add the rice, stir, bring back to a boil, cover the pan with a lid, reduce the heat to low and cook for 15 minutes, or until the rice is cooked, but still al dente. When cooked, remove the rice, place it in a large shallow bowl and spread it to cool off faster.

Place the oil and butter in a medium skillet and add the chopped vegetables and cubed pork lion. Season with the remaining teaspoons of salt and pepper, and sauté, mixing often over medium heat for about 10 minutes. Then add the juices from the cooked squab to the vegetables, stir and continue cooking until all the liquid is absorbed.

Add the beaten eggs and parmesan cheese to the rice bowl and mix thoroughly until blended. Then add the pork-vegetables mixture and mix.

Butter a 6-cup mold. Pour the rice mixture into it, pressing it down and smoothing the top evenly. Place the mold in the preheated 350° F. oven for 30 to 40 minutes. When done, remove the mold from the oven and let it sit for about 15 minutes. Gently insert a spatula around the edge of the mold and turn it out onto a large preheated platter. Cut each squab in half and place them on top of the mold. To serve place some rice on each of 6 plates and place 2 squab halves on top of each serving of rice.

Asparagi alla Parmigiana
Asparagus Parma Style

Serves 6

3 pounds fresh asparagus
1 teaspoon salt
*3/4 cup freshly grated Parmesan
    cheese*

*1/2 teaspoon freshly ground black
    pepper*
4 tablespoons unsalted butter

Cut off the tough asparagus ends. Peel the asparagus with a sharp knife or a potato peeler. Rinse the asparagus under cold water and tie them, not too tight, with kitchen string or rubber bands, in several bunches. This will keep them from falling apart when cooking.

Place 3 inches of water in a tall stock pot. Bring the water to a boil over medium-high heat, add the salt and asparagus, and cook, covered, until tender, about 5 to 8 minutes, depending on the size of the asparagus,. Remove the asparagus from the pot, cut off the strings or rubber bands, and pat them dry with paper towels. Transfer the asparagus to 6 individual plates.

Sprinkle the green tips with parmesan cheese and season with black pepper. Melt the butter in a small saucepan, over medium heat until light brown and pour it over the asparagus and serve immediately.

Ciambella Bolognese
Bolognese Cake

Serves 6 to 8

4 large eggs
1 cup granulated sugar
4 cups all purpose flour
5 teaspoons baking powder
6 tablespoons unsalted butter,
   softened
1 cup milk
1/2 teaspoon vanilla extract
1/4 teaspoon salt

6 tablespoons pine nuts
6 tablespoons almonds, peeled,
   toasted, coarsely chopped
1/2 cup golden raisins, soaked in
   Marsala wine, squeezed dry,
   dusted with flour
Butter for bundt pan
4 tablespoons granulated sugar, to
   sprinkle over cake

Beat 3 of the eggs with the cup of sugar in a large bowl until thick. Sift the flour and baking powder into a bowl, then add it gradually to the egg mixture and beat it with an electric mixer, until well blended.

Cut the butter into small pieces and add it to the batter beating until well blended. While still beating add the milk, vanilla extract, salt, pine nuts, almonds, and raisins. Mix thoroughly until completely blended and pour the batter into a buttered bundt pan. Beat the remaining egg, and using a small brush, brush it on top of the batter. Then sprinkle with the 4 tablespoons of sugar.

Bake the in a preheated 350° F. oven for 35 to 45 minutes, or until a cake tester inserted in the center of the cake comes out clean. Cool the cake on a wire rack and then remove it from the pan.

This cake can be served either slightly warm or cold with a glass of sweet wine, some whipped cream, or sliced seasonal berries. A scoop of ice cream would also go nicely with the cake.

Un Compleanno Speciale
A Special Birthday

Serves 12

Finocchi al Formaggio
Fennel in Cheese Sauce

Tagliatelle con Salsiccia e Funghi
Tagliatelle with Sausage and Mushrooms

Scaloppine di Vitello alla Bolognese
Veal Scallops Bologna Style

Pure di Patate
Potato Puree

Melanzane Fritte
Fried Eggplant

Torta di Nocciole e Cioccolata
Hazelnut Chocolate Torte

Caffè
Coffee

A Special Birthday

Birthdays are very special and for one of my good friend's birthday recently I decided to honor her with a grand affair. I chose an elaborate menu based on the foods of Emilia-Romagna and prepared my dining room for an elegant celebration.

To start the dinner I served fennel with cheese as an antipasto, a typical dish of Emilia-Romagna. The mildness of this dish complemented the pasta course which followed. The tagliatelle, a flat long pasta, featured mushrooms and mild sausage in a cream sauce.

For the main course I prepared veal scallops with prosciutto and Parmesan cheese in the style of Bologna. The veal was served with a potato puree and fried eggplant. A decadent hazelnut chocolate torte ended this festive birthday feast.

Preparations

Much of the preparations can be done ahead for this meal. Prepare the fennel for the antipasto in the morning. Place the parboiled fennel in a casserole and refrigerate it. Bring the casserole to room temperature before adding the cheese and milk and then bake it in the oven that evening.

The sauce for the tagliatelle is best if made just before your guests arrive. However, you could sauté the mushrooms and the sausage separately; then place them together in one skillet and set them aside. That evening reheat the sausage, add the cream and nutmeg while the pasta is cooking. Drain the pasta and combine it with the sauce.

Late in the afternoon start to prepare the veal scallops. Brown them and place them in a baking pan. Make the Marsala and chicken sauce and set it aside. Assemble the veal scallops with the sauce just before finishing the cooking.

The potato puree can be made ahead. Place the puree in an oven proof bowl with few pieces of butter on top and reheat it in a 350° F. oven in the evening. The eggplant has to be fried that evening to be crisp, but it can be sliced and prepared in the late afternoon except for frying.

The hazelnut chocolate cake can be made the day before and refrigerated. Bring it to room temperature and whip the cream just before serving.

Finocchi al Formaggio
Fennel in Cheese Sauce

Serves 12

6 large fennel bulbs
1 teaspoon salt
4 tablespoons unsalted butter
1/2 teaspoon freshly ground black
    pepper

6 slices Fontina cheese, cut into thin
    strips
1/4 teaspoon grated nutmeg
1/2 cup milk

    Wash and clean the whole fennel bulbs. Discard the tough outer layers and cut off the top stalks and the hard base. Cut each fennel bulb into 4 wedges.

    Boil the fennel wedges with 1 teaspoon salt in water for 10 minutes or until the bulbs are tender, but crisp; then dry them with paper towels. Butter an oven proof casserole and add the fennel wedges. Season the fennel with salt and pepper. Place the strips of cheese over the top of the fennel wedges and sprinkle nutmeg over them. Pour the milk over the fennel and dot with the remaining butter cut into small pieces.

    Bake the fennel in a preheated 425° F. oven for about 15 minutes. Serve 2 fennel wedges per person.

Tagliatelle con Salsiccia e Funghi
Tagliatelle with Sausage and Mushrooms

Serves 12

1 1/2 pounds brown crimini or white champignon mushrooms
8 tablespoons unsalted butter
2 garlic cloves, smashed
Salt
6 mild Italian sausages, casing removed and crumbled

2 cups whipping cream
3 tablespoons chopped fresh parsley
2 pounds Tagliatelle pasta, dry or fresh
1 cup freshly grated Parmesan cheese

Clean and slice the mushrooms. Melt 4 tablespoons of the butter in a large saucepan over medium heat. Add the garlic and sauté until browned. Discard the garlic and add the sliced mushrooms. Sprinkle with some salt and sauté for 10 minutes or until the liquid from the mushrooms has almost evaporated.

In another saucepan melt the remaining 4 tablespoons of butter over medium heat. Add the crumbled sausages and sauté until browned, about 4 minutes, separating the sausages with a fork. Add the cooked mushrooms with their juice to the sausage and then add the cream. Stir thoroughly until the cream starts to thicken. Remove from heat, sprinkle with parsley, and mix again.

Cook the pasta until it is al dente. If using fresh pasta, remember it will be ready almost as soon as the water comes back to a boil. When the pasta is tender, drain it, and add it to the pan with the sausage, and toss. Add the Parmesan cheese and serve immediately.

Scaloppine di Vitello alla Bolognese
Veal Scallops Bologna Style

Serves 12

12 large, thin slices of veal scallops
3/4 cup all purpose flour
4 large eggs, beaten with a pinch of
Salt
6 tablespoons olive oil
6 tablespoons unsalted butter

Salt and finely ground black pepper
8 tablespoons dry Marsala wine
1 1/2 cups chicken broth
12 thin slices prosciutto crudo (raw parma ham)
12 teaspoon grated Parmesan cheese

Flatten the veal slices by placing the scallops between two sheets of wax paper and pounding them gently until they are flattened. Dip the veal slices in flour, shake off any excess, and then dip them in the beaten eggs.

Heat the oil and butter in a large heavy frying pan over medium-high heat. When the butter begins to bubble, add the veal scallops and sauté the slices quickly on both sides for a few minutes until tender and golden brown, about 2 minutes per side. (May have to be done in several batches with additional oil and butter.) Transfer the veal slices to a baking pan and season with salt and pepper. Add the Marsala wine and chicken broth to the skillet and boil for a few minutes stirring with a spoon to deglaze the pan.

(If preparing the dish ahead, make the recipe up to this point and stop. When ready to continue, warm the sauce, then pour it over the veal scallops and place the prosciutto and sprinkle the cheese on top of the meat.)

Pour the wine-chicken broth mixture over the veal scallops. Place a slice of prosciutto on each slice of veal and sprinkle each with one teaspoon of grated Parmesan cheese. Place the baking pan in a preheated 425° F. oven for just long enough to melt the cheese. Remove the veal from the oven and serve immediately while hot.

Pure di Patate
Potatoes Puree

Serves 12

4 pounds baking potatoes
1 cup milk
6 tablespoons unsalted butter, cut
   into pieces

Salt and freshly ground black
   pepper

Peel the potatoes and cut them into 4 pieces. Place the potatoes in a large saucepan over high heat with sufficient salted water to cover all the potatoes. Bring to a boil, cover, and cook over medium heat for 20 to 30 minutes. Use a fork to see if the potatoes are done. When the potatoes are tender, drain them, and while hot pass them through a food mill, use a potato masher, or an electric hand mixer to mash them. Place the mashed potatoes in a large saucepan over low heat.

Heat the milk to just below boiling and remove it from the heat. Add the butter to the potatoes and mix thoroughly with a wooden spoon. When all the butter is absorbed by the potatoes, add the hot milk little by little, stirring constantly with the wooden spoon. This procedure will made the puree soft and foamy. When the potato puree starts to boil, remove the saucepan from the heat. Use a metallic beater or a hand-held electric mixer to whip the potatoes until the puree is soft and smooth.

Melanzane Fritte
Fried Eggplant

Serves 12

2 medium, long eggplants
1/2 cup all purpose flour
4 large eggs, beaten and salted
2 cups fine bread crumbs

3/4 cup olive oil
Salt and freshly ground black
   pepper

Peel the eggplants and cut them lengthwise into thin slices. Dredge the slices in the flour, then dip each slice in the beaten eggs, and finally into the bread crumbs.

Heat the oil in a large skillet over medium-high heat. When the oil is hot add the eggplant slices and fry them on both sides for about 2 minutes per side. Remove the eggplant slices to paper towel to absorb the oil. Serve while hot and crispy with the veal.

Torta di Nocciole e Cioccolata
Hazelnut Chocolate Torte

Serves 12

1 cup chopped toasted hazelnuts
2 sticks (1 cup) unsalted butter, at
*   room temperature*
6 large egg yolks
1 large whole egg
1 cup granulated sugar
6 ounces semisweet chocolate, finely
*   chopped*

1/4 cup dark rum
2 cups all purpose flour
6 large egg whites
2 tablespoons confectioner's sugar
1 cup heavy whipping cream
1/2 teaspoon instant expresso coffee
*   powder*

Butter and flour a 10-inch springform pan and shake off any excess flour.

Place the hazelnuts on an ungreased baking sheet and bake in a preheated 350° F. oven for 4 minutes or until lightly golden in color. Then place them on a kitchen towel and rub off the skins. Chop the hazelnuts coarsely in a food processor, so that small pieces, not powder remain.

In a large bowl with an electric mixer at high speed beat the butter with the egg yolks, whole egg and sugar until thick and pale yellow. Add the chopped hazelnuts, chocolate, and rum and mix to blend. Slowly add the flour, beating gently to blend.

Beat the egg whites until stiff peaks form. Fold them into the chocolate mixture until well blended. Pour the batter into the prepared cake pan, smooth the top with a spatula, and bake in a preheated 350° F. oven for 35 to 40 minutes, or until a toothpick inserted in the center of the cake comes out only a little moist.

Let the cake cool on a wire rack. Remove the cake from the springform pan and sprinkle it with confectioner's sugar.

Whip the cream with the instant coffee powder until into stiff peaks form. Serve a dab of whipping cream next to each slice of cake.

Tuscany

Tuscany, situated in the central part of Italy's western coast, is surrounded by five regions Liguria, Emilia-Romagna, Marche, Umbria, and Lazio. It is a land of hills, mountains, and beaches. The favorable Mediterranean climate of the Tuscan region has made a great variety of agriculture possible. Although Tuscan soil is not very rich, it has been enhanced by the use of fertilizers and nutrients. The Tuscan peasant has worked diligently to make this beautiful and rugged region productive with vineyards and olive groves.

Over the centuries the Italian peninsula was a most desired area and was invaded many times. Since Tuscany is in the center of the country, it became the focal point of armies going both north and south. Thus the Tuscany area was the target of many invasions. In addition there were local wars between the Tuscan provinces. These local wars were inspired by the desire for independence or for economic supremacy.

The Goths, Arabs, Normans, Spaniards, Austrians and French were some of the peoples who have invaded and occupied Tuscany. Each time these various people came to Tuscany they took away some of the culture but they also left some of their own behind. That is why it is not always easy to trace the exact origin of a particular dish of Tuscan cuisine.

Tuscans love simple dishes based on fresh ingredients. They do not use elaborate sauces and gravies to disguise the flavors of food. Tuscan meat entrees are usually either roasted or grilled. Fruits and some vegetables are often consumed raw. Tuscan cooking can be described as *Una cucina povera*, which means a cuisine without elaboration or frills. In other words, just plain, simple cooking.

Tuscan cooks are famous for their soups, which are nourishing and thick — full of vegetables, beans, herbs, and olive oil. Much of their cooking is based on a love of wine, extra virgin olive oil, and bread. The prominence of bread and olives in Tuscan cooking dates back to the Etruscans who were indigenous to Tuscany prior to the Romans. Bread continues to be the mainstay of Tuscan cuisine. Throughout the centuries garlic, onions, and leeks were traditionally eaten with bread.

Pan sciocco is the classic local, country-style bread. This unsalted bread is a perfect combination when served with country ham (prosciutto), sheeps' milk cheese, and salami. A slice of this bread, toasted over the fire, then rubbed with garlic and sprinkled with good olive oil is fantastic, either when eaten alone, or accompanied by meat, vegetables, fish, and soups.

Bread is never thrown away in Tuscany. Leftover bread is the basic ingredient in several dishes. For example, *ribollita* is a thick soup made with bread, green vegetables, beans, black cabbage, and olive oil. *Panzanella* is a summer salad made with stale bread, tomatoes, onions, basil, and olive oil. *Pappa al pomodoro*, one of the famous Florentine soups, is traditionally made in late summer when tomatoes and fresh basil are readily available. It is made with fresh tomatoes, oil, garlic, stale Tuscan bread, hot peperoncino, bouillon, and salt and pepper.

Olive oil is also vital to Tuscan cooking, particularly extra virgin olive oil. The olives used for making extra virgin olive oil must be picked very carefully. Traditionally they should never touch the ground. They are hand picked and large tarpaulin are placed under the trees to catch any that fall to the ground. The olives must be dry and pressed immediately after harvesting. In Tuscany, the town of Lucca is the center of the olive oil trade. Its olive oil is exported all over the world.

In Tuscan cooking there are only a few traditional recipes for pasta. These include *pappardelle con la lepre*, which is a dish consisting of wide noodles with hare. *Sienese pinci* is a type of thick, fresh spaghetti from Montalcino. Another typical Tuscan pasta is ravioli filled with spinach and ricotta and in Lucchesia there is a meat-filled pasta called *tordelli*.

Herbs are a very important part of Tuscan cooking. Sage, rosemary, parsley, thyme, marjoram, and bay leaves are the primary herbs. The Etruscans of pre-Roman times introduced bay leaves and parsley as a flavor enhancement to their foods.

As mentioned earlier Tuscan cooking features fried or grilled foods and roasts without sauces. Many of the meats are roasted or grilled with rosemary or fennel such as *bistecca alla Fiorentina*. Almost all over Tuscany, meat is grilled over open fires. Restaurants in Tuscany typically have large roasting spits called *girarrosto*, which are loaded with chickens, pork, suckling pigs, guinea fowls and all kinds of game from birds to boar. Also chickens are simply fried or sautéed in the skillet with olive oil.

Salumi (which is known in this country as cold cuts) is a Tuscan specialty. It includes *finocchiona*, *salame Toscano*, prosciutto, and salami made from wild boar. These meats make a perfect *spuntino* (snack) accompanied by some good local unsalted bread. They are also used as an antipasto.

Along the Tuscan coast the most traditional dishes are made with fish. The Tyrrhenian Sea between the Italian peninsula and the islands of Sardinia and Corsica contain many types of fish in great abundance. The sea faring Tuscans along the coast claim that they created the oldest Italian recipe for fish soup, which is actually a rich and thick stew rather than soup. This fish stew has every imaginable kind of fish and shellfish in it. It also contains chili pepper, which is called *zenzero* in Tuscany and is quite popular. At least five different fish are a requirement for this stew.. The result is a spicy stew which is served in a deep dish over slices of toasted bread.

Other traditional Tuscan fish dishes feature *cefalo* (gray mullet), *triglie* (red mullet), butterfish, and octopus. *Fritto del mare* is a dish that consists of a mixture of small fried fish. Another specialty is *cieche*, which is based on tiny baby eels caught at the mouth of the Arno River near Pisa. These eels are cooked live in very hot oil and flavored with garlic and sage.

Tuscany has an excellent cheese called, pecorino, which is made from sheeps' milk. It is produced around Arezzo, Volterra, Chianti and Pienza. Tuscan dinners often end with a slice of pecorino and some fruit. In the spring this cheese is frequently eaten with young raw fava beans.

Tuscan desserts are less extravagant than those of other Italian regions. Florence is famous for *zuccotto*, a pound cake with a custard-like filling in the center containing chocolate and nuts. Siena is the home of *panforte*, a delicious Christmas cake made with flour, almonds, hazelnuts, cocoa, spices, and fruit. *Castagnaccio*, another traditional Tuscan cake, is a simple chestnut-flour cake covered with pine nuts, raisins, and rosemary. *Brigidini* are small spiced, wafer-like pastries which are sold at markets and country fairs.

Wines

Tuscany is one of the most famous wine regions of Italy. Wine grapes are grown throughout the region. The well-known Chianti is primarily made from the Sangiovese grape with some Trebbiano, Malvasia, and Canaiolo Nero added for complexity.

Although Chianti has become the best known of the Tuscan wines, other famous wines are: Vernaccia di San Gimignano, a golden yellow wine; Procancio, a red wine with a faintly licorice taste; Brunello , a traditional Tuscan red wine; and Moscadello di Montalcino, which is made from the muscat grape. There is also Vinsanto (holy wine), which takes a long time to mature, becoming darker and sweeter the longer it is kept in the barrel. It is served for dessert with biscotti or also in the morning to stimulate the appetite.

Vineyard and winery in Tuscany.
Photo courtesy of Tom Vano.

Una Cena d'Estate alla Griglia
A Summer Barbecue

Serves 6

Gamberetti all'Agro e Fettunta
Marinated Shrimp and Garlic Toasts with Olive Oil

Pappardelle al Sugo Finto
Wide Noodles with Fake Sauce

Tagliata di Manzo al Rosmarino
Sliced Grilled Beef with Olive Oil and Rosemary

Fagiolini in Umido
Green Beans with Tomato Sauce

Patate Arrostite
Roasted Potatoes

Pesche al Vino Rosso con Biscotti
Peaches in Red Wine with Biscotti

Caffè
Coffee

A Summer Barbecue

Summer usually signifies casual entertaining with numerous barbecue dinners for friends and family. To me barbecues mean that I will be able to prepare dishes ahead of time. I can even get the meat ready for my husband to barbecue. This means that I will have time to relax and enjoy our guests.

In planning a Tuscan summer barbecue menu I take advantage of the many seasonal vegetables as they do in Italy. My Tuscan barbecue starts with an antipasto of marinated shrimp with garlic bread — an aromatic and tasty combination.

The pappardelle (wide noodles) with a sauce based on fresh tomatoes makes a very colorful and flavorful dish.

In this barbecue menu the grilled beef is drizzled with the olive oil after cooking. The oil is flavored with garlic and rosemary. The green beans, a summer favorite, are prepared with onions and tomatoes in a typical Tuscan dish. Crispy, roasted potatoes also accompany the beef.

Fresh peaches with wine served with traditional biscotti provide a cooling and refreshing ending to this summer barbecue. Biscotti dipped in the tangy peach juice and red wine combination is an extra taste treat.

Preparations

Boil the shrimp in the morning, marinate them with the lemon juice, salt, and pepper and then place them in the refrigerator to marinate. Finish preparing the shrimp just before dinner. The garlic toast should be served warm with the shrimp. Grill the bread on the barbecue with the beef, then rub it with garlic and add the oil.

Prepare the sauce for the pappardelle several days ahead, refrigerate it, and then reheat it while cooking the pasta just before dinner.

The steaks are to be grilled after your guests arrive. While the meat is cooking they may enjoy an aperitif and the shrimp antipasto.

The green beans with the tomato sauce can be made a day ahead and then reheated before serving. By doing this the beans will have a chance to absorb more flavor while staying in the sauce.

The peaches should be prepared in the early afternoon so that they can soak in the wine. The peaches will not discolor, they will absorb some of the color of the wine, which adds to their flavor. The biscotti may be made several days ahead and stored in a cookie tin.

Gamberi all'Agro
Marinated Shrimp

Serves 6

2 pounds medium shrimp, unshelled
Water
1 tablespoon coarse salt
Juice of 2 lemons
1/2 teaspoon salt

1/2 teaspoon freshly ground black
    pepper
2 tablespoons fresh chopped Italian
    parsley
1/4 cup extra virgin olive oil

Bring a large saucepan of cold water to a boil and add the coarse salt. Then add the shrimp, cover and bring to a boil over medium-high heat. When the water starts to boil again, remove the cover and continue boiling the shrimp for 3 minutes. Remove from heat, drain and cool the shrimp under running cold water.

Shell and devein the shrimp and place them in a bowl. Pour the lemon juice over them and season with salt and pepper. Mix well, cover, and marinate the shrimp in the refrigerator for 4 to 6 hours, turning them occasionally.

Before serving drain the shrimp and place them in a bowl. Then sprinkle them with the chopped parsley and pour the olive oil over them. Mix gently and serve with the toasted bread.

Fettunta
Garlic Toast with Olive Oil

Serves 6

6 large thick slices coarse Italian
    bread (or 12 small slices)
1 large garlic clove,, cut in half

6 tablespoons extra virgin olive oil
Salt and freshly ground pepper

Grill the bread slices on a charcoal grill or use a preheated to 375° oven. Toast the bread on both sides until golden in color. While the bread slices are hot, rub them with the cut garlic on one side only. Place the bread slices on a serving dish. Drizzle the oil onto each bread slice and sprinkle each with salt and pepper. Serve with the shrimp.

Pappardelle al Sugo Finto
Wide Noodles with Fake Sauce

Serves 6

This sauce is called "Fake" because it is similar to the typical Tuscan meat sauce but does not have meat. It is also similar to many Italian tomato sauces, but it is not made exclusively with tomatoes. This "Fake" sauce does not take long to prepare.

4 tablespoons extra virgin olive oil
1 medium onion, finely chopped
1 carrot, finely chopped
1 garlic clove, finely chopped
2 celery stalks, finely chopped
2 tablespoons chopped fresh Italian parsley
1/2 cup dry red wine
2 pounds fresh ripe tomatoes, peeled and chopped or 4 cups canned

chopped Italian tomatoes with juice
6 fresh basil leaves, coarsely chopped
1 teaspoon salt
1 teaspoon freshly ground black pepper
1 pound dry pappardelle pasta or any wide, flat pasta
1/2 cup freshly grated Parmesan cheese

Heat the olive oil in a medium-size saucepan over medium heat. Add the chopped onion, garlic, carrot, celery and parsley and sauté for about 7 minutes, stirring often. Add the wine and let it evaporate over high heat, then add the chopped tomatoes and basil and stir. Season with salt and pepper and stir again. Cook over low heat until the sauce has thickened and most of the liquid has evaporated, about 20 minutes.

(This sauce can be made several days ahead and stored, covered, in the refrigerator. Before using, reheat the sauce over low heat.)

Cook the pasta in a large pot of boiling salted water until tender but firm to the bite, al dente. Drain the pasta and transfer it to a serving bowl. Pour over the hot sauce over the pasta and sprinkle it with the Parmesan cheese. Toss thoroughly and serve immediately.

Tagliata di Manzo al Rosmarino
Sliced Grilled Beef with Olive Oil and Rosemary

Serves 6

Florence is the only place in Italy where you can get a genuine beefsteak. A Florentine beefsteak usually comes from the special Chianina breed of beef cattle that is found only in the Valley of Chiana near Florence. This beef is so scarce that is available only in Florence. A Florentine beefsteak is the same cut as the American T-bone or Porterhouse.

3 large Porterhouse or T-Bone
  steaks, each 2 inches thick and
  weighing at least 1 1/2 pounds
  each
1/2 cup extra virgin olive oil

3 garlic cloves, peeled and sliced
4 sprigs fresh rosemary
1/2 teaspoon salt
1/2 teaspoon freshly ground black
  pepper

When it is time to cook have the steaks at room temperature. Preheat the barbecue or grill to very hot before placing the steaks on it.

Pour the olive oil into a small saucepan, add the sliced garlic and the rosemary sprigs. Sprinkle in salt and pepper and mix. Cook gently over low heat for about 5 to 8 minutes, stirring occasionally. Do not let the garlic brown. Keep the olive oil mixture warm over very low heat.

Place the steaks on the hot grill or barbecue and cook for about 5 minutes, turn and cook for 5 minutes on the second side. Cook the first side for 5 more minutes and then remove the steaks and place them on a wooden carving board. The steaks should be rare inside. Cut the steaks into long thin slices and place them on a preheated serving platter.

Remove the sliced garlic and rosemary sprigs from the olive oil. Then pour the flavored oil over the sliced beef.

Serve the beef immediately with green beans and roasted potatoes.

Fagiolini in Umido
Green Beans with Tomato Sauce

Serves 6

Long narrow beans, known as Chinese long beans, are also excellent cooked in this tomato sauce. In Tuscany, these long narrow beans are called St. Anna beans. You can often find these long beans in a Chinese market. When I was growing up in Tuscany my mother made these beans every Sunday in the summer for dinner to accompany meat.

2 pounds string beans
1/4 cup extra virgin olive oil
1 small onion, finely chopped
1 small carrot, finely chopped
3 garlic cloves, left whole
1 pound fresh ripe tomatoes, peeled,
seeded, and chopped or 3 cups
canned Italian tomatoes, chopped
6 fresh basil leaves, coarsely chopped
1 teaspoon salt
1 teaspoon freshly ground black
pepper

Remove the ends and any strings from the string beans. Then soak them in a large bowl of cold water for 30 minutes.

Heat the oil in a 3-quart saucepan over medium heat, add the chopped onion, carrot, and whole garlic cloves. Sauté until lightly golden, about 7 to 8 minutes, then remove the garlic.

Add the chopped tomatoes, basil, and string beans. Season with salt and pepper and mix well. Cover the saucepan and simmer the beans slowly for 30 minutes. Do not add any liquid because the beans shed lots of water while cooking. The beans should be cooked, but still firm. Taste for salt and pepper, add if needed. Cook the beans for a few more minutes, without the cover, and then transfer them to a serving dish.

Patate Arrostite
Roasted Potatoes

Serves 6

2 pounds potatoes
2/3 cup olive oil
6 garlic cloves, unpeeled and left
   whole

3 tablespoons fresh rosemary leaves
Salt and freshly ground pepper,
   to taste

Peel the potatoes, cut them in half lengthwise, then in half again. Warm the olive oil in a roasting pan over medium heat. Add the potatoes, the whole garlic cloves, and rosemary, and stir to coat all the ingredients with the olive oil. Season with salt and pepper. Sauté for a few more minutes and then place the casserole or roasting pan in a pre-heated 350° F. oven. Roast the potatoes, turning often, until golden in color, about 40 minutes. When cooked, remove the potatoes from the oven and discard the garlic. Use a slotted spoon to remove the potatoes and place them in a warm serving dish. Serve with the beef.

Pesche al Vino Rosso
Peaches in Red Wine

Serves 6

6 large firm, ripe peaches
Juice of 1 lemon
1/2 cup sugar

3 cups dry red wine (Chianti
   Classico)

Rinse the peaches and pat them dry. Do not peel them. Cut the peaches in half, remove the pit and cut the peach halves into slices. Place the sliced peaches into a serving bowl. Squeeze the lemon over the peaches and sprinkle them with the sugar. Pour the wine over the peaches and mix well.

Cover the bowl and place in the refrigerator for at least 6 hours.

Before serving the peaches, gently mix them. Serve the peaches with some of the wine and some Biscotti to dip into the juice.

Biscotti
Cookies

Makes 6 dozen cookies

Biscotti are dry, crunchy, hard cookies because they are baked twice. They will soften up immediately when dipped into a liquid such as wine. They are also tasty when dipped in coffee. Kept in a cookie tin, the Biscotti will last for months.

3 cups all-purpose flour
1 1/2 teaspoons baking powder
1/4 teaspoon salt
4 eggs
1 cup sugar
1 teaspoon vanilla extract
1 teaspoon almond extract

3 tablespoon Amaretto liqueur or
*   brandy*
8 tablespoons (1 stick) unsalted
*   butter, melted*
1 cup walnuts, almonds, or hazel
*   nuts, coarsely chopped*

Pour the flour in a mound on a work surface or in a big bowl. Make a well in the center and place the baking powder and salt in the well.

Beat 3 of the eggs in a medium bowl and add the sugar, vanilla and almond extracts, Amaretto or brandy, and the melted butter. Add this mixture to the center of the well. Gradually work the flour into the ingredients in the well and mix with your hands or a wooden spoon until smooth. Knead in the nuts thoroughly and keep kneading, sprinkling additional flour, if necessary. Place the dough in the refrigerator for about 15 minutes.

Butter and flour two baking sheets. Divide the dough into quarters. Roll each piece of dough on a floured surface into a 2- to 3-inch wide log and place the logs at least 3 inches apart of the baking sheets.

Beat the remaining egg and brush it over the tops of the dough logs. Bake in a preheated 350° F. oven for 20 minutes. Remove the logs from the oven and reduce the heat to 325° F. Cut the logs diagonally into 1-inch slices and lay them cut side up on the baking sheets. Return to the oven for another 15 minutes. Cool on racks. Store the Biscotti in a cookie tin.

Una Cena Invernale in Campagna
A Winter Dinner in the Country

Serves 8

Salumi
Cold Cuts

L'Infarinata
Vegetable Soup with Polenta

Bistecche di Maiale con Cavolo
Pork Chops with Cabbage

Castagnaccio
Chestnut Cake

Caffe
Coffee

A Winter Dinner in the Country

I was raised on a farm in Tuscany and when I was a child my parents frequently invited friends for dinner on Sundays. Dinner was served in our big kitchen, which was the largest room in the house, and had a huge fireplace. This fireplace was our only source of heat in the winter. Thus all of our winter activities were centered in the kitchen.

I have choosen typical Tuscan winter menu that I remember from my childhood. The dinner starts with few slices of *salumi* (assorted cold cuts) to whet your appetite.

This is followed by L'Infarinata, a vegetable soup, which is thickened with cornmeal. The entree consists of pork chops, flavored with fennel seeds and cooked with cabbage in a tomato sauce.

The dinner concludes with a typical Tuscan chestnut cake.

Preparations

All of the items of this menu are very easy to prepare and can be made ahead of time.

The sliced meats for the *salumi* are purchased at an Italian delicatessen or in the deli department of the supermarket. Have them sliced at the market on the day of the party or the day before to your desired thickness. The meats are usually wrapped in special paper to keep them fresh. In addition you may store them in platic bags in the refrigerator.

Make the vegetable soup days ahead of your dinner and keep it covered in the refrigerator. That evening bring the soup to a boil, slowly add the cornmeal and cook for about 6 minutes.

The main course can be prepared in the morning or early afternoon. The longer the pork chops stay in the tomato sauce with the fennel seeds, the more flavor they will absorb. Boil the cabbage, drain ,and set it aside. That evening reheat the pork chops, then add the cabbage to the sauce and cook for 10 minutes.

Bake the chestnut cake in the morning and then reheat it that evening. It may be served with some creamy ricotta, as is traditional in Florence.

Salumi
Cold Cuts

Serves 8

*8 slices of finocchiona (coarse-
grained pork sausage)*
8 slices of Toscano salame
8 slices prosciutto
*8 slices coppa (cured, rolled pork
shoulder)*

8 slices mortadella
8 small curls of unsalted butter
1 large loaf of crusty bread, sliced
8 small sprigs of fresh parsley

Place a slice of each meat, rolled cigar-like, if desired, on each of 8 plates, add a small curl of butter and garnish the dish with a sprig of parsley. Serve with sliced bread.

L'Infarinata
Vegetable Soup with Polenta

Serves 8

L'Infarinata is a specialty dish of the Garfagnana, the mountainous region of the province of Lucca in Tuscany. This classic and traditional dish is a simple one. However, it takes time and patience to prepare, but the effort is well worth it. This dish may be made with white or red beans depending on your preference and availability. Dry lima beans may also be used.

As a little girl in Italy, I frequently ate *L'Infarinata* in the winter. It is a hearty and filling soup, which gives one a feeling of warmth in cold weather. My mother often added an additional garnish of chopped red onion on top of the soup. She would also sprinkle extra virgin olive oil on top of each serving of soup.

1 1/2 pounds fresh or dried white or
  red beans
4 quarts water
Few pieces of pork rind or 1 ham
  hock
1 teaspoon salt
1 large onion
1 large garlic clove
1 carrot
3 celery stalks
1 sprig rosemary
2 medium potatoes
1 bunch of kale

1 small head green cabbage
1 slice smoked pancetta (about 2
  ounces) or bacon
3 tablespoons extra virgin olive oil
1 cup chopped tomatoes with their
  juice
1 teaspoon fennel seeds (mashed)
4 cups chicken broth, or more,
  if needed
1 1/2 cups instant yellow
  cornmeal (polenta)
Salt and freshly ground pepper

Shell the beans if fresh and if dried soak them overnight in luke-warm water. Place the beans in a large saucepan with the water and bring to a boil. Then cook over low heat until the beans are done but still firm, al dente, 40 minutes to an hour. Toward the end of cooking time add the salt.

In the meantime, chop the onion, garlic, carrot, celery and parsley. Peel the potatoes and dice them. Cut the kale and cabbage into thin strips, removing the tough stalks from the kale and the hard core from the cabbage. Chop the pancetta or bacon into small pieces.

Just before the beans are done, place the oil into a large pot, add the chopped pancetta, onion, garlic, carrot, celery and rosemary and saute over medium heat, stirring often, for 5 minutes.

When the beans are cooked, remove the pork rind or ham hock and add the beans with all of their liquid and the chicken broth to the sauteeing vegetables. Add the strips of kale and cabbage, mix and cook for 40 minutes over medium-low heat. While the vegetables are cooking, add the crushed fennel seeds to the pot.

When all the vegetables are cooked, check to see if more liquid is needed. You should have at least 2 quarts of liquid, if not add more chicken broth to bring it to that amount. The soup should not to be too thick, because the cornmeal is still to be added. Add salt and pepper, if needed.

Slowly add the cornmeal to the boiling vegetable soup pouring it in a steady slow stream with one hand while stirring with the other, so that no lumps are formed. Then cook slowly on low heat for 5 minutes. Laddle the hot soup into individual soup dishes and sprinkle each with some freshly ground black pepper.

If there is any soup left over, place it in the refrigerator. It will be firm by the next day. Then slice it and fry it in oil or grill it, similar to leftover polenta. Serve with Parmesan cheese.

The leftover soup can also be thinned with more chicken broth and served hot with sliced fried bread placed in the soup bowl.

Bistecche di Maiale con Cavolo
Pork Chops with Cabbage

Serves 8

For this recipe the Tuscans use cavolo nero, black cabbage, which is actually a dark green color. It tastes slightly bitter and is available primarily in winter. Kale is very close in taste to the Tuscan cabbage and is available in all the supermarkets. Green cabbage, which is a little sweeter, may also be used.

4 pounds Italian black cabbage, kale or green cabbage
1/3 cup olive oil
4 large garlic cloves, crushed
8 pork chops
1/4 teaspoon salt

1/2 teaspoon freshly ground black pepper
2 tablespoons fennel seeds
2 tablespoons tomato paste diluted in 1 cup water or 1 (8-ounce can) tomato sauce

Rinse the cabbage leaves one by one, remove the hard stalk that forms the center of each leaf and then cut each leaf into thin strips. If using green cabbage cut out the hard core in the middle.

Use a large frying pan that will accommodate all the pork chops, if not brown the chops in two batches. Place the olive oil in the frying pan over medium heat, and add the crushed garlic cloves. When the garlic is golden in color, add the pork chops and sprinkle them with the salt and pepper and fennel seeds. Brown the pork chops on both sides until golden brown and then add the diluted tomato paste and stir. Cover the frying pan and cook for about 30 minutes over low heat.

Boil the strips of cabbage in sufficient salted water to cover for 5 minutes. Then drain and squeeze out any water. Remove the pork chops to a preheated platter and keep them warm. Add the boiled cabbage to the frying pan, stir thoroughly and cook over medium-low heat for 10 to 15 minutes. If the cabbage looks too dry add a little warm water. Add salt and pepper, if needed. Serve one pork chop per person with some cabbage arranged around each chop.

Castagnaccio
Chestnut Cake

Serves 8

Chestnut flour was once an important part of the winter diet of the workers in the Garfagnana mountains of Tuscany. They used it as a base for a nourishing polenta which was eaten with biroldo, a Tuscan pork sausage and accommapied by local wine.

In Florence Castagnaccio is eaten with creamy ricotta cheese. It can also be eaten cold but do not store the cake in the refrigerator.

3 tablespoons golden seedless raisins
1/2 cup lukewarm milk
4 cups chestnut flour
6 tablespoons extra virgin olive oil
3 tablespoons sugar
1/2 teaspoon salt
2 to 2 1/2 cups cold water
3 tablespoons pine nuts or walnuts
2 tablespoons fresh rosemary leaves

Soak the raisins in lukewarm milk for 20 minutes. Drain and pat dry.

Place the chestnut flour in a large bowl, and stir in 2 tablespoons of the oil, sugar and salt. Mix thoroughly. Then gradually add the water, stirring constantly with a wooden spoon to prevent lumps from forming, resulting in a fairly thin, smooth batter.

Pour the remaining 4 tablespoons olive oil into a 9-inch cake pan with 2-inch sides, tipping the pan to coat the bottom and sides evenly with the oil. Pour the batter into the pan and sprinkle the surface with pine nuts, golden raisins and rosemary leaves. Although there may seem to be an excess of oil, it is needed for the cake to bake properly.

Bake the cake in a preheated 400° F. oven for 50 to 60 minutes or until the top of the cake is crisp and covered with tiny cracks and a toothpick inserted into the middle comes out clean. Remove the cake from the oven and pour off any excess oil.

Loosen the cake with a knife and with a spatula transfer it to a serving dish. Let the cake rest 15 to 20 minutes before serving. Serve while still warm.

The Marches

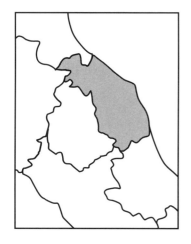

In medieval times the region, today known as The Marches, was three areas, each governed by a representative of Rome. These areas were named Marca di Camerino, Marca di Ancona, and Marca di Fano. Modern spelling and pronunciation have changed the name to The Marches.

The Marches, located in the middle of the east coast of Italy, are beautifully situated along the Adriatic Sea with craggy mountains that taper down to rounded hills as they approach the sea. The area surrounds the republic of San Marino. The region has many deep narrow valleys which have been cut by rivers. Breezes from the sea combined with cool mountain air give The Marches a moderate temperature. However, winters in the mountains can be harsh.

The infertile, rocky soil of much of the region limits the amount and variety of agriculture. Sugar beets, fennel, barley, and cauliflower are the prime crops. With limited commercial agriculture the cooking styles of the Marchigiani depends on the harvest of vegetables and meats from individual farms and gardens. A variety of fish is caught along the coastline, including all kinds of crustaceans, even lobster, which is a rarity in other parts of the peninsula.

Brodetto is the finest fish soup of the region. *Brodetto Marchigiano* traditionally contains eight varieties of shell- and fin-fish. The *brodetto* from Ancona, the capital of The Marches, is frequently made by fishermen on their boats. It contains up to thirteen varieties of seafood. This soup is flavored with white wine, vinegar, and saffron and is served over slices of toasted bread.

Fin fish is usually grilled, fried, or boiled, and seasoned with herbs and olive oil. The Marchigiani dry fish for later use. This dried fish is called *stoccafisso*. In Umido this dried fish is cooked with tomatoes, onion, carrots, and celery and seasoned with oil. Another popular dish using dried fish is flavored with rosemary and garlic, while still another consists of the dried fish baked in layers with potatoes.

The cuisine of The Marches is hearty. Many of the meats and fish are stuffed, generously seasoned with herbs, and cooked in wine. Olives are stuffed and served as a separate course. In the town of Ascoli Piceno huge green olives are stuffed with ground meat, egg, and pecorino, then dipped in batter and bread crumbs. They are fried and served hot.

One of the traditional dishes of The Marches is a tender young pig that is boned and stuffed with garlic, fennel, and rosemary. After being marinated in white wine, the pig is cooked on a spit. This dish, called *porchetta*, is usually featured at celebrations.

The beef of The Marches is lean yet flavorful. In Pesaro, the birthplace of Rossini, a chef created a dish called *Medaglioni alla Rossini* in honor of the composer. This dish consists of beef tournedos cooked with prosciutto, wild mushrooms, cheese, parsley, lemon, and pepper. When in season, grated white truffles are sprinkled over the meat before serving.

The white truffles of The Marches, although not as famous as those of Alba in Piedmont, are of excellent quality. Most truffles are found in the Valley of Metauro, which is particularly known for its brown and black truffles.

Chickens and lamb raised by the local population are plentiful. Game such as rabbit, quail, guinea hen and pigeon are found in the hills and become the basis of many local dishes. Typically they are seasoned with marjoram or rosemary. The game is usually either roasted or grilled.

A well known baked pasta dish of The Marches is *vincisgrassi*, a lasagna layered with mushrooms, chicken livers, prosciutto, and truffles. Bechamel

The town of Fossombrone Ovest, The Marches. Photo courtesy of Walter Bibikow

sauce binds the ingredients. The dish was named for an Austrian general who fought Napoleon in the region.

The Marches region is famous for its cured pork products. The prosciutto is washed with vinegar, rubbed with black pepper, and then smoked. Three well-known sausages of the region are *cotechino*, made with pork and flavored with cloves and cinnamon; *coppa Marchigiana*, made with pork, almonds, pine nuts, and orange rind; and *ciasculu*, made with finely ground lean pork mixed with spices and cooked in wine.

The Marchigiana prepare many of their vegetables in an elaborate manner. Heads of cauliflower are coated with a light batter of egg, flour and wine, and then fried. Zucchini are stuffed with bread crumbs and parsley and then baked. Vegetable dishes usually include tomatoes, bell peppers, fennel, cabbage, broad beans, and green peas.

Fresh fruit often ends a Marchigian meal. Peaches, figs, apples, and cherries abound from spring through autumn. Cheese always appears on the table at the end of a meal. Pecorino, made from sheep's milk, is the main cheese of the region. Fresh or aged, it is served with fruit and fresh breads.

Wines

Verdicchio is the most famous wine of The Marches. It is yellowish-green in color, extremely dry, and goes well with seafood. Two good table wines are Verdicchio Castelli di Jesi and Verdicchio di Montanello. Verdicchio di Matelica, a rarer wine, is considered to be the best of the variety. A sparkling Verdicchio Pian delle Mura pairs well with pasta dishes. Red wines include Sangiovese and Rosso Canero. The latter is a very robust dry red.

Un Pranzo nel Giardino
Dinner in the Garden

Serves 4

Olive al Forno
Baked Green Olives

Spaghetti al Guanciale
Spaghetti with Pancetta

Coniglio in Potacchio
Rabbit in Casserole

Funghi in Umido
Sautéed Mushrooms

Insalata di Finocchio e Arugula
Fennel and Arugula Salad

Frutti di Bosco
Wild Berries

Caffe
Coffee

Dinner in the Garden

It was a perfect evening for a garden dinner since the weather was warm and there was a slight breeze. I decided to serve a typical Marche dinner which started with huge green olives that grow in the Marche region. I used large olives, removed the pits, then wrapped them with bacon and baked them in the oven.

For the first course I chose spaghetti with pancetta, a typical Marche dish. This pasta combines tomatoes and pancetta, which are cooked in red wine.

There is an abundance of wild game in the mountains of this region, therefore I chose rabbit cooked in a casserole with fresh herbs and chili peppers for the entree. Sautéed mushrooms pair well with the rabbit. A crunchy salad of sweet fennel and slightly bitter arugula — two flavors that complement each other — provided an interlude between the entree and the dessert.

Fresh berries were served with a combination of mascarpone and whipped cream for a very light, refreshing end to this tasty meal.

Preparations

This Marche dinner is simple and easy to prepare. In the morning assemble the olives completely, then cover them with plastic wrap and refrigerate. In the evening bring the olives to room temperature before baking them in the oven.

The pancetta, or bacon sauce, for the spaghetti can be made in the morning or even a day ahead and refrigerated. In the evening simmer the sauce while the spaghetti is boiling.

In the morning or even the day before cook the rabbit in the casserole completely The rabbit will be more tasty and tender if it is allowed to sit in the sauce. After cooking refrigerate the rabbit, then reheat it slowly on the evening of the dinner. Early in the afternoon cook the mushrooms completely and reheat them before serving.

Prepare the ingredients for the salad in the morning. Rinse the fennel bulbs and the arugula and pat them dry. Cut the fennel bulbs in slices and chop the arugula. Then make the oil-lemon dressing. Toss the salad that evening just before serving.

In the afternoon clean the berries for the dessert and place them in a bowl. Add the sugar and lemon juice and refrigerate. Beat the cream, mascarpone and sugar to stiff peaks, then cover and refrigerate. Assemble the dessert just before serving it.

Olive al Forno
Baked Green Olives

Serves 4

These olives are traditionally served as an antipasto.

16 large green olives in brine   *Olive oil*
8 slices bacon, cut in half   *4 sprigs parsley, for garnish*

Remove the pits from the green olives carefully by using a small sharp knife to cut around the pit in a circle. If you do not break the olive spiral you can reform the olive into the original shape.

Wrap each olive with a half slice of the bacon and secure two olives together with toothpicks. Oil an ovenproof dish, place the olives in it and bake them in a preheated 375° F. degree oven until the bacon fat has been rendered and the bacon is crispy, about 15 minutes.

Place the cooked olives on a serving dish and serve 4 per person as an antipasto with some crusty Italian bread.

Garnish each dish with one sprig of parsley.

The cooked olives may also be placed on a small platter and passed as an accompaniment to some wine before dinner.

Spaghetti al Guanciale
Spaghetti with Pancetta

Serves 4

3 tablespoons olive oil
1 medium onion, finely chopped
1 celery stalk, finely chopped
1 small carrot, finely chopped
1/4 pound pancetta or bacon, diced
1 tablespoons chopped fresh parsley
1 pound tomatoes, peeled and
    chopped or 3 cups canned

crushed Italian style tomatoes
1/2 teaspoon salt
1/2 teaspoon freshly ground black
    pepper
1 cup red wine
1 pound spaghetti
1/2 cup freshly grated pecorino
    cheese

Heat the oil in a medium saucepan. Add the chopped onion, celery and carrot and sauté over medium heat, until the onion is pale yellow. Add the cubed pancetta and chopped parsley and sauté until the pancetta is lightly colored. Then add the tomatoes and their juice. Simmer the mixture and season it with salt and pepper.

After 10 minutes of cooking, add the red wine. Continue cooking for 15 to 20 minutes or until the sauce is of a medium-thick consistency.

Bring a large pot of salted water to a boil, add the spaghetti and cook until al dente. Drain the pasta thoroughly and place it in a warm deep bowl. Add the cooked pancetta sauce and grated pecorino cheese, then toss until mixed.

Coniglio in Potacchio
Rabbit in Casserole

Serves 4

1 (3 to 3 1/2 pound) rabbit , cut in
    pieces
1/2 cup wine vinegar
1/2 cup water
2 cloves garlic, crushed
2 large rosemary sprigs
1/4 teaspoon chopped hot pepper

flakes or 1 small piece of hot chili
    pepper, finely chopped
6 tablespoons extra virgin olive oil
1/2 teaspoon salt
1/2 teaspoon ground black pepper
1 cup dry white wine
1/2 cup chicken broth

Wash the rabbit pieces in the wine vinegar and water mixture, then wipe them dry with paper towels.

Place all of the rabbit pieces into a large bowl and add the crushed garlic, rosemary sprigs, chili pepper, olive oil, and sprinkle with salt and pepper. Cover the bowl and place it in a cool place or in the refrigerator to marinate for 10 to 12 hours, turning the rabbit pieces occasionally.

Place the rabbit pieces with the garlic, rosemary sprigs, chili pepper and oil into a casserole or Dutch oven. Sauté the rabbit pieces over medium heat on all sides until browned. Discard the garlic. Add the wine. Cover the casserole and cook over low heat for about 40 minutes, or until the rabbit pieces are tender. Add the broth, a little at a time, while the rabbit is cooking.

Serve the rabbit with some of the pan juices poured over them.

Funghi in Umido
Sautéed Mushrooms

Serves 4

Use a mixture of mushrooms such as oyster, crimini, champignon or portabello mushrooms to make this flavorful dish.

1 1/2 pounds mushrooms
4 tablespoons olive oil
1 small onion, chopped
2 tomatoes, chopped
1 bay leaf

2 fresh small rosemary sprigs
1/4 teaspoon salt
1/4 teaspoon freshly ground black
  pepper

Wipe the mushrooms with a damp paper towel to remove any dirt and then slice them.

Heat the olive oil in a large skillet over medium-high heat. Add the chopped onion and sauté until the onion starts to color, then add the chopped tomatoes, bay leaf, and rosemary sprigs. Cook for a few minutes and then add the sliced mushrooms. Continue cooking, over medium heat, for 10 to 15 minutes, stirring occasionally.

Season the mushrooms with salt and pepper and then serve them with the pieces of cooked rabbit.

Insalata di Finocchio e Arugula
Fennel and Arugula Salad

Serves 4

2 large or 4 small fennel bulbs	Juice of 1/2 lemon
2 bunches arugula, chopped	1/4 teaspoon salt
3 tablespoons extra virgin olive oil	1/4 teaspoon ground black pepper

Remove the outside leaves of the fennel and cut off the stalks and feathery tops. Cut the fennel bulbs lengthwise into quarters, then slice them into very fine lengthwise slices.

Place the sliced fennel and chopped arugula in a large bowl. Combine the olive oil, lemon juice, salt and pepper in a small bowl. Pour the dressing over the salad, toss thoroughly, and serve on individual plates.

Frutti di Bosco
Wild Berries

Serve 4

In the summer in Italy one can find wild berries in almost every region. Most of our berries, however, are cultivated and are quite good. For this recipe use either one kind of berry or a mixture of berries. These berries may also be served with whipped cream or a scoop of ice cream.

4 cups berries	1 cup mascarpone cheese
4 tablespoons sugar	1/3 cup heavy cream
2 tablespoons lemon juice	1/4 cup sugar

Clean the berries with a damp paper towel. If using wild berries, rinse them first.

Place the berries in a bowl, add the 4 tablespoons sugar and lemon juice and mix slowly. Cover the bowl and place in the refrigerator.

In a small bowl beat the cream until soft peaks form.

With a whisk beat together the mascarpone, cream, and sugar in a bowl until the mixture has stiff peaks. Divide the berries evenly among 4 dishes. Then top the berries with the whipped mascarpone mixture.

Una Cena al Caminetto
A Dinner by the Fireside

Serves 4

Stracciatella
Broth with Egg

Pollo con le Olive
Chicken with Green Olives

Carciofi Dorati
Fried Artichokes

Torta di Riso
Rice Tart

Caffè
Coffee

A Dinner by the Fireside

Winter brings cold temperatures and periods of rain to The Marches region. Sitting by a crackling fire and enjoying a delicious meal takes the chill out of even the coldest day.

For this fireside dinner I chose some typical dishes of The Marches. To enhance the warm feeling I have selected a soup to start the meal, light chicken broth with egg.

In the entree I combined the green olives that typically grow in The Marches with chicken cooked in wine. Chili peppers, which are a predominant seasoning of The Marches, are used to flavor the chicken along with rosemary. The olives provide a tangy undertone for this dish. I have selected fried artichokes to accompany this chicken dish.

An interesting and unusual rice tart with the intriguing flavors of pine nuts, cocoa powder, lemon rind, vanilla, and rum ends this fireside dinner

Preparations

Make the broth for the soup days ahead and refrigerate it. On the morning of the dinner mix the eggs, salt, Parmesan cheese, bread crumbs, flour, and lemon peel together in a small bowl. Cover and refrigerate. That evening, bring the broth to a boil and pour in the egg mixture.

Early in the afternoon of the meal prepare the chicken with olives. After adding the olives to the chicken, remove it from the heat and finish cooking the dish in the evening.

Cut and clean the artichokes early in the afternoon and keep them soaking in water. Beat the eggs with salt, pepper and parsley and set aside.

In the evening just before your guests are to arrive, fry the artichokes, place them on a plate with paper towels and keep them warm in a 200° F. oven or place them in a warming drawer.

The rice tart for the dessert can be made a day ahead or on the morning of the party.

Stracciatella
Broth with Egg

Serves 4

This soup is similar to *minestra del paradiso,* paradise soup from Emilia-Romagna region and also the *stracciatella alla Romana,* the Roman soup of the Lazio region. A very pleasant light soup, it is especially good when made with a homemade broth.

4 eggs	1 tablespoon all purpose flour
Pinch of salt	Grated peel of half lemon
4 tablespoons freshly grated Parmesan cheese	5 cups homemade chicken or beef broth
2 tablespoons bread crumbs	1 tablespoon finely chopped parsley

In a bowl beat the eggs and the salt with a fork. Then add the cheese, bread crumbs, flour, and grated lemon peel and mix thoroughly until well blended. Bring the broth to a boil, pour in the egg mixture, and stir with a whisk. Lower the heat and keep whisking for 1 minute. Serve while hot and sprinkle a little parsley over each serving.

Brodo
Broth

The Italians usually make homemade broth. It is either used as a broth for soup, a broth to be added when making risotto, or a broth for braising meats or vegetables. It is also used to make some sauces.

There are two kinds of broth used in Italian cooking. *Brodo di carne,* meat stock, and *brodo di verdura,* vegetable stock. The latter is a light, fresh flavored stock.

Stock is made with an assortment of bones from beef, veal, or chicken with some scraps of meat, and some vegetables and herbs to give flavor.

The vegetable stock is made with potatoes, carrots, onions, leeks, parsley, turnips and dried or fresh mushrooms. The vegetables are cooked in cold water over low heat for about 3 hours. The strained liquid is then used in vegetable soups, fish soups, or sauces.

Makes about 10 cups of broth

3 pounds bones and meat scraps
   from beef, chicken, or veal
1 medium onion, cut in half
2 celery stalks cut, in large pieces

2 carrots, cut into large pieces
2 medium tomatoes, cut in half
1/2 cup loosely packed parsley
1 tablespoon salt

Place the bones and meat scraps and the rest of the ingredients in a large stock pot. Add sufficient cold water enough to cover the ingredients by 2 inches (about 4 quarts). Cover the stock pot and bring to a boil over medium heat. As soon as the liquid starts to boil, lower the heat to low and simmer for 2 and 1/2 to 3 hours. Skim the surface foam that floats to the top occasionally. When cooked strain the broth into a bowl. Cool the broth completely, cover and then refrigerate long enough for any fat to come to the surface and solidify. Remove the fat and pour the clear broth into a plastic container or into ice-cube trays. Freeze until needed.

Pollo con le Olive
Chicken with Green Olives

Serves 4

2 1/2 to 3 pounds chicken, cut up
1/2 cup all purpose flour
3 tablespoons olive oil
2 garlic cloves, crushed
1/2 teaspoon salt
2 teaspoons fresh rosemary, coarsely
   chopped

1/2 teaspoon hot chili pepper, finely
   chopped
1 cup dry white wine
1 1/2 cups of green olives, pits
   removed
1/2 cup broth, if needed

Rinse the chicken pieces and pat them dry with paper towels,. Then dust them with flour.

Heat the olive oil in a large casserole or deep skillet over medium heat. Add the garlic cloves and sauté until they begin to brown. Discard the garlic, add the chicken pieces, and sauté until brown on all sides.. Sprinkle the chicken with salt, add the sprig of rosemary and the chopped chili pepper. Pour the wine over the chicken and let it reduce a little. Then add the broth. Cover the casserole and cook slowly over low heat for about 45 minutes. Fifteen minutes before the chicken is cooked, add the pitted olives. Check to see if more broth is needed and continue cooking, until the chicken is tender.

Carciofi Dorati
Fried Artichokes

Serves 4

4 large artichokes
1 lemon, cut in half
2 large eggs, beaten
Salt and freshly ground black
    pepper

2 tablespoons chopped fresh parsley
1/2 cup all purpose flour
Olive oil for frying
Lemon wedges

Cut the stems off the artichokes and remove the hard outer leaves with your fingers until only the pale leaves with green at the tips remain at the base of the artichokes. Cut off about 1 inch from the top, eliminating all the dark green parts of the leaves. Rub the cut edges with the lemon half. Cut the trimmed artichokes into quarters. Using a paring knife scrape away the inner choke and curly prickly leaves. Slice the quarters again in half and sprinkle with a little lemon juice. Place the artichoke pieces in a bowl with cold water and the remainder of the lemon juice fro 10 minutes. Drain the artichokes and pat them thoroughly dry with paper towels.

Beat the eggs with salt and pepper and the chopped parsley. Dip the artichoke pieces first into the flour and then into the beaten eggs.

Place the olive oil in a large frying pan over medium heat. When the oil is hot, add the artichoke pieces, letting the excess egg drip off. Cook them for about 10 minutes or until golden brown and cooked through, turning the artichoke pieces several times during cooking.

If necessary, cook the artichokes in batches. Do not cook them overlapping. When cooked place the artichoke pieces on a plate covered with paper towels to let excess oil drain off. Then place them on a platter and serve while hot with some lemon wedges.

Torta di Riso
Rice Tart

Serves 6 to 8

4 cups milk
2 cups arborio Italian rice
1 tablespoon unsalted butter
Pinch of salt
1 teaspoon vanilla extract
4 tablespoons pine nuts
1 1/4 cups sugar

1/3 cup cocoa powder
1 tablespoon rum
Grated rind of 1/2 lemon
3 eggs
Butter to grease pan
Fine dry bread crumbs

Bring the milk to a boil in a heavy saucepan, add the rice, butter, pinch of salt, and vanilla and cook covered for 15 minutes or until the rice is tender and the milk is absorbed. Let the rice cool.

In a large bowl mix together the pine nuts, sugar, cocoa powder, rum, grated lemon rind and rice. Beat the eggs and add them to the rice mixture.

Butter a 10-inch spring form pan and coat it with bread crumbs.

Pour the rice mixture into the pan and bake in a preheated 325° F. oven for about 50 minutes to 1 hour or until the top is brown.

Let the cake cool before removing from the pan and dust the top with confectioner's sugar.

Umbria

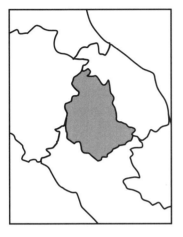

Umbria is a mountainous, land-locked region in central Italy. It is surrounded by Tuscany, The Marches, and Lazio regions. Umbria has a soft, typical Italian landscape that has kept beauty intact throughout the centuries. Its green valleys have many springs, rivers, and lakes. There are still walled towns and cities of rose-colored stones which are unchanged since Medieval times.

Being inland and mountainous, winters in Umbria are cold and summers are pleasant with moderate temperatures. Snow prevails on the high mountains in winter.

Etruscans, who once inhabited the area taught the Umbrians the art of roasting meats on a spit. These Etruscans were good hunters and fishermen and were also experienced in agriculture.

However, agriculture is not an important part of the Umbrian economy, because now the land is divided into many individually-owned small plots. The principal crops are wheat, sugar beets, olives, and grapes. As the terrain of Umbria is mountainous, most of the agriculture is devoted to the raising of animals, primarily beef cattle and pigs. Umbria has good beef because the Umbrian breed has been crossed with the famous Chianina breed.

Meat is very important in Umbrian cooking. Umbrians slaughter their own pigs and prepare prosciutto and various type of *salumi*. The prosciutto is lean and sweet. *Capocollo*, also a preserved meat, is made from the neck of the pig and is flavored with wild fennel. Fresh and dried sausages, as well as the well-known mortadella are made by the Umbrians.

The meat of the Umbrian pigs is very tasty because the pigs roam in the mountains and feed on wild plants, herbs, and even truffles. *Porchetta*, a milk fed piglet, is roasted on the spit and served whole.

Recently wild boar has become very popular in Umbria. The Umbrian people say that some wild boar must have escaped from a Tuscany reserve and reproduced quickly because there are many wild boar in Umbria. When making prosciutto from wild boar the butchers leave a little fur on the hams so that they can be easily recognized.

Lamb is another specialty of the Umbria region. There are entire towns inhabited only by shepherds. These shepherds make cheese from sheeps' milk and sell their cheeses to the men of Norcia, the gastronomic capital of Umbria, where sausage is made. These men age the shepherds' cheeses along with their sausages. The shepherds also exchange their cheese with peasants for wine, olive oil, and *salumi*.

One of the specialties of the Umbria region is *tartufi neri di Norcia*, black truffles from Norcia. The black truffles are one of the backbones of Umbria cooking. Meat and fish dishes are prepared with them all over the region. Truffles are also used in pasta and egg dishes and fine slivers of the black truffles are used in salads. In Umbria a plain risotto made with butter and Parmesan cheese is often topped with slivers of black truffles. Many Italians prefer the black truffles of Umbria over the famous white truffles of Alba in Piedmont.

The fish eaten in Umbria comes primarily from the rivers and from Lake Trasimeno. Carp, tines, and perch are prepared with sage and olive oil. Eels found in the lake are prepared in a variety of ways.

The pasta dishes of Umbria are similar to those of their neighboring regions, but the Umbrians have three pasta specialties of their own. *Strascinati* and *umbrici* are long, thick spaghetti. *Ciriole ternana* are wide thick tagliatelle that are often served with olive oil, garlic, and a touch of chili pepper.

Every feast in Umbria has its specialty. At Christmas time there are *pinocchiate*, which are lemon or orange-flavored biscuits with pine nuts. There is also a sweet tagliatelle made with sugar, walnuts, raisins, and chopped dried figs. At Easter time there is the *crescia di pasqua* which is a savory brioche that is eaten for breakfast with hard boiled eggs and prosciutto.

At Carneval time, the Umbrians make fritters in the shape of small chestnuts,. The dough for these fritters is made with wine. The finished fritters are dipped in honey with few drops of liqueur before serving.

Misty lanscape in Umbria.
Photo courtesy of Frank Spadarella.

Rocciata is a strudel-type roll filled with dried figs, prunes, almonds, pine nuts and hazelnuts. The strudel may also be filled with fresh apples or pears and nuts and seasoned with nutmeg and cocoa. These strudels may be eaten cold or hot.

Torciolata is a chocolate and apple strudel in the shape of a coil. It has this shape because it resembles the rolled cloth women used to put on their heads when carrying heavy things.

Some of the world's best chocolates are made in Perugia, the capital of Umbria. The company whose name is Perugina is famous for its chocolate *baci* (kisses) as well as its many other chocolate creations.

Wines

There not many wines from the Umbrian region. Orvieto, the most significant producer, makes two types of wine. One is slightly sweet and is served as a dessert wine, and the other is a dry white wine, which is good with fish.

Red Torgiano from near Perugia is known as Rubesco, the name of the main producer. It is a superb aged wine. Torgiano Bianco, also known as Torre di Giano, is a tart, fruity white wine. Montefalco is a dark, strong full-bodied red with a scent of blackberries.

Vin Santo, a strong, very rich, usually sweet wine is also made in Umbria. Sometimes it is made as a dry wine, golden amber in color.

E l'Ora di Pranzo
It's Dinner Time

Serves 4

Crostini di Olive
Olive Crostini

Acquacotta dell'Umbria
Tomato-Onion Soup from Umbria

Filetti di Maiale con Capperi
Pork Fillets with Capers

Fave con Pancetta
Broad Beans with Pancetta

Torcolo Perugino
Perugian Cake

Caffè
Coffee

It's Dinner Time

This is a tasty dinner and easy to prepare.

In planning this menu I decided to feature olives, which are grown in Umbria, in the crostini appetizers. The olives are mixed with anchovies, capers, garlic and oil to make a delicious spread for the crostini.

The tomato-onion soup has a mild acidic taste and is a colorful start to this meal. It is also good reheated the following day.

The entree consists of pork fillets which are sautéed in olive oil and then braised with red wine, lemon juice and capers. Broad beans with pancetta and scallions accompany the pork fillets.

The Perugian cake, which has a very pleasing flavor of orange, lemon and anise, finishes this meal. The leftover cake may be served with coffee for breakfast the next day for an additional taste treat.

Preparation

Make the olive mixture several days ahead and refrigerate. This will give the ingredients a chance to blend together and enhance the flavor.

Use good ripe tomatoes and a high quality olive oil to pour over the bread in the tomato-onion soup, Make the soup a day ahead or early in the morning. Toast the bread slices and set them aside. The evening of the dinner, heat the soup to boiling. Assemble the bread in the dishes with the oil, pour the soup over the bread and add the Parmesan cheese.

I recommend preparing the pork fillets the evening of the dinner. Just before your guests are to arrive, cook the pork fillets completely, cover, and set aside. Reheat them for a few minutes before serving.

The broad beans with the pancetta can be cooked completely ahead of time and reheated in the evening.

Make the Perugian cake a day ahead, and set it aside. Slice it that evening and put some whipping cream on top of each slice.

Crostini di Olive
Olive Crostini

Serves 4

To make this olive spread use olives of a very good quality, such as the Italian gaetas.

1 medium coarse loaf of bread, cut into slices
I cup pitted black olives
4 anchovies packed in olive oil, drained and chopped

2 tablespoons capers, drained
2 garlic cloves, cut into pieces
6 tablespoons extra virgin olive oil

Place the slices of bread flat on a cookie sheet and toast them in a 350° F. oven until golden in color.
Put all the remaining ingredients in a food processor and blend until the anchovies, capers, and garlic are finely chopped, but not mashed.
Spread the olive mixture on the toasted bread and serve.

Acquacotta dell'Umbria
Tomato-Onion Soup from Umbria

Serves 4 to 6

This is a thick and tasty soup, which is made with leftover bread.

1/4 cup extra virgin olive oil
4 onions, thinly sliced
6 fresh mint leaves
2 pounds ripe tomatoes, peeled and seeded or 1 (35 ounce) can peeled tomatoes, chopped
2 cups or more vegetable broth made with 1 bouillon cube
1 teaspoon salt

1/2 teaspoon freshly ground black pepper
6 thick slices country-style bread, stale if possible, if not toasted
6 tablespoons extra virgin olive oil
Salt and black pepper
1/2 cup freshly grated Parmesan cheese

Place 1/4 cup olive oil and the onion in a soup pot and sauté over medium heat until the onion is soft. Add the mint leaves, tomatoes, and vegetable broth. Season with salt and pepper and cook slowly , covered, over low heat for about 30 minutes. If the soup mixture becomes too thick and dry, add some broth. Toast the slices of bread in the oven, and then place a slice of toasted bread in each soup bowl.

Cover each slice of bread with 1 tablespoon of olive oil and season with a little salt and pepper. Pour the tomato soup into the bowls, sprinkle with Parmesan cheese and serve.

Filetti di Maiale con Capperi
Pork Fillets with Capers

Serves 4

3 tablespoons extra virgin olive oil	*1 teaspoon salt*
8 fillet slices of pork tenderloin	*1/2 teaspoon freshly ground black pepper*
1 cup dry red wine	
Juice of 1/2 lemon	*1 tablespoon capers, drained*

Place the oil in a casserole or skillet large enough to accommodate all of the fillets of pork in one layer. Heat the olive oil over medium-high heat, add the pork slices and sauté them on both sides until golden in color, about 10 minutes.

Add the red wine and lemon juice and season with salt, and pepper. Then add the drained capers and continue cooking, covered, over low heat until the wine has almost evaporated and the meat is cooked, about 20 minutes.

Serve 2 pork slices with sauce per person.

Fave con Pancetta
Broad Beans with Pancetta

Serves 4

1 pound fresh broad (fava) beans
Salt for water
3 tablespoons extra virgin olive oil
1/2 cup chopped pancetta or bacon

1/2 teaspoon salt
1/2 teaspoon freshly ground black
   pepper
2 scallions, finely chopped

     Shell the beans and cook them in a saucepan with lots of boiling salted water, over medium heat. Cook the beans slowly and as soon as they are tender, drain them.

     Place the oil in a small saucepan over medium heat. Add the chopped pancetta and sauté until the pancetta turns golden in color. Add the cooked fava beans, season with salt and pepper and add the chopped scallions. Stir thoroughly and cook for a few minutes. Then serve the fava beans with the pork slices.

Torcolo Perugino
Perugian Cake

Serves 8 to 10

     This is a classic sweet dessert from Perugia. It is traditionally served at the feast San Costanzo, the patron of the city of Perugia. In some other areas, olive oil and pine nuts are add to this dessert.

1/2 cup milk
3 1/2 ounces raisins, to be soaked in
   lukewarm water
2 egg yolks
3/4 cup sugar
2 egg whites

2 cups all purpose flour
1/4 cup candied orange and lemon
   peel, chopped
1 tablespoon anise seeds
1 egg yolk

Place the milk in a saucepan over medium heat; do not let the milk boil. When the milk is hot, add the butter and stir until the butter is melted.

Soak the raisins in lukewarm water for 15 minutes.

Beat the egg yolks with the sugar until pale yellow. Beat the egg whites until stiff, then fold them into the beaten egg yolks.

Place the flour in a bowl, add the egg mixture and mix thoroughly. Add the squeezed raisins, mix again and then add the milk mixture, the candied peel and the anise seeds. Mix thoroughly and work the dough with your hands until it is light and soft. If needed, add a little more milk.

Butter a bundt pan and place the dough into it. Use a pastry brush dipped in the beaten yolk and brush the egg yolk over the top of the dough.

Place the cake pan in a preheated 375° F. oven for about 30 minutes, or until baked and golden brown in color.

Cool the cake and then remove it from the pan. Serve each slice of cake with some whipped cream.

Festa del Raccolto
Umbria Harvest Festival

Serves 6

Tagliatelle con Olive e Funghi
Tagliatelle with Olive and Mushroom Sauce

Polletti alle Erbe
Cornish Hens with Herbs

Verdure all'Agro di Limone
Vegetables with Oil and Lemon Dressing

Torta di Mele Rustica
Upside Down Apple Tart

Caffè
Coffee

Harvest Festival

Olives and a variety of mushrooms are in abundance in the Umbria region. Thus I have chosen tagliatelle with a mushrooms and olive sauce as a first course for this harvest dinner. Cream and cheese are added to the sauce for a creamy texture and a more complex flavor.

The main course consists of Cornish hens marinated with herbs and then grilled. The herbs add a pleasing aroma and flavor to the birds. Mixed boiled vegetables, each with its own distinctive flavor, are seasoned with an oil vinaigrette, and are a mild accompaniment to the Cornish hens.

The rustic apple tart with its flavors of cinnamon, nutmeg, and almonds is a great ending to the harvest festival.

Preparations

You can make most of the dishes in this menu ahead of time.

On the morning of the dinner clean the Cornish hens by removing extra fat and rinsing them under cold water; then pat them dry. Season the Cornish hens with salt and pepper and brush them with the marinade sauce, then pour the remaining sauce over them. Cover the hens with plastic wrap and refrigerate them all day, basing them several times during the day. One hour before you are going to grill the hens, bring them to room temperature.

You can completely cook the sauce for the tagliatelle one hour before your guests are to arrive. However, clean the mushrooms and remove the pits from the olives ahead of time. Also chop the garlic and parsley.

In the morning clean and cut all of the vegetables. Cook them about 40 minutes before guests are to arrive. Then season the vegetables with the oil, lemon juice, salt and pepper. Just before you are going to serve the vegetables, toss them gently and serve.

The dessert can be made a day ahead. It can be served at room temperature or reheated for a few minutes.

Tagliatelle con Olive e Funghi
Tagliatelle with Mushrooms and Olive Sauce

Serves 6

4 tablespoons extra virgin olive oil
3/4 pound mushrooms, thinly sliced
2 garlic cloves, finely chopped
3 tablespoons fresh chopped parsley
3/4 cup black olives (gaetas or
    Kalamata) pitted and chopped
    coarsely
1 1/2 cups whipping cream

1/4 teaspoon freshly ground black
    pepper
1/4 teaspoon ground chili pepper
1 pound dry tagliatelle or fettuccine
    pasta
1/2 cup freshly grated Parmesan
    cheese

Heat the olive oil in a skillet over medium-high heat. Then add the mushrooms and sauté for about 5 minutes, stirring often. Add the chopped garlic and parsley and sauté for another 3 to 4 minutes. Do not burn the garlic.

Add the chopped olives, the whipping cream, and the black and chili peppers. Simmer over low heat, stirring occasionally for few minutes or until all is incorporated.

Boil the tagliatelle or fettuccine pasta in lots of boiling salted water until the pasta is cooked, but al dente to the bite. When cooked, drain the pasta thoroughly and place the pasta back into the pot in which it was boiled. Add the mushrooms-olive sauce to the pasta and stir. Sprinkle with the Parmesan cheese, toss again, and serve while hot.

Polletti alle Erbe
Cornish Hens with Herbs

Serves 6

Partridge, squabs, guinea hen, quail, or pheasant may be substituted for the domestic-raised Cornish hens, if desired. All of these birds are caught in the Umbria region.

The Cornish hens can either be cooked under the broiler, on the grill, or in a large heavy skillet.

3 large Cornish hen (about 2 pounds or more each) or 6 small Cornish hens	*6 tablespoons olive oil*
	4 garlic cloves, thinly sliced
	3 sprigs rosemary, stems removed
2 teaspoons salt	*2 tablespoons dried ground sage or*
2 teaspoons freshly ground black pepper	*16 fresh sage leaves, coarsely chopped*
Juice of 2 large lemons	*Lemon wedges, for garnish*

Have your butcher butterfly the Cornish hens and then cut them in half lengthwise. You can cut the hens yourself lengthwise along the entire backbone. Then open out the Cornish hens until flat, and cut in-between the two breasts, making two halves of each hen.

Place each half hen, skin side down, on a cutting board and with a meat pounder or a large cleaver, beat the hens without breaking the bones to flatten them. Rinse and dry them with paper towels. Season each half with salt and pepper. In a small bowl combine the lemon juice, olive oil, garlic, rosemary, and sage and mix until blended.

Then place the Cornish hens in a large shallow bowl and brush each half with the oil mixture. Pour the remaining oil mixture over them. Let the hens marinate for at least 2 to 3 hours, best if marinated all day; basting the hens several times with the oil mixture.

Preheat a broiler, grill, or barbecue. Place the Cornish hens with the skin side facing the heat in a broiler pan and broil for 5 minutes, then turn and baste with the marinade. Keep turning and basting then hens. Cook for about 20 minutes, or until the hens are tender and brown in color. If cooking the hens in a large skillet, place the hens and the marinade in the skillet and cook over medium heat, turning the birds often for about 15 to 20 minutes, or until the hens are tender and golden brown.

Serve 1/2 or 1 Cornish hen per person with a few lemon wedges.

Verdure all'Agro di Limone
Vegetables with Oil and Lemon Dressing

Serves 6

1 large fennel bulb
2 medium potatoes
2 or 3 carrots
1/4 pound small string beans
3 zucchini

1 tablespoon fresh chopped parsley
Salt
Freshly ground black pepper
1/4 to 1/3 cup extra virgin olive oil
Juice of 1 lemon

Cut off the long stalks and outside bruised leaves of the fennel. Slice the end off and rinse the fennel. Cut the fennel into quarters

Nearly fill a large saucepan with water, add some salt and bring to a boil over medium-high heat.

First cook the potatoes, which will take longer to cook, about 20 to 25 minutes. After 10 minutes, as the potatoes are cooking, add the carrots and fennel for about 10 to 15 minutes. When cooked remove the carrots and fennel wedges and slice the carrots into 1/4-inch rounds. Cut each fennel wedge in half.

Place the carrots and fennel in a salad bowl. Check to see if the potatoes are done. Add the beans and zucchini to the saucepan and cook them for about 5 to 10 minutes. Drain the beans and the zucchini and cut the zucchini into 1/4-inch rounds. Add beans and zucchini to the salad bowl. Peel the potatoes while hot and let them cool for about 20 minutes before cutting them into 1/4-inch slices.

The vegetables should be boiled to a crisp tenderness. Taste the vegetables while cooking to check if done

Add the potatoes to the salad bowl and sprinkle the vegetables with the chopped parsley. Season with salt and pepper. Gradually pour the olive oil and lemon juice over the vegetables and toss gently. Serve hot or at room temperature with the Cornish hens.

Torta di Mele Rustica
Upside Down Apple Tart

Serves 6 to 8

Apples have been a traditional fruit all over Italy and grow in abundance in Umbria. Ground almonds are used in the tart dough which is the base for sliced, tart apples seasoned with cinnamon and nutmeg.

8 tablespoons (1 stick) unsalted
   butter
1 1/4 cups all purpose flour
2 teaspoons sugar

1/2 cup blanched ground almonds
1 egg yolk
3 tablespoons ice water

Cut the butter into the flour in a bowl until the mixture resembles fine crumbs. Stir in the ground almonds and sugar. Combine the egg yolk and water and slowly stir into the flour mixture with a fork. Stir well to combine. Then using your hands, shape the dough into a ball. Place the dough between two large sheets of plastic wrap and with a rolling pin, roll the dough 1 inch larger than a 9-inch round cake pan. Carefully place the dough in the refrigerator for 20 minutes, while preparing the apples.

Apple Topping

3 tablespoons unsalted butter
1/4 cup sugar
5 large tart apples, peeled, cored,
   and thinly sliced

1/2 teaspoon cinnamon
1/2 teaspoon nutmeg
Whipped cream, for garnish

Place the butter and sugar in a 9-inch round cake pan and melt the mixture over low heat. Continue cooking, stirring constantly, with a wooden spoon, until the mixture is a light golden brown. Remove from heat, cool slightly, and add the apple slices, making sure that the top is reasonably flat. Sprinkle the apples with the cinnamon and nutmeg. Unwrap the pastry and fit it over the apples, tucking the edges under the crust. Bake in a preheated 400° F. oven for 30 to 35 minutes, or until the crust is lightly browned.

After removing the tart from the oven, immediately turn it upside down on a serving plate. Leave the pan on the tart for a few minutes to let all of the juice permeate the crust, Serve warm or cool with whipped cream, if desired.

Lazio

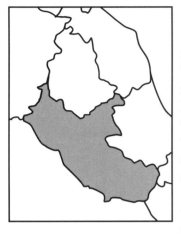

Lazio was originally called Latium, as the first people to inhabit the area were called Latins. This was long before Rome existed. Later, as the influence of Rome spread, the inhabitants became known throughout Italy as Romans. They were then and still are very proud people who defend their traditions. Romans are very friendly and treat strangers with familiarity. Above all, they love pleasure and good food.

The region of Lazio, with Rome as its center, occupies a large belt of land along the west coast of Italy and extends from the Appennines in the east to the Tyrrhenian Sea in the west. To the north it touches Tuscany and to the south, the region surrounding Naples, called Campania.

Lazio is the division between northern and southern Italy. Consequently the region's cooking is a combination of southern and northern Italian dishes.

Rome is the center and capital of the Lazio region today as it has been for 2000 years. The cuisine of Lazio, therefore, is basically that of Rome. No other city in Italy has as many restaurants, trattories, and inns serving food.

Lazio is a sun-scorched land of volcanic origin although it has many different types of land. There are mountains, lakes of volcanic origin, very fertile valleys, and sandy beaches along the coast. Some of the mountains are bare of trees while others are covered with forests and olive groves.

The climate of Lazio varies. Near the coast the winters are mild and the sea refreshes the suffocating heat of summer. The middle of the region experiences hot summers and cold winters. Rain is scarce near the coast and in the valleys, but abundant in the mountains, particularly in winter and spring.

The Roman countryside with its volcanic soil is ideal for growing vegetables because the mineral content of the soil enhances the flavor and the quality of the vegetables. Lazio is known throughout Italy for its crisp lettuce, celery, cabbage, cauliflower, tomatoes, carrots, , zucchini, pumpkin, and artichokes

Along the coast of Lazio, red mullets, squid, and octopus, as well as shellfish are harvested. Eels are found in some of the volcanic lakes. In the countryside farmers raise sheep, suckling pigs and lamb for their own table.

Because of the abundance of vegetables in and around Rome, the Romans use a large amount of raw vegetables in their cuisine. In the spring and summer they serve *pinzimonio*, raw vegetables dipped in olive oil, lemon juice, salt, and pepper. Another dish with raw vegetables is *panzanella*, which consists of stale bread soaked in water and served with fresh raw tomatoes, red onion, celery, basil, and parsley dressed with olive oil, vinegar, salt and pepper.

Asparagus has long been another favorite of the Romans. As soon as spring arrives, they enjoy the young, very thin and tender, wild asparagus shoots.

Since ancient times artichokes have been a Roman favorite. One of the best loved artichoke dishes is *carciofi alla giudea* (artichokes Jewish style). Many artichoke dishes in Rome originated in the restaurants of the old Jewish ghetto. In this recipe artichokes are flattened out and deep fried. Another favorite is *carciofi alla Romana*, which is an artichoke stuffed with bread crumbs, parsley, anchovies, and salt and pepper.

Other vegetable dishes of Lazio are spinach with pine nuts and raisins; stuffed tomatoes with rice; peas with onion and prosciutto; broccoli with sausages; peppers with bacon; mushrooms with garlic and mint; and zucchini stuffed with ground beef. Roman frittates are made with vegetables and eggs or cheese such as ricotta, mozzarella, or pecorino.

There are many classic Roman pasta dishes. A number of these pasta dishes are made with spaghetti, the best known of which is *spaghetti carbonara*. This dish is believed to have originated in the neighboring Umbria region and was brought to Lazio by Umbrian coal miners, called carbonari.

Other popular Lazio pasta dishes are *pasta all'amatriciana* made with fried, cured pork meat, chili peppers, tomatoes and pecorino cheese; *pasta all'arrabbiata* made with hot red peppers; and *pasta alla carrettiera* made with tuna and mushrooms.

Used in a variety of dishes, sheep, suckling pigs and lamb abound in the countryside. The most famous lamb dish is *abbacchio*. It is a suckling lamb that has not eaten any grass, only dry feed, and is killed when it is just 3 weeks old. The lamb usually weighs about 20 pounds. It is roasted either in the oven or over an open spit with pork fat and seasoned with garlic, sage, and rosemary. The lamb is often served with a sauce containing anchovies, olive oil, vinegar, garlic, and rosemary.

Pork is also a very important ingredient of Roman cooking. Until recently *strutto*, pork fat, was the prime fat used in cooking, but health conscious Romans now prefer olive oil. As in other regions a well-known dish is *porchetta*, a pig that is killed when it is six or seven months old, boned, flavored with herbs and then roasted, preferably on a spit.

Another popular meat dish is beef stew made with celery. One of the most famous Roman meat dishes is *saltimbocca* which means "jump in the mouth," because it is so good. *Saltimbocca* is made with thin slices of veal scaloppini topped with prosciutto and sage. *Pollo coi peperoni*, a popular chicken dish, is made with peppers and tomatoes, garlic, and white wine.

Organ meats have been a staple of peasants for centuries. Oxtail, tripe, and *pagliata* are still popular dishes made with organ meats. *Pagliata* is made from part of the intestine of a calf or an oxen. It is a traditional peasant dish of the Roman countryside. *Pagliata* can be grilled or cooked in a tomato and wine sauce spiced with rosemary, cloves, and chili peppers.

Romans make a variety of soups. However, the most famous is *stracciatella alla Romana*, a very simple, delicate soup prepared with homemade broth, Parmesan cheese, and eggs. The latter two are combined and beaten into the broth. The soup is flavored with nutmeg. Other soups are made with peas, fava beans, and potatoes. There is also one based on lentils and another made with whole wheat berries that dates from Roman times.

Romans do not put a great emphasis on desserts but there are several traditional ones of note. At carnival time before Lent, fried pastries dusted with powdered sugar, are popular traditional sweets. *Crostate* and tarts are also typical desserts of the area. Ricotta is used to make ricotta pudding and also ricotta fritters. *Zuppa Inglese*, similar to English trifle, is popular in Lazio.

Wines

The best wines of Lazio are grown on the volcanic slopes of Castelli Romani, hills southwest of Rome. Primarily dry and sweet white wines are produced from these grapes, including Frascati, which has been made since Roman times.

A variety of wines are also produced in other areas of the Lazio region. One of the most popular of these Roman wines is Falerno, a wine which was a favorite in the days of the Caesars. Most of these local wines are consumed in Lazio, leaving little to be exported.

Other wines of Lazio are the golden-yellow Frascatis; Colli Albani, a dry white wine; and the excellent white wines of Marino.

Dessert wines include Aleatico of Gradoli from near Viterbo district, a sweet aromatic red; Cesanese from near Sabina; and Ciociaria.

The Fountain of Trevi in Rome.
Photo courtesy of Frank Spadarella.

Buon Viaggio
Bon Voyage

Serves 10

Spaghetti alla Carbonara
Spaghetti with Pancetta and Cheese

Involtini di Vitello con Prosciutto e Vino Bianco
Veal Rolls with Prosciutto and White Wine

Piselli e Carciofi
Peas and Artichokes

Patate Arrostite al Rosmarino
Roasted Potatoes with Rosemary

Insalata Mista
Mixed Salad

Dolce di Ricotta
Roman Cheesecake

Caffe
Coffee

Bon Voyage

If you are planning a trip to Europe, especially to Italy, here are some Roman dishes you may want to try prior to your trip to give you a little taste of Roman cuisine.

Spaghetti with an egg and ham sauce starts the meal. This light and flavorful pasta is the one of the most famous pastas of the Rome.

The entree of veal rolls stuffed with prosciutto and sage and cooked in white wine is a version of the classic Roman dish, saltimbocca. The veal rolls are accompanied by a combination of peas and artichokes. Both vegetables are typical of Roman cuisine. Roasted potatoes also accompanies the veal rolls.

The slight sharpness of arugula in the mixed salad of spring greens provides a pleasing interlude and palate cleanser before the dessert of a Roman cheesecake. This cheesecake is made entirely of ricotta without a crust.

Preparation

In the morning, cut the pancetta into cubes, crush the garlic and chop the parsley for the spaghetti sauce. Place these ingredients in the refrigerator for later use. In the evening while the spaghetti are cooking make the sauce and then assemble the pasta and sauce.

Also in the morning prepare the veal rolls layering the veal slices with the prosciutto and sage and then rolling up the meat. Cover the veal rolls with plastic wrap and place them in the refrigerator. Sauté the veal rolls before your guests arrive and make the sauce with the wine. Then cover them and set them aside until ready to serve. Reheat, if necessary, and serve.

Make the peas and artichokes vegetable dish in the morning up to adding the prosciutto and peas with the broth. Then stop the cooking, cover, and set the vegetables aside.

That evening cook the vegetables for 5 to 6 minutes. In the early afternoon peel and cut the potatoes in pieces lengthwise and keep them in cold water. Rinse the rosemary sprigs. Forty-five minutes before dinner, cook the potatoes.

In the morning or afternoon rinse the mixed salad greens, pat them dry with paper towels and refrigerate them in a plastic bag. Make the lemon dressing for the salad and set it aside.

Make the cheesecake in the morning, cover it, and refrigerate.

Spaghetti alla Carbonara
Spaghetti with Egg and Bacon Sauce

Serves 10

6 tablespoons olive oil
1 cup pancetta or bacon, diced
2 garlic cloves, crushed
Salt
2 pounds spaghetti
4 eggs
1/2 cup freshly grated Parmesan
 cheese

1/2 cup freshly grated pecorino
 cheese
6 tablespoons whipping cream
1 tablespoon freshly ground black
 pepper
2 tablespoons chopped fresh parsley

Heat the oil in a small sauté pan over medium heat and sauté the pancetta or bacon and the crushed garlic. When the garlic starts to turn brown, discard it.

Bring a large pot of salted water to a boil over high heat, add the pasta and cook until al dente.

While the pasta is cooking, beat the eggs in a large bowl with a little salt, the Parmesan and pecorino cheese, whipping cream and freshly ground black pepper. As soon as the pasta is cooked, drain it and place it back into the pot. Add the egg mixture and the bacon with its cooking fat. Then cook over very low heat, stirring constantly for a few minutes to heat the eggs completely.

Sprinkle the parsley over the pasta, toss again and serve immediately while hot.

Involtini Di Vitello
Con Prosciutto e Vino Bianco
Veal Rolls with Prosciutto and White Wine

Serves 10

20 slices of veal scaloppine
20 thin slices of prosciutto
24 fresh sage leaves

1/2 teaspoon freshly ground black
   pepper
6 tablespoons unsalted butter
1 cup dry white wine

Lay the scaloppine flat on a work surface and cover each with a slice of prosciutto, place a sage leaf on top and sprinkle with some black pepper. Roll up the scaloppine and fasten each one with a round toothpick, inserting it lengthwise so that it is parallel to the roll.

Choose a skillet large enough to accommodate ten rolls at a time in a single layer without overlapping or cook them in several batches. By not crowding the rolls they will brown better. Add the butter to the skillet and melt over medium heat. When the butter foam begins to subside, add the veal rolls and the remaining 4 sage leaves. Sauté over medium-high heat, for about 5 to 7 minutes, turning the veal rolls until they have become a golden color all over, then transfer them to a plate. Add the wine to the skillet and scrape loose any cooking residue with a wooden spoon. Reduce the wine by half, then return all the rolls to the skillet turning them often in the pan juices for a few minutes. Turn off the heat, add one tablespoon of butter and incorporate it with the juices.

Remove the toothpicks before serving and serve 2 veal rolls per person with some of the pan juice.

Piselli e Carciofi
Peas and Artichokes

Serves 10

2 pounds fresh peas, or frozen,
  thawed
2 pounds baby artichokes, or 6
  medium
1 lemon, cut in half
1/4 cup extra virgin olive oil
1 large onion, finely chopped

1 teaspoon salt
1 teaspoon freshly ground black
  pepper
1 cup dry white wine
1/2 cup chopped prosciutto
1 cup chicken broth

Shell the peas, if using fresh ones. Cut off the stems of the artichokes and remove the hard outer leaves with your fingers, until only the pale leaves with green at the tips remain at the base of the artichokes. Cut off one inch off the top of each artichoke, making sure that all of the dark green parts of the leaves have been eliminated.

Rub the cut edges with the lemon half. Cut the trimmed artichokes into quarters. Using a paring knife scrape away the inner choke and curly prickly leaves. Slice each artichoke quarter in half and sprinkle with a little lemon juice. If using the small artichokes, do the same as above except cut the artichokes only in quarters. Place them in a bowl of cold water with the remaining lemon juice for 10 minutes. Drain the artichokes and pat them dry with paper towels.

Place the olive oil in a large sauté pan over medium heat. When the oil is hot add the chopped onion and sauté until soft. Then add the artichokes and sprinkle them with some salt and pepper. Stir and turn the artichokes 3 or 4 times and cook them for about 10 minutes. Then add the wine and let it evaporate for 1 minute. Cover the pan, reduce the heat to low and cook the artichokes until they are almost tender, about 5 minutes. Add the chopped prosciutto, peas and broth. Stir and cook covered on low heat for 5 to 6 minutes. (If using fresh petite peas, cook them only 2 to 3 minutes.) Season with salt and pepper, mix well and serve.

Patate Arrostite al Rosmarino
Roasted Potatoes with Rosemary

Serves 10

3 pounds potatoes
3/4 cup olive oil
6 sprigs rosemary
10 garlic cloves with skin

1 tablespoons salt
1 teaspoon freshly ground black
   pepper

Peel the potatoes and cut them into pieces lengthwise. Place the olive oil in an oven proof dish. Arrange the potatoes in one layer and roll them in the oil until well coated. Add the rosemary sprigs and the garlic cloves. Sprinkle the salt and pepper over the top. Stir all the ingredients together and place the dish in a preheated 350° F. degree for 40 to 45 minutes, depending on thickness of the potatoes. Stir the potatoes several times during roasting. Before serving, remove the rosemary and garlic. Transfer the potatoes to a warm serving dish and serve with the veal rolls.

Insalata Mista
Mixed Salad

Serves 10

1 pound mixed spring salad greens
2 bunches of arugula
6 tablespoons extra virgin olive oil
Juice of 1 lemon

1 teaspoon salt
1/2 teaspoon freshly ground black
   pepper

Rinse the mixed spring salad greens and the arugula, dry well. Cut the arugula coarsely. Place the greens and arugula in a large bowl.

To make the dressing, whisk together the olive oil and lemon juice in a small bowl. Season with salt and pepper. Pour the dressing over the salad and toss thoroughly. Serve immediately.

Dolce di Ricotta
Roman Cheesecake

Serves 10

Ricotta, the great cooking cheese of Italy, is used in many Roman dishes from first course to dessert. In this dessert, ricotta is the base of a delicious cheesecake.

1 pound ricotta	*2 teaspoons ground cinnamon*
4 eggs, separated	*Grated rind of 2 lemons*
3 tablespoons flour	*5 tablespoons rum*
1 cup sugar	*Confectioner's sugar*

Mash the ricotta and beat it well with the egg yolks. Stir in the flour, sugar, cinnamon, grated lemon rind, and rum and mix well.

Beat the egg whites until stiff, and fold them into the ricotta mixture. Pour the batter into a buttered and floured 10-inch cake pan. Bake in a preheated 350° F. oven for about 40 minutes or until the cheesecake is firm. Remove the cheesecake from the oven and place it on a wire rack to cool. Then sprinkle the top with confectioner's sugar. Serve at room temperature or cold.

Una Celebrazione
A Celebration

Serves 10

Bruschetta al Pomodoro
Toasted Bread with Tomato and Mozzarella

Penne all'Arrabbiata
Angry Penne Pasta

Grigliata Mista di Carne
Mixed Grilled Meats

Broccoli a Crudo
Broccoli Sautéed with Wine and Garlic

Peperoni alla Pancetta
Peppers with Pancetta

Zuppa Inglese
Italian Trifle

Caffe
Coffee

A Celebration

There are many festivals and feast days that feature gastronomic traditions in Italy, especially in the Lazio region.

One of the festivals celebrated in Lazio is the Feast of the Befana on January 6th when children traditionally receive presents. This Feast was named for a toothless old woman, La Befana, who is the Italian equivalent of Santa Claus. She often brings sweets, called *befanini*, to the children. Another festival, Ferragosto, the Feast of the Assumption of the Virgin Mary, on August 15th is a celebration often associated with fish and fishermen because legend has it that Naples fishermen, thinking they had found a treasure, brought up a picture of the Madonna. To celebrate this event cooks fry large amounts of fish in gigantic pans.

I planned this Lazio menu for a big celebration. A typical antipasto of Roman cuisine — toasted bread with mozzarella, tomato, olive oil and a pinch of oregano — starts this menu.

Penne all'Arrabbiata, angry pasta, is made with fresh peas, mushrooms, pancetta, hot pepper flakes, and a little tomato sauce. This pasta, with its burst of color and a slight sharpness, is a very tasty dish. There is no record as to why the name angry pasta. I do know that eating this pasta evokes a very satisfying experience.

For the main course I selected a mixed grilled of lamb, veal, and pork, a typical dish of Lazio. Two vegetable dishes — broccoli with wine and garlic and the peppers cooked with pancetta — complements the mixed grill.

A scrumptious Zuppa Inglese, Italian trifle, finishes the meal of this celebration.

Preparation

There are several easy and simple preparations for this dinner that can be made ahead.

In the morning prepare the bruschetta with the tomato and mozzarella. Place the assembled bread slices on a dish, cover them, and refrigerate. In the evening place the bread slices on a baking sheet and bake them in the oven.

Make the sauce for the penne in the morning or even a day ahead and refrigerate it. In the evening while the pasta is cooking, simmer the sauce.

Prepare the 3 marinades for the meat early in the afternoon and pour the appropriate sauce over each of the meats, so that they can marinate for several hours. Bring the meats to room temperature before cooking them.

Also in the afternoon, prepare the broccoli by cutting off the stems. Then cut the broccoli into individual florets and place them in water. Chop the garlic and set it aside. Cook the broccoli in the evening,. This is a quick preparation, taking only 7 minutes.

Prepare the peppers a day ahead and refrigerate them. They may be served warmed or at room temperature.

Zuppa Inglese, an Italian version of English trifle, can be prepared a day or two ahead and refrigerated.

Bruschetta al Pomodoro
Roasted Bread with Tomato and Mozzarella

Serves 10

1 loaf country or French bread, cut into slices
2 garlic cloves, peeled
6 ripe Roma tomatoes, peeled and sliced lengthwise
Extra virgin olive oil
Salt
Freshly ground black pepper
2 (4 ounce) balls mozzarella cheese, thinly sliced
Pinch of oregano

Toast the slices of bread on a grill on in the oven, on both sides, until golden in color.

Rub garlic on one side of the bread only,. Place a tomato slice on each piece of bread, then sprinkle some oil over the tomato and season it with salt and pepper. Add a thin slice of mozzarella over each tomato and sprinkle with a pinch of oregano. Place the slices of bread on a baking sheet and place them in a preheated 350° F. oven for 10 minutes, or until the mozzarella has stated to soften.

You can serve the bruschetta as an antipasto at the dinner table or you can pass a tray of bruschetta while your guests are having drinks.

Penne all'Arrabbiata
Angry Penne

Serves 10

4 tablespoons unsalted butter
1 pound fresh mushrooms, cleaned
  and sliced
1/2 teaspoon salt
1/2 teaspoon freshly ground black
  pepper
2 tablespoons fresh chopped parsley
3 tablespoons olive oil
2 garlic cloves, finely chopped
1 cup cubed pancetta or bacon

1/4 teaspoon hot red pepper flakes
2 cups fresh shelled peas, or frozen
  peas, thawed
1 (28 ounces) can peeled Italian
  tomatoes, chopped, with their
  juice
2 tablespoons basil leaves, chopped
2 pounds penne rigate
1 cup freshly grated pecorino
  cheese

Place 3 tablespoons of the butter in a small sauté pan over medium heat. When the butter starts to foam add the sliced mushrooms and season them with salt and pepper. Add the chopped parsley and cook over low heat until the mushrooms start to brown.

Place the olive oil with the remaining 1 tablespoon of butter in a large saucepan over medium heat and add the chopped garlic. Sauté until the garlic starts to color, then add the cubed pancetta and the pepper flakes. Mix thoroughly and cook for a few minutes, or until the pancetta start to color. Add the peas, chopped tomatoes, and basil and mix well. Season with salt and cook slowly over low heat for about 20 minutes. Add the cooked mushroom mixture to this sauce and mix thoroughly

Boil the penne rigate in a large pot of boiling salted water until cooked, but still al dente. Drain the pasta and place it back into the pot. Add the sauce, sprinkle with the pecorino cheese and toss thoroughly until the cheese is melted. Serve while hot.

Grigliata Mista di Carne
Mixed Grilled Meat

Serves 10

Abbacchio allo Scottadito
Lamb Chops

10 lamb chops
8 tablespoons olive oil
4 garlic cloves, chopped
2 sprigs marjoram, finely chopped
2 tablespoon chopped parsley

2 sprigs rosemary
1/2 cup dry white wine
Juice of 1 lemon
Salt and freshly ground black
  pepper

Place the lamb chops on a platter. Combine all the remaining ingredients except the salt and pepper in a small bowl and then pour the mixture over the lamb chops. Marinate for at least 3 hours, or longer to enhance the flavors.

Costolette di Vitello All'erbe
Veal Chops

10 veal chops
8 tablespoons olive oil
4 garlic cloves, chopped

4 tablespoons chopped fresh rosemary
2 tablespoons chopped fresh sage
1/2 cup dry white wine

Place the veal chops on a platter. Combine all of the ingredients in a small bowl and pour the mixture over the veal chops. Marinate for at least two hours.

Braciole di Maiale con la Panuntella
Pork Chops with Grilled Bread Slices

Panuntella is the name given to the bread that absorbs the juices from the pork.

10 pork chops	1/2 teaspoon freshly ground black
1/2 cup olive oil	pepper
1 teaspoon salt	10 slices country bread

Place the pork chops on a platter. Combine the olive oil, salt and pepper in a small bowl. Pour the mixture over the pork chops just before you are going to grill them.

To Cook the Mixed Grill

Make sure the grill has been properly heated before adding the meats.

Cook the pork chops first since they take longer to cook than the other meats, about 15 minutes or about 7 minutes per side, depending on the thickness of the meat.

After the pork chops have cooked on one side, turn them and place a slice of bread over the cooked side of each pork chop to absorb any juices. Continue grilling the pork chops until golden in color and cooked through.

Place the bread slices on a platter, sprinkle each with some pepper and then place a pork chop on each bread slice. Serve each person a bread and pork chop.

The lamb and veal chops should be added to the grill just before turning the pork chops since their cooking time is about 8 minutes, or 4 minutes per side, depending on thickness and desired doneness. While the meats are cooking, brush them with some of their marinade. After they are cooked seasoned the meats with salt and pepper.

Broccoli a Crudo
Broccoli Sautéed with Wine and Garlic

Serves 10

2 1/2 to 3 pounds broccoli
Salt
6 tablespoons olive oil

3 large garlic cloves, finely chopped
Freshly ground black pepper
1 cup dry white wine

Clean the broccoli, discard any coarse leaves, and remove the hard stalks. Cut the broccoli into individual florets and rinse them under cold water. Then place them in a bowl with cold salted water until ready to be cooked. Before cooking drain the broccoli well and pat it dry with paper towel.

Heat the oil in a large sauté pan over medium heat and when hot add the broccoli florets, season with salt and pepper and sauté for 5 minutes, stirring often. Add the chopped garlic and continue to sauté for 2 more minutes. Add the wine, bring to a boil, and cook slowly over low heat, stirring often, until the florets are cooked but still al dente.

Peperoni alla Pancetta
Peppers with Pancetta

Serves 10

8 large sweet red bell peppers
4 tablespoons olive oil
3 tablespoons unsalted butter
1 large onion, thinly sliced

1/2 cup cubed pancetta or bacon
1 teaspoon salt
1/2 teaspoon freshly ground black
  pepper

Cut the peppers in half and remove the seeds. Wash the peppers and dry them with paper towels. Place them, cut side down, on a baking sheet and roast them under the broiler until the skin begins to blister and is dark brown. (The peppers may also be roasted over an open flame of a gas cook top.) Remove the peppers from the oven and place them in a brown paper bag. Close the bag and set aside for at least 10 minutes. Remove the peppers from the bag and peel the skin. Cut the peppers into 1-inch wide strips and set aside.

Heat the oil and butter in a large frying pan over medium heat. When the oil is hot and the butter foams, add the sliced onions and the cubed pancetta and sauté until the onion is limp and the pancetta is almost transparent. Add the peppers, season with salt and pepper, mix thoroughly and cook for 15 minutes. Serve either hot or at room temperature with the grilled meats.

Zuppa Inglese
Italian Trifle (English Soup)

Serves 12

We will probably never know why this popular dessert is called *zuppa inglese*, meaning English soup. One theory is that it is called soup because when the cake is soaked in custard it has the consistency of bread soaking in peasant soups. Just like soup, it is eaten with a spoon. In Italy *zuppa inglese* is traditionally flavored with rum and alchermes, a lightly spiced red liqueur, which is not available here.

5 cups custard
2 (10 ounce) pound cakes, cut into
   1/4 inch thick slices
4 tablespoons cognac
8 tablespoons Cherry Brandy

4 tablespoons Drambuie
2 tablespoons rum
4 ounces semi-sweet chocolate
   squares

Mix all of the liqueurs together in a small bowl.

Custard

6 egg yolks
2/3 cup sugar
10 tablespoons flour

4 cups milk
Grated peel of 1 lemon

Place the egg yolks and sugar into a heavy saucepan or in a double boiler. Beat the eggs until pale yellow and creamy. Add the flour slowly, beating in 1 tablespoon at a time.
Bring the milk to the point of boiling in another saucepan and then add the hot milk gradually to the egg mixture. Stir constantly to avoid lumps.

Place the saucepan over low heat, or if using a double boiler over simmering water in the bottom pan. Cook for about 5 minutes, stirring constantly with a wooden spoon. Do not let the mixture come to a boil. The custard is done when it clings to the spoon with a creamy coating.

Remove the custard from the heat and stir it for a few minutes to cool it a little. Then mix in the grated lemon peel.

To assemble the trifle, choose a deep trifle dish or a large bowl from which you will be serving the zuppa. Barely cover the bottom of the dish with 4 tablespoons of the hot custard.

Line the bottom of the dish with a layer of sliced pound cake. Dip a pastry brush into the liqueur mixture and brush the layer of pound cake with some of the liqueur. Cover the layer of pound cake with one-third of the custard. Add another layer of pound cake slices over the custard, and brush it with the liqueurs.

Place the chocolate squares into a small saucepan and melt over low heat.

Divide the remaining custard into two parts. Mix the melted chocolate into one and spread it over the cake in the bowl. Add another layer of sliced pound cake to the dish, brush it with the liqueurs and then cover it with the remaining custard.

I decorated the trifle with fresh sliced strawberries, covering the top of the trifle completely. The top of the trifle may also be decorated with 3/4 cup of sliced almonds.

Refrigerate the trifle for 2 to 3 hours before serving. If refrigerated for a longer period, cover the dish with plastic wrap. It can be refrigerated up to 3 days.

Abruzzi and Molise

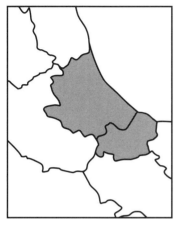

Abruzzi and Molise are situated next to each other on the east coast of Italy. They straddle the imaginary line that separates northern and southern Italy. The region has a typical Mediterranean climate of warmth toward the seashore and cold in the mountains. The Abruzzi and Molise region has some of the tallest peaks in the Apennines. Many are covered with snow almost all year.

Abruzzi and Molise became one region when Italy was unified in 1860, but the two regions were broken apart again in 1963. Except for administrative purposes, however, they are still considered to be one.

The cooking of the region emphasizes the dishes of the south, with accents on tomatoes and chili peppers. It is a simple cuisine primarily based on the availability of local ingredients and the meat raised by the local inhabitants. The cooks of Abruzzi and Molise have preserved their old recipes and still make many of the traditional dishes as they were prepared centuries ago.

There are two cuisines of Abruzzi and Molise. One is of the coast, featuring primarily fish. The other is of the interior and mountainous areas which is based on pork with some lamb, veal, and poultry. Although Abruzzi and Molise is not as poor as regions further south, it is not overly rich in food ingredients. Meat is not eaten often and is reserved for special occasions. If animals are raised by a family, the choice cuts are sold and the less-desirable and organ meats are kept by the family. The seacoast and interior areas of the region have pasta and vegetable dishes in common.

The most famous pasta dish of the region is *maccheroni alla chitarra*. Described as guitar macaroni, it is made with a dough consisting of flour, egg, and a little olive oil. Invented in Abruzzi, this pasta is made by stretching the thin dough over a rectangular wooden frame with steel guitar-like strings stretched across it. A rolling pin forces very thin strips of dough through the frame resulting in a square spaghetti, although the name *maccheroni* would indicate a hollow pasta. (In Abruzzi, like many regions, the term maccheroni encompasses all types of long pasta.) *Maccheroni alla chitarra*, like many pasta in Abruzzi, is still made at home.

Maccheroni alla chitarra is usually served with a tomato-meat sauce and freshly grated pecorino cheese. Small meat balls or chicken giblets are added to the sauce when a fancier dish is desired. This pasta is also frequently served with a tomato sauce flavored with sweet peppers and smoked fat pork, then topped with pecorino cheese. If mutton is available, cooks might top the *maccheroni alla chitarra* with *ragu di pecora* or mutton sauce. *All'amatriciana* is another sauce which consists of bacon, olive oil, and pecorino cheese.

Hot red chili peppers, known as *diavolillo*, are typically used in varying quantities. They are the prime seasoning of most pasta sauces in Abruzzi and Molise and are also used in non-pasta dishes. An example of the spiciness of Abruzzi food is a popular dish along the coast called *polpi in purgatorio*. It is cuttlefish cooked in a rich tomato sauce with garlic and liberally seasoned with peppers, thus the reference to purgatory in its name.

Shepherds tend sheep in the mountains of Abruzzi and Molise, as they did centuries ago. Lamb is a specialty of the region and is prepared in various ways. It is fried, roasted, or cooked *alla cacciatore* with tomatoes and red peppers. The less tender cuts of lamb are often cooked in a fricassee with an egg and lemon sauce.

Besides tending the sheep, the shepherds also make excellent cheese from the ewe's milk. In this region, as in many others, pecorino is the prime cheese followed by ricotta. Scamorza, a soft cheese, is made from the milk of cows who graze in mountain pastures. Scamorza is typically prepared for eating in an old Abruzzi manner. Several of the cheeses are threaded on a stick and laid on burning embers. The stick is turned often until the cheeses are an amber color and the inside is very creamy.

Pigs roam freely in the mountains with the sheep. Being the staple meat of the region, every part of the pig is used. The best known sausage is *ventricina*, which is made with pork, sweet peppers, fennel, and orange. The local prosciutto is made primarily in the mountains in Aquila and is similar to the famous Spanish *jamon serrano* (mountain ham). The Spanish occupied this area from the 1200s through the 1500s and taught the local mountain inhabitants how to cure ham in the Spanish style. *Porchetta*, suckling pig, is a specialty that is shared by many of the regions of central Italy. The local mortadella is different in that it has a piece of lard in the center.

A variety of fish is harvested along the coast of Abruzzi and Molise. One of the most famous seafood dishes of the region is *scapece*. For this dish, the fish is first fried and then preserved in white vinegar flavored with saffron. The recipe for *scapece* is of Greek origin and came to the region when the Greeks occupied it 200 years ago. Saffron, which is used extensively in Greek cooking, was introduced to Abruzzi by the Spanish when they occupied the area. Strangely the local fish soup, *brodetto alla pescarese*, does not use saffron as do the fish soups of neighboring regions. This Abruzzi fish soup is prepared with tomatoes, garlic, onion, bay leaf, red pepper, and a touch of white vinegar.

There are also fresh water fish in the interior of Abruzzi. Trout is the best known and most abundant. Trota del vera is a dish that consists of trout cooked in olive oil with tomatoes, parsley, and garlic. Another trout dish is baked in the oven with garlic, parsley, and capers, topped with bread crumbs.

Being a very mountainous region, game of all types can be found and is used as the basis of many local specialties. One of the most popular is rabbit, which is often skewered with sausages and grilled, Rabbits are also stuffed and cooked with eggs and lemon.

Other meat dishes of Abruzzi and Molise include goat, which is roasted, cooked on the spit, or cooked in a casserole with olive oil and wine. Ducks are cooked with lard and lemon juice or with local truffles and bacon. Chicken is often prepared with tomatoes and bell peppers as well as hot peppers.

Turkeys are raised by many of the local inhabitants. The turkeys are fed walnuts and tended with special care until they are ready to eat. One of the popular turkey dishes is *tacchino alla Canzanese* named after the small town of Canzano. This dish features a boned turkey that is cooked in the oven with salt and pepper, bay leaves, rosemary, sage, and carrots. Calves or pigs feet are added along with some water to keep the turkey moist during cooking. The turkey is served cold along with some of the jellied broth. *Tacchino alla nerese* consists of roasting a turkey on a spit.

Although fruit is the preferred everyday dessert of the region, there are many sweet specialties of Abruzzi and Molise. One of the most famous is *parrozzo*, a dessert from Pescara, a coastal town of Abruzzi. *Parrozzo* used to mean a poor man's bread made with cornmeal and boiling water. Today the name *parozzo* has been transferred to a cake made with flour, crushed almonds, butter and sugar with a chocolate frosting.

In Aquila, the capital of Abruzzi, a traditional Italian nougat is made with honey, sugar, almonds, egg whites and chocolate. Other sweets include *cicerchiata*, a confection made with honey and shaped to look like chick peas.

Town of Gildone. Photo courtesy of Frank Spadarella.

Fiadone and *siffioni* are Easter cakes filled with ricotta. There is also *pizza ripiena alla crema e marmellata di lamponi*, which is a unique sweet pizza filled with fresh custard and raspberry jelly.

Villa Santa Maria, a mountain village among the highest peaks of the Apennines in Abruzzi, is known all over Italy for its cooking school where many of Italy's and Europe's best chefs have received their education. For that small village the interest in cooking began in the sixteenth century when the princes of Naples came to Villa Santa Maria to hunt. The princes liked the way that the young men of Villa Santa Maria cooked game and eventually took these cooks back to their palaces near Naples.

Since then almost every young man in Villa Santa Maria has become a cook. First they cooked for the noble families of Naples and later for royalty all over the world. In 1939 a cooking school was established in Villa Santa Maria and in 1962 it was transformed into a culinary institute with an adjoining hotel. Today many chefs come to this school for one or two week courses taught by some of the most famous chefs of Italy and Europe.

Wines

The rocky slopes of much of Abruzzi and Molise are not easily conducive to the cultivation of wine grapes. However, there are some notable wines produced there, none of which are exported out of the region.

The best red wine is the Montepulciano d'Abruzzi. Cerasuolo d'Abruzzi is a lighter cherry-pink version of the same Montepulciano grape. It is usually served with soups, vegetables and roasted Scamorza cheese. Montepulciano d'Aquila pairs well with roasts and porchetta. Marsicano is also a pleasant dry red wine from the region. Trebbiano d'Abruzzi is a very dry white wine and is often served with fish.

There are various liqueurs made from herbs gathered in the woods and mountains. The best known is Centerbe. The name means a hundred herbs. It is emerald green in color and is made in two strengths of alcoholic content. The lighter version is served as an after-dinner drink. Other liqueurs are made with anise seeds, wormwood, and mountain herbs.

Una Cena per le Laureate
A Dinner for the Graduate

Serves 6

Fettuccine all'Abruzzese
Fettuccine Abruzzi-Style

Coniglio alla Molisana
Skewers of Rabbit and Sausages

Peperoni Arrostiti
Roasted Peppers

Funghi Arrostiti
Roasted Mushrooms

Parrozzo
Almond and Chocolate Cake

Caffe
Coffee

A Dinner for the Graduate

Graduation is a time when family and friends gather to honor the graduate. Since most graduations take place in the summer when the weather is warm I have chosen an Abbruzi menu that can be partially cooked ahead and then eaten outside.

The fettuccine Abruzzi-style is a piquant first course, which has a slight spicy saltiness from the pancetta and pecorino cheese.

For the entree, rabbit is seasoned with rosemary and sage and cooked with Italian sausage. The combination is prepared on the grill. A colorful platter of marinated bell peppers is served with the grilled meats, as well as roasted portabello mushrooms which are seasoned with hot chili peppers.

A rich almond and chocolate cake is a fitting ending for this dinner honoring the graduate.

Preparations

Several dishes on this menu can be prepared ahead. However, since the fettuccine does not take long to prepare and the sauce is best served fresh, make this dish just before dinner. The pancetta, onion, garlic, and parsley for the fettuccini can be chopped in the morning and refrigerated. In the evening sauté all these ingredients while the pasta is cooking and then chop the basil (if done earlier the basil will turn dark).

In the morning cut the rabbit into pieces. Chop the parsley and rosemary and assemble the rabbit, sausages and sage leaves onto the skewers, place them on a platter and refrigerate. Bring the meats to room temperature one hour before grilling. The roasted peppers and mushrooms can be prepared in the morning and served at room temperature.

Bake the cake the day before.

Fettuccine all'Abruzzese
Fettuccine Abruzzi-Style

Serves 6

1 pound fettuccine
1/4 cup extra virgin olive oil
4 slices pancetta or bacon, cut into
    small cubes, about 1 cup
1 small onion, finely chopped
3 garlic cloves, finely chopped
2 tablespoons chopped fresh parsley

6 basil leaves, finely chopped
Salt
1/2 teaspoon freshly ground black
    pepper
1/2 cup freshly ground pecorino
    cheese

Boil the fettuccine in a large amount of salted water until al dente. While the pasta is cooking, heat the oil over medium heat in a small saucepan. Add the pancetta, onion, and garlic and sauté. After a few minutes of sautéing, add the chopped parsley and basil and season with salt and pepper. Cook until the onions and garlic turn light gold. Remove pan from the heat.

Drain the pasta and return it to the pot in which the pasta was cooked. Add the sauce and the grated pecorino and toss them together for a few minutes, so that the sauce and cheese blend together with the fettuccine.

Coniglio alla Molisana
Skewers of Rabbit and Sausages

Serves 6

1 large (3 1/2 to 4 pound) rabbit
Salt and pepper
3 tablespoons fresh chopped parsley
2 rosemary sprigs, leaves finely
   chopped

12 thin slices of prosciutto, about
   1/4 pound
12 sage leaves
6 Italian sausages
1/2 cup olive oil

Remove the bones from the rabbit, keeping the pieces of meat as large as possible. Then cut the meat into 12 even-sized pieces. Wipe the rabbit meat with a damp cloth and then flatten the meat pieces slightly so they can be rolled. Sprinkle the rabbit pieces with salt and pepper, and then with some chopped parsley and rosemary.

Place a slice of prosciutto over each flattened piece of rabbit, then roll the rabbit up tightly. Sprinkle with salt and pepper. Place the 12 rabbit rolls on a platter, cover, and refrigerate.

This recipe can be made up to this point and finished later.

Using 6 skewers, thread them with the rabbit and the sausage in the following manner: Place one rabbit roll on a skewer. Then add a sage leaf, a sausage, another sage leaf, and finally another rabbit roll. Brush the skewers with oil and cook them on a barbecue grill or broil in the oven. Baste the skewers occasionally with the oil and turn them often. Cook for 15 to 20 minutes, depending on the size of the rabbit.

Peperoni Arrostiti
Roasted Peppers

Serves 6

These peppers can also be served as a snack, served on toasted slices of French bread, or as an antipasto dish.

6 large bell peppers, yellow, orange, red and green
2 large garlic cloves, finely chopped
4 tablespoons fresh chopped basil
1/2 teaspoon salt

1 teaspoon dried crushed hot chili pepper
6 tablespoons extra virgin olive oil
1 basil sprig for decoration

Cut the peppers in half and remove the seeds. Wash the peppers and dry them with paper towels. Place them cut side down, on a baking sheet and roast them under the broiler until the skin begins to blister and is dark brown (The peppers may also be broiled on the grill over high heat, turning them often.)

Remove the peppers from the oven and place them in a brown paper bag. Close the bag and set aside for 10 minutes. Remove the peppers from the bag and peel the skin, then cut them into 1/2-inch strips.

Arrange the pepper strips on a medium platter so that they overlap. Combine the garlic, basil, salt and chili pepper in a small bowl. Add the oil and mix well. Pour this dressing over the peppers and marinate. Refrigerate for several hours to absorb the flavors. To serve, bring the peppers to room temperature and garnish with a sprig of basil placed in the center.

Funghi Arrostiti
Roasted Mushrooms

Serves 6

The people of Abruzzi use wild mushrooms that grow in the region for this recipe and grill them over charcoal. Portabello, a large cultivated mushroom, is also ideal for this recipe.

These mushrooms are also delicious served as an antipasto. For an hors d'oeurve with cocktails, use smaller mushrooms and cook them for a shorter time.

*6 medium-size Portabello mush-
    rooms, stems removed and
    cleaned with a damp cloth*
3 garlic cloves, finely chopped
4 tablespoons finely chopped parsley

Salt
*1 teaspoon dried crushed hot red
    chili pepper*
1/4 cup extra virgin olive oil

Place the mushrooms with the stem side up in a large shallow baking pan. In a small bowl mix the garlic, parsley and season with salt and chili pepper. Pour the olive oil over it and mix thoroughly. With a soup spoon spread the mixture evenly over each mushroom. Place the baking pan under a preheated broiler and broil under high heat for about 10 minutes. Serve while hot, or at room temperature.

Parrozzo
Almond and Chocolate Cake

Serves 6

This dessert from the town of Pescara was originally a rough bread of the peasants, which contained cornmeal. Now it is a delicate dessert made with almonds and chocolate and has no resemblance to the original cake. The word *parrozzo* means rough bread, but there is nothing rough about this cake.

1 cup almonds, blanched and peeled
2/3 cup granulated sugar
Butter and flour, for the cake pan
1/2 cup all purpose flour
1/2 cup potato flour
5 tablespoons unsalted butter

5 large eggs, separated
2 teaspoons vanilla extract
4 (squares) ounces semisweet
   chocolate
1 tablespoon unsalted butter

After blanching the almonds make sure they are completely dry and place them in a food processor. Add 3 tablespoons of the sugar and process until the almonds are reduced to powder.

Grease and flour a 9-inch cake pan, shaking off any excess flour.

In a bowl mix together the almond powder with the flour and potato flour. Melt the butter and let it cool. Place the egg yolks, vanilla extract, and the remaining sugar in a large mixing bowl and beat vigorously until creamy and fluffy. Add the flour mixture a little at a time, beating thoroughly between each addition. Then beat in the butter.

In another bowl, beat the egg whites until stiff and fold them gently into the batter. Pour the mixture into the prepared cake pan and bake in a preheated 350° F. oven for about 40 minutes or until the cake has risen and the top is firm and golden. Let the cake cool on a wire rack. Remove it from the pan and place it on a serving dish.

Break the chocolate into small pieces and melt it with 1 tablespoon of water, in the top of a double boiler over hot water. Then stir in the butter. Quickly pour the chocolate glaze over the top of the cake, spreading it evenly over the top and sides of the cake with a spatula dipped in hot water. Let the chocolate dry. Then decorate the top of the cake with chocolate slivers or with whipped cream flavored with Amaretto liqueur.

Slice the cake into wedges and serve with coffee.

Incontriamoci
Let's Get Together

Serves 6

Crostini con Melanzane
Eggplant Crostini

Brodetto di Pesce alla Marinara
Fish Soup

Bruschetta
Slices of Toasted bread

Insalata di Cicoria e Pomodori
Salad of Curly Endive and Tomatoes

Pizza Ripiena di Crema e Marmellata
Sweet Pizza Filled with Custard and Raspberry Jelly

Caffe
Coffee

Let's Get Together

I planned this ladies' luncheon as a get-together for friends who have not seen each other for a while. It is an opportunity to visit and catch up on the latest news. For this luncheon I chose a light menu, which is appropriate for a mid-day meal.

The luncheon starts with crostini topped with a zesty eggplant mixture. The entree is a fish stew typical of those served in the coastal regions of Abruzzi and other eastern regions of Italy. The stew consists of fin and shell fish cooked in a broth flavored with basil and a small amount of chili peppers, which are the typical seasoning used in Abruzzi. Toasted, garlic-infused bread slices accompany the stew.

A refreshing salad of endive, bell peppers, and tomatoes provides a palate cleanser. An elegant fruit tart with a custard filling ends this get-together luncheon.

Preparations

Some of the preparations for this luncheon can be done ahead, most are done in the morning before the luncheon. The eggplant mixture for the crostini can be made even days ahead, and then refrigerated. However, the bread slices (crostini) should be toasted in the morning before the luncheon.

On the morning of the luncheon, clean the mussels and clams, shell the shrimp, and cut the fish and the lobster. Then prepare the stock. About 10 minutes before your guests are due to arrive, start cooking the fish, shrimp and lobster and then remove the fish soup from the heat and let it sit until ready to serve. Finish making the bruschetta.

Prepare the lettuce, bell peppers and tomatoes for the salad and place them in the refrigerator. Also make the dressing for the salad and set it aside. Toss the salad after the fish stew has been eaten. Toast the bread in the late morning and set it aside. Finish making the bruschetta just before the guests arrive.

Also in the morning, make and bake the tart shell for the dessert and set it aside to cool. Make the custard and then assemble the tart with the fruit and jam. Serve the dessert with a cup of coffee and then enjoy your guests.

Crostini con Melanzane
Eggplant Crostini

Serves 6

1 pound eggplant
Salt
6 tablespoons extra virgin olive oil
2 medium size onions, chopped
2 large yellow bell peppers, cut into
   thin strips
2 large fresh tomatoes, peeled,
   seeded, and cut into thin strips

1/4 teaspoon salt
1/2 teaspoon freshly ground black
   pepper
2 tablespoons chopped fresh basil
2 tablespoons chopped fresh parsley
2 garlic cloves, finely chopped, plus
1 garlic clove, cut in half
1 French baquette, sliced thin

Wash and cut the eggplant into small cubes, without peeling it. Place the eggplant in a colander, sprinkle with salt, and let it stand for 20 minutes. Rinse the eggplant and pat it dry with a paper towel. This procedure will remove the bitter juice from the eggplant.

Heat 4 tablespoons of the oil in a large frying pan over medium heat. Add the chopped onion and sauté until the onions are limp. Then add the cubed eggplant, the strips of bell peppers, and the tomatoes and season with salt and pepper. Mix and cook for 10 minutes over medium-high heat, stirring often. Then add the chopped basil, parsley, chopped garlic, and the remaining 2 tablespoon of oil. Mix thoroughly and cook uncovered over medium heat for 40 minutes, stirring often.

Toast the bread slices, in the oven under the broiler on both sides until golden in color. Rub one side of each bread slice with the cut side of the garlic.

The eggplant may be served either hot or cold. Serve it hot on a platter surrounded by toasted bread. The cold eggplant may be served on toasted bread as a Crostini for an appetizer. Refrigerate any leftover eggplant mixture in a container. Add a little olive oil on top of the eggplant before refrigerating. It lasts for more than a week.

Brodetto di Pesce alla Marinara
Fish Soup

Serves 6

This recipe for fish soup was created by Italian fishermen at sea. It was usually prepared at midmorning, using the fish that were just caught. Although containing a variety of fish pieces this dish is eaten with a spoon, like soup.

1/2 cup extra virgin olive oil
4 garlic cloves, cut in half
1 medium onion, chopped coarsely
1/2 teaspoon dried crushed hot pepper flakes
4 tablespoons chopped fresh parsley
6 cups water
2 teaspoons salt
3 pounds chowder fish for stock (mixed fish with bones cut into large pieces), rinsed
4 tablespoons white wine vinegar
1 pound clams, cleaned and rinsed
1 pound mussels, cleaned, rinsed

1 pound halibut, cut into large pieces
1 pound swordfish, cut into large pieces
1 pound large shrimp, shelled and deveined
1 lobster tail, shell removed and flesh cut into 6 pieces
1 squid, cleaned, cut into 1/2-inch rings
2 cups fresh cubed tomatoes
1/2 teaspoon freshly ground black pepper

Place the olive oil in a large pot over medium heat. Add the garlic, onion, and hot pepper flakes and sauté until the onion is limp and the garlic is golden in color, stirring often. Add 2 tablespoons of the chopped parsley and sauté for 1 minute. Then add the water, chowder fish, and the salt. Cover the pot and simmer for 30 minutes, stirring occasionally.

Add the vinegar, clams, and mussels and cook for 5 minutes. Remove the clams and mussels, discarding any unopened ones and set them aside.

Strain the broth through a fine sieve into a bowl and discard the fish bones and garlic. Add more salt to the broth, if necessary.

The broth may be made ahead to this point and refrigerated.

Pour the broth back into the pot and bring it to a boil. Add the fish pieces — halibut, swordfish, large prawns, and lobster — to the pot. Cook covered over medium heat, for 7 to 10 minutes. Add the squid and cook 1 minute. For the last 5 minutes of cooking, add the cubed fresh tomatoes and continue cooking. Then add the cooked clams and mussels and the pepper. Let the soup rest for 5 minutes.

Using a perforated spoon distribute the fish and seafood evenly among 6 soup bowls. Place the clams, mussels and lobster on top of the fish. Spoon the broth over the seafood and then sprinkle with the remaining parsley. Serve the fish soup with the bruschetta (toasted bread).

Bruschetta
Slices of Toasted Bread

Serves 6

1 long coarse loaf of Italian bread, cut into slices
3 to 4 garlic cloves, slightly crushed

Extra virgin olive oil
Salt and pepper

Do not use a pre-sliced or packaged bread, a rough country bread is best.

Toast the slices of bread on the grill or in the oven until golden brown and crisp. While hot, rub one side of the toasted bread with the crushed garlic. Arrange the toast slices on a plate, brush them lightly with oil, and sprinkle with salt and freshly ground pepper.

Serve at once with the fish stew. Another way to serve the fish soup is to place two slices of bread on the bottom of the soup plate, then pour the fish soup on top.

Insalata di Cicoria e Pomodori
Salad of Curly Endive and Tomatoes

Serves 6

1 large head of curly endive
4 small scallion, thinly sliced
2 large red or yellow bell peppers, or 1 of each, seeded and cut in strips
3 to 4 Roma tomatoes, seeded and cut into wedges

5 tablespoons extra virgin olive oil
2 tablespoons wine vinegar
1/2 teaspoon salt
1/2 teaspoon freshly ground black pepper

Cut the curly endive into thin strips and soak it in salted water for 1 hour to eliminate the bitterness, then spin dry.

Place the dry curly endive, onion, peppers, and tomatoes in a large salad bowl. Make the dressing by mixing together the olive oil and vinegar and season with salt and pepper. Pour the dressing over the salad just before serving.

Pizza Ripiena di Crema e Marmellata
Sweet Pizza Filled with Custard and Raspberry Jelly

Serves 6

The people of southern Italy have given the name sweet pizza to traditional tarts prepared for village feasts or saints' days. These tarts are made with various fresh fruits, depending on the season. Many types of fruit can be used for this tart. Peel, remove seeds and slice fruit is necessary. Choose a compatible jelly for the glaze.

Pastry

2 1/2 cups all purpose flour	*3 large egg yolks*
1/2 cup sugar	*2 tablespoons ice water*
1/2 cup unsalted butter, cut into	*1 egg white, slightly beaten*
* pieces*	

Combine the flour and sugar in a bowl. With a pastry blender or 2 knives cut in the butter until the mixture resembles small pebbles. Mix in the egg yolks and then the ice water, 1 tablespoon at a time, until a soft dough is formed.

Add some flour to a wooden board and roll out the dough with a floured rolling pin. Cover a 13-inch tart pan with the rolled dough and pat it into place. With the rolling pin roll over the top of shell to trim the dough flush with rim. Using a fork prick the bottom all over to prevent puffing. Place a piece of aluminum foil, shiny side down, over the bottom of the tart shell. Fill the shell with dry beans and bake in a preheated 400° F. oven for 10 minutes. Remove the tart shell from the oven and remove the beans and the foil. Then brush the tart shell with the egg white to seal the crust and bake for another 10 minutes or until is light golden in color. Set the shell aside to cool.

Custard

1 cup sugar
5 egg yolks
2/3 cup flour
2 cups milk

2 to 3 baskets of raspberries, rinsed
and drained
1 cup raspberry jelly, for the glaze

Beat the sugar with the egg yolks in a medium bowl until light and pale, then gradually add the flour and continue beating. In a small saucepan bring the milk to a boil over medium-high heat. Then pour it slowly into the egg mixture a little at a time, beating vigorously, until blended.

Pour the mixture into a heavy bottom saucepan and slowly bring to a boil, stirring constantly. When it starts to boil, reduce the heat and simmer over low heat for 3 minutes, stirring occasionally, until the custard is smooth. Let the custard cool before placing in the pastry shell.

Place the cleaned and dried raspberries on top of the custard spreading them evenly. Melt the raspberry jelly with a few tablespoons of water in a saucepan and then spoon it over the fruit for a light glaze.

You can choose from many kinds of fruit for this tart. When necessary peel, remove seeds, and pits, and slice the fruit.

Campania

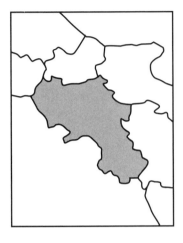

The cuisine of Campania is not fancy, but it is complex as it has been influenced by the foreign peoples who have occupied the region over the centuries. These include the Romans from the north, the Greeks from the east, the Arabs from Africa, as well as the French and Spanish. The cuisine is also influenced by the great variety of vegetables and fruit grown in the rich volcanic soil on the slopes of Mount Vesuvius.

East to west the Campania region extends from the Apennines to the Tyrrhenian Sea. From north to south it lies between the region of Lazio and that of Basilicata. The most famous features of Campania are Naples, Mount Vesuvius, the Bay of Naples, the island of Capri, and the Amalfi coast.

The Campania region has many beautiful panoramas, lush vegetation, and a mild climate, all of which make this region one of the most favorite nature spots in Europe. The soil in the valleys is very fertile as the result of repeated volcanic eruptions. Combined with a near-perfect climate, they produce among the best fruits and vegetables in Italy, both in quantity and quality. The beauty of the region also makes it one of the favorite tourist areas in Europe, as it was for the early Romans.

The Romans quickly learned to appreciate the richness of the soil, the beauty of the landscape, and the dry mild climate of Campania. The region became the playground for the Roman nobility and wealthy. They vacationed there and built huge villas, particularly in and around Pompeii. Agriculture and tourism are still the prime attractions and industry of the Campania region.

Campania, particularly Naples, is known for two foods — pizza and pasta. Food historians say that pizza is a direct descendent of an ancient Roman breakfast dish — bread with a relish topping.

Pizza was originally sold at street stalls and consumed while walking along the streets of Naples. Later pizza moved indoors and special restaurants, called pizzeria, were created.

The traditional pizza of Naples is *pizza alla napoletana*. It is a round leavened dough, brushed with olive oil, and topped with chopped fresh tomatoes or tomato sauce, cubed mozzarella cheese, oregano or basil, garlic, and anchovy fillets.

Perhaps the most famous Neapolitan pizza is *Pissa Margherita*. It was created in honor of the first queen of Italy during a visit to Naples with her husband King Umberto. A local pizzeria owner combined the colors of the flag by using red tomatoes, white mozzarella cheese and green basil. Mozzarella is, of course, one of the main traditional ingredients of pizza.

Today the typical pizza of Naples is made with olives, mushrooms, artichokes, sausages, salami, and various kinds of seafood. It has become a popular lunch dish for the Neapolitans. Herbs, olives, mushrooms, artichokes, sausages, various kinds of fish and shellfish, etc. are just a few of the other ingredients used in making pizzas today.

Pasta, originally brought to Sicily by the Arabs, came to Naples in the form of hollow macaroni in the 1400s. Later the term macaroni encompassed all types of long round pasta — macaroni, spaghetti and *bucatini*. Eventually short tubular pasta, such as rigatoni, penne, and *maltagliati* (long narrow triangles) were included in this definition.

Originally pasta was made by hand and hung outside on clothes lines to dry. The long tubular macaroni were shaped around knitting needles to create a hollow center. Early-on pasta was a luxury item eaten only by the affluent. Commoners enjoyed it only on special occasions. It did not take long. however, for pasta to become an everyday food. Eventually it, like pizza, was sold on the street in stalls. By the late 1700s, historians say there were more than sixty shops selling pasta in Naples.

The classical pasta sauce that made Neapolitan cooking famous is called *pommarola*. It consists of tomatoes, a little olive oil, and basil. Seafood and vegetables also provide the basis for Neapolitan pasta sauces. For the Neapolitan, a day without pasta is like a day without sunshine and there are very few non-sunny days in the Naples area.

Over the years other more elaborate pasta sauces have evolved, including *ragus* containing meat called *ziti al ragu*. This dish is traditionally prepared on Sunday in Neapolitan homes.

Mozzarella cheese is an essential ingredient in most Campanian cuisine. Originally made from buffalo milk, it is now also made from cow's milk. The buffalo mozzarella is still made and enjoyed today. These Italian buffalo are descended from the Indian water buffalo and were im-

Furore Fishing Village on the Amalfi Coast.
Photo courtesy of Frank Spadarella.

ported into Italy in the early 600s. Years ago herds of buffalo roamed along the Campania coast, but they have moved inland as the herds diminished in size. Thus buffalo mozzarella has become somewhat of a rarity.

Mozzarella is frequently eaten plain with a touch of olive oil. It is also fried with an egg and bread crumb coating. Mozzarella is a popular toping for crostini along with anchovies and tomatoes.

Other cheeses of the Campania region made from cow's or sheep's milk include provolone, either smoked or fresh; caciocavallo, a semi-hard cheese that is hung on poles to age; scamorza, a soft cheese; and pecorino. All of these can be eaten fresh or aged.

The people of Campania are not great meat eaters. One dish that is a specialty of the area features veal. This dish consists of small slices of veal that are rolled and stuffed with cheese, garlic, golden raisins, and pine nuts, and then simmered in wine with tomato paste. Typically pasta is served with the sauce of the veal and the meat becomes a second course.

The absence of meat in the Neapolitan diet is compensated by the abundance of fish caught along the coast of Campania. *Fritto di pesce*, a favorite of mine, consists of the catch of the day that might include fish, shrimp, mussels, clams, squid, and octopus. These are quickly sautéed in a frying pan and served with a bit of lemon juice. Neapolitan cooks frequently prepare octopus with garlic, olives, capers, parsley, and oil in sealed earthenware pots.

Dessert is served only on special occasions at Neapolitan tables. When served they are usually rich and elaborate, and related to religious feasts. One such dessert is a pastry called *struffoli*, which means little wads of cotton. This pastry consists of balls of light dough flavored with grated lemon and orange peels, fried and then dipped in honey. It is traditionally served at Christmas. Another popular Neapolitan dessert is *pastiera*, which is a crumbly cake filled with ricotta cheese and candied fruit.

Wines

The best wines of Campania come from the islands of Capri and Ischia. The white Capri wine is considered to be one of the best of Italy and is particularly enjoyed with fish. It improves with age up to five years. White Piedimonte, red and white Epomeo and Fiorio d'Ischia are all wines from the island of Ischia. White, red and rose Ravello are wines found along the coast of Amalfi and the red Gragnano is found on the Sorrento peninsula.

The wines of Campania that were served in ancient Rome are still served today. The famous Falerno wine drunk by Romans is still produced in Campi Flegrei, the volcanic fields west of Naples. Asprino wine is produced in Caserta. It is essentially a local wine since it should be drunk as soon as it is made.

There are many legends about the wines of Campania. The most famous concerns the ancient wine called Lacryma Christi, or Tear of Christ. The name comes from a legend that a tear of Christ, shed over the sinning of the people of Naples, watered the wine grapes growing on the slopes of Vesuvius.

Una Festa di Paste
A Pasta Feast

Serves 12

Crostini di Melanzane
Crostini with Eggplant Puree

Crostini alla Napoletana
Neapolitan Crostini

Spaghetti con le Vongole e Cozze in Bianco
Spaghetti with Clams in White Sauce

Spaghetti alla Puttanesca
Spaghetti with Hot Chili

Ziti con Salsa Genovese
Ziti with Genovese Sauce

Insalata Verde
Green Salad

Torta Caprese
Capri Chocolate Torte

Caffe
Coffee

A Pasta Feast

The Neapolitans love to eat pasta and have become known for their many pasta dishes. Thus I decided to plan a meal featuring a variety of pastas — a meal sure to please pasta lovers.

As eggplant is one of the many vegetables grown in Campania, I chose to use it in a puree for crostini to start this pasta dinner. Along with the eggplant crostini I decided to serve a Neapolitan crostini made with mozzarella, tomato, anchovy, and oregano. Both pair well with drinks before dinner.

The three pasta dishes for the entree are typical of the cooking of Campania. The seafood spaghetti made with clams and mussel has a white sauce. The clams are cooked in oil, with garlic, parsley and black pepper. The spaghetti with hot chili sauce adds a spicy complexity to the menu. The ziti pasta has a typical Genovese sauce which is prepared with meat — prosciutto and salami — and chopped vegetables. This pasta dish is particularly easy to prepare.

A green salad follows the three pasta dishes and provides a palate refresher. The dinner concludes with a chocolate torte dessert that originated in Naples near the place where the boats leave for Capri.

Preparations

Several of the preparations for this dinner can be done ahead. The crostini can be made hours ahead. The eggplant mixture can even be made a day ahead and refrigerated. The Neapolitan crostini can be prepared and assembled in the afternoon and then baked that evening.

Both the meat sauce and the chili sauce can be prepared 3 to 4 days in advance, stored in the refrigerator, and reheated on the evening of the party. The clam sauce, however, should be prepared in the late afternoon of the party. After the sauce is finished, it can be covered, set aside, and then reheated before serving.

Prepare the various salad greens in the morning and store them in plastic bags in the refrigerator. Before dinner assemble the salad and make the dressing.

The Capri chocolate cake can be made up to 2 days ahead and kept, covered, at room temperature.

The evening of the party warm the sauces over low heat while cooking the pastas. Cook the ziti pasta first as it takes the longest. To cut down on the number of pots, boil the spaghetti for the two recipes in one large pot.

After the pastas are cooked, combine them with their respective sauces and cheese, where called for. Then toss each pasta thoroughly and serve immediately. Place a bowl of additional grated Parmesan cheese on the table. The clam sauce does not require cheese.

The three pasta dishes combined will each serve 12. However, if planning to use just one of the recipes, it will be sufficient for 4 to 6 people, depending on what else is being served.

Crostini di Melanzane
Crostini with Eggplant Puree

Serves 12

1 pound eggplant	*Salt and pepper*
3 tablespoons extra virgin olive oil	*1 French baguette bread, sliced*
Juice of 1 lemon	

Wash, peel and cut the egg plant into small cubes. Place the cubes of eggplant in a skillet with the olive oil, salt and pepper. Sauté over medium heat for a few minutes, cover and reduce the heat to low. Cook for 15 minutes, mixing once in a while and adding some water a little at a time, if necessary. Do not let the eggplant mixture dry out.

When the eggplant pieces are very soft, whip them and add the lemon juice and mix. Add salt and pepper, if needed.

Toast the slices of bread and serve them with the eggplant puree.

Crostini alla Napoletana
Neapolitan Crostini

Serves 12

These crostini with the mildness of mozzarella cheese and the saltiness of anchovies pair well with before-dinner-drinks.

*12 slices white sandwich bread, a
    few days old*
Unsalted butter
*1 1/2 pounds mozzarella cheese,
    thinly sliced*
8 small ripe tomatoes, thinly sliced
Salt

Freshly ground black pepper
1 tablespoon dried oregano, crushed
*2 ounces anchovy fillets in oil,
    drained and each fillet sliced
    lengthwise*
3 to 4 fresh basil sprigs, for garnish

Cut the crusts off of each slice of bread and then cut each slice diagonally. Spread one side of each triangle with the butter. Cover each triangle with a slice of mozzarella cut a little smaller than the bread, then top this with a slice of tomato. Sprinkle with salt, pepper, and oregano and add a piece of anchovy on top.

Grease a large baking sheet with the butter and place the bread triangles on it. Bake in a preheated 350° F. oven until the cheese is golden in color, about 8 to 10 minutes.

Place the crostini on a warmed platter, garnished with basil sprigs, and serve immediately while hot.

Spaghetti con le Vongole e Cozze In Bianco
Spaghetti with Baby Clams and Mussels in White Sauce

Serves 4 to 6 or 12 in a pasta dinner

2 pounds baby clams
2 pounds mussels
8 tablespoons olive oil
4 large garlic cloves, 2 cloves
crushed, 2 cloves finely chopped

2 tablespoons fresh chopped parsley
1 teaspoon freshly ground black
pepper
1 pound spaghetti

Scrub the clams and mussels with a brush, then place them in a large bowl with salted water to cover for 1 hour. Then wash the clams and mussels several times under running cold water and wipe them clean.

Place 3 tablespoons of the olive oil in a large saucepan over medium heat; add the 2 crushed garlic and sauté until brown. Discard the garlic, add the clams and mussels to the pan and cook, covered, for 5 to 7 minutes over medium-high heat, shaking the pan once in a while. Remove the clams and mussels that did not open and throw them away. Remove the pan from the heat. Then remove the clams and mussels from their shells, placing them in a bowl with their juice. Let the juice settle down to the bottom of the bowl, then strain it with a sieve.

Heat the remaining 5 tablespoons of olive oil in a saucepan. Add the remaining 2 chopped garlic and sauté until golden, then add the clams and mussels with their juices the chopped parsley and season with pepper. Cook over low heat for a very few minutes, no longer, or the clams and mussels will toughen.

Boil the spaghetti in boiling salted water and cook until al dente. Drain the pasta thoroughly and mix it with the seafood sauce in a large warm bowl. Serve while hot. This dish is served without cheese.

Spaghetti alla Puttanesca
Spaghetti with Hot Chili

Serves 4 to 6 or 12 in a pasta dinner

The title of this recipe means spaghetti in the manner of a prostitute. The sauce which is made very quickly originated in the slums of Naples, an area frequented by sailors looking for female companions.

1/4 cup olive oil

3 cloves garlic, 2 cloves crushed, 1 cloves, finely chopped

3 cups fresh tomatoes, peeled and finely chopped or 3 cups canned Italian whole tomatoes, chopped with their juice

2 tablespoons capers, drained

1 cup black pitted olives, chopped coarsely

1/4 teaspoon hot pepper flakes

1 teaspoon fresh chopped oregano or 2 teaspoons dried oregano

1/2 teaspoon. freshly ground black pepper

4 anchovies packed in olive oil, drained, finely chopped into small pieces

2 tablespoons finely chopped fresh parsley

1 pound spaghetti

1/2 cup freshly grated Parmesan or pecorino cheese

Heat the olive oil in a large frying pan over medium heat. Add the crushed garlic and sauté until golden in color. Discard this garlic and add the finely chopped garlic, tomatoes, capers, olives, pepper flakes, oregano, and black pepper. Mix well and cook for 20 minutes, stirring occasionally. Then add the finely chopped anchovies and smash them to a paste with a fork thoroughly mixing them into the sauce, then add parsley. Cook slowly for 2 more minutes over low heat and add salt, if necessary.

Bring a large pot of salted water to a boil, add the pasta and cook the spaghetti until al dente. Drain well and mix the pasta with the sauce and cheese. Serve immediately while hot.

This recipe makes about 4 cups of sauce.

Ziti con Salsa Genovese
Ziti with Genovese Sauce

Serves 4 to 6 or 12 in a pasta dinner

Ziti is another name for maccheroni, long hollow pasta. This shape of pasta is prevalent in southern Italy and Sicily. In this country ziti often refers to short pieces of the traditional thick, hollow macaroni.

This recipe is said to have originated in the sixteenth century when Genovese merchants used to meet in the central square of Naples and purchase pasta with this sauce from the local street vendors. Although the sauce is Neapolitan it was given the name Genovese. This recipe has been handed down from generation to generation with very little changes.

1/4 cup olive oil
1 pound lean ground beef
2 teaspoons salt
2 large onions, finely chopped
2 celery stalks, finely chopped
3 medium carrots, finely chopped
1/4 cup diced salami
1/4 cup diced prosciutto
3 cups canned Italian whole tomatoes, chopped with their juice

1 1/2 cups water
1 cup dry white wine
Broth
1 teaspoon freshly ground black pepper
1 pound ziti pasta
1/2 cup freshly grated Parmesan cheese

Place the olive oil in a large heavy saucepan. Add the ground beef and 1 teaspoon of the salt, onion, celery, carrots, salame, prosciutto, tomatoes, and water. Mix well and cook over medium-low heat, partially covered, for 1 hour, or until the water has evaporated.

Then add the wine and continue cooking on very low heat for 1 additional hour, uncovered, stirring occasionally. If the sauce gets too dry, add some broth. When cooked, the sauce should be smooth and thick. Then add the remaining teaspoon of salt and pepper and stir well.

Cook the ziti pasta until it is al dente, drain, and place it on a heated platter, add the sauce and toss. Add the parmesan cheese and serve immediately.

This recipe makes about 6 cups of sauce. Freeze the extra sauce for later use. Any large shaped pasta may be substituted for the ziti.

Insalata Verde
Green Salad

Serves 12

2 heads butter lettuce
2 bunches red lettuce
2 large bunches arugula
2 bunches watercress, large stems
   removed

1/2 cup extra virgin olive oil
4 tablespoons red wine vinegar
1 teaspoon salt
1/2 teaspoon freshly ground black
   pepper

Trim, rinse, and dry the salad greens and tear them into bite-sized pieces. Place all the greens in a large salad bowl. In a small bowl combine the oil, vinegar, salt and black pepper and whisk to blend. Pour the dressing over the salad greens and toss thoroughly until well blended.

Food Note

When boiling pasta, always use a large pot with plenty of water. When cooking 1 pound of pasta you will need about 4 quarts of water. When the water boils, add the salt and pasta.

Cooked pasta should be al dente, tender but firm to the bite. It continues to cook even after it is drained. Never rinse cooked pasta unless making lasagna or cannelloni.

When adding sauce to the pasta, add half of the amount and add more if needed. The Italians never oversauce their pasta.

I like to under-cook my pasta a little more because I toss the pasta with the sauce over the heat for a few minutes. By doing this, the pasta will be completely coated with the sauce and be very hot.

Torta Caprese
Capri Chocolate Torte

Serves 12

Capri Chocolate Torte is named for the famous resort island in the Bay of Naples. This chocolate nut cake is one of southern Italy's few chocolate desserts. It is a specialty of Chiaia, a district of Naples, from where the ferries leave for Capri.

1 1/2 cups almonds (about 7 ounces)
1/3 cup all purpose flour
8 ounces bittersweet or semisweet
    chocolate, chopped
1/2 cup (1 stick) unsalted butter, at
room temperature
14 tablespoons sugar
7 large eggs, separated, at room
    temperature
Confectioner's sugar, for garnish

Butter a 9-inch springform pan with 3 inch high sides. Line the bottom of the pan with waxed paper.

Finely grind the almonds with the flour in a food processor and set aside. Melt the chocolate in top of a double boiler over simmering water, stirring until the chocolate is melted and smooth. Remove the double boiler from the water and cool the chocolate slightly.

Using an electric mixer, beat the butter and 7 tablespoons of the sugar, in a large bowl until the mixture is light and fluffy. Beat in the melted chocolate. Add the egg yolks one at a time, beating well after each addition. Continue beating until smooth and light, about 3 minutes. Mix in the ground almond mixture.

Using the electric mixer with clean and dry beaters, beat the egg whites in another large bowl, until soft peaks are beginning to form. Slowly add the remaining 7 tablespoons of sugar and beat to soft peaks. Fold 1/4 of the beaten egg whites into the batter to lighten it. Fold in the remaining beaten egg whites.

Pour the batter into the prepared pan and smooth the top. Bake the cake in the middle of a preheated 350° F. oven until a cake tester or toothpick inserted in the center comes out with some moist crumbs, about 40 minutes. Cool the cake in the pan on a rack for 10 minutes. Run a sharp knife around the pan sides to loosen the cake. Release the pan sides and cool the cake completely. (Cake will fall as it cools.)

Cover the cake with plastic wrap and let it stand at room temperature. Transfer the cake to a platter, and sift some confectioner's sugar over the top. Cut into wedges and serve.

Si Mangia la Pizza
Let's Eat Pizza

Serves 6

Antipasto di Frutti di Mare
Seafood Antipasto

Pizza Margherita
Tomato and Mozzarella Pizza

Pizza alle Salsicce
Sausage Pizza

Pizza ai Funghi
Mushroom Pizza

Insalata di Arugula e Indivia
Arugula and Endive Salad

Granita di Fragole
Strawberry Ice

Let's Eat Pizza

In Campania pizza is eaten in the street during a walk or after the cinema. It is seldom made or eaten at home. Pizza is the favorite food at soccer matches in Italy. When planning this menu I decided that a variety of pizzas is an ideal way to entertain at home while watching a soccer match or football game on television

This Campania dinner starts with an elegant antipasto of mixed seafood seasoned with olive oil, lemon juice, salt, pepper, and a few hot pepper flakes for a hint of sharpness.

Each of the three pizzas has a different topping — cheese, mushrooms, and sausage — to satisfy a variety of tastes.

A refreshing and tangy arugula salad follows the pizza.

A light, cooling and refreshing dessert of strawberry ice ends this fun and relaxing Campania pizza party.

Preparations

In order to enjoy watching the game on television, prepare the seafood antipasto in the morning. Then refrigerate it so that it is ready to enjoy during the game.

Prepare the pizza sauce a day or two ahead and refrigerate it. Make the different toppings for the pizzas the day before. Place each topping in its own container and then refrigerate it. Bring the toppings to room temperature before assembling the pizzas. Make the pizza dough early in the afternoon and assemble the three pizzas with the toppings that evening. Then bake the pizzas just before you are to serve dinner.

Clean the arugula, endive, and radishes for the salad that morning, place them in a bowl and refrigerate.

Make the strawberry ice in the morning and freeze it. Four hours before the game, crush the strawberry ice cubes in an ice crusher or blender and return the mixture to the freezer. Serve the ice in the evening.

Antipasto di Frutti di Mare
Seafood Antipasto

Serves 6

3 pounds mussels
2 1/2 pounds clams
1/2 cup extra virgin olive oil
2 garlic cloves, coarsely chopped
1/4 teaspoon crushed hot pepper
   flakes
2 pounds octupus, cleaned

2 pound shrimps with shells
3 tablespoons fresh chopped parsley
1 teaspoon salt
1 teaspoon freshly ground black
pepper
Juice of 2 lemons

Wash the mussels and clams in water and scrub them with a brush, removing the beard.

Place 3 tablespoons of the olive oil into a large saucepan over high heat and add the mussels, clams, garlic, and pepper flakes. Cook, covered, over medium-high heat for about 10 minutes, shaking the pan often. When the shells are all open, take the mussels and clams out, and discard any unopened ones. Strain the liquid and set it aside.

Take the cleaned octupus and place it into a large saucepan, add the strained liquid from the shellfish and cook, covered, slowly over low heat for about 40 minutes. Add the shrimp and cook for another 2 to 3 minutes or until the shrimp have turned pink and are done. Remove the octupus and shrimp from the saucepan. Shell and devein the shrimp and cut the octupus into small pieces.

Place all of the seafood on a large platter. Add the chopped parsley and season the seafood with salt and pepper. Then add the olive oil and lemon juice and mix thoroughly. The seafood antipasto can be served while it is still hot, or it can be served warm or cold. If serving the seafood antipasto cold, refrigerate it after it is made until ready to serve.

Pizza

The authentic Neapolitan pizza is baked in wood-fired brick ovens, giving the pizza crust a unique taste and aroma. Unfortunately this method is not possible in home kitchens, but this recipe makes a reasonable facsimile.

This dough will make three round 12-inch pizzas, however, other size pizza baking pans may be used to conform to the amount of dough. Either canned or fresh tomatoes, finely chopped and drained of its liquid, may be used in making a pizza.

The following pizza sauce can be made ahead. It makes about 6 cups of sauce, which is enough sauce for three pizzas with some leftover to be used for pasta or for more pizza.

Salsa Pizzaiola
Pizza Sauce

4 tablespoons olive oil
1 large onion, finely chopped
3 garlic cloves, finely chopped
4 cups canned Italian whole
   tomatoes, coarsely chopped with
   their juice
1 (6 ounce) can tomato paste
1 tablespoon dried oregano,
   crumbled

1 tablespoon finely chopped fresh
   basil or 1 teaspoon dried basil,
   crumbled
1 bay leaf
2 teaspoons salt
1 teaspoon freshly ground black
   pepper

Heat the olive oil in a large stainless-steel saucepan over medium heat, add the chopped onion and sauté, stirring often, for about 5 to 7 minutes or until the onions are soft and transparent. Then add the chopped garlic and cook for a few minutes more, stirring often. Add the chopped tomatoes and their liquid, tomato paste, dried oregano, basil, bay leaf, 1 teaspoon of the salt and pepper.

Bring the sauce to a boil, then reduce the heat to low and simmer uncovered, stirring once in a while, for 30 to 40 minutes. When the sauce is cooked it should be thick and partially smooth. Remove the bay leaf, taste, and season the sauce with the remaining salt and a little more black pepper, if necessary.

If a smoother sauce is preferred, puree it through a food mill, rub it through a sieve with the back of a large wooden spoon, or puree it in a food processor.

Pizza Dough

2 packages or cakes of yeast
1 1/2 cups lukewarm water
1/4 teaspoon sugar

3 1/2 cups all purpose flour
1 teaspoon salt
2 tablespoon olive oil

Dissolve the yeast and sugar in a bowl in the lukewarm water and let it stand for 2 to 3 minutes, then stir until the yeast and sugar are completely dissolved. Add about 1 cup of flour to make a soft, smooth dough. Cover the bowl and leave it in a warm place to rise (a turned off oven would be best) about 10 to 15 minutes or until the yeast bubbles up and the mixture almost doubles in volume.

Sift the flour and salt together into a large mixing bowl. Make a well in the center of the flour and pour the yeast mixture that has risen into it. Add 1 tablespoon of the olive oil and mix well with a fork or your fingers until the dough forms a ball. Place the dough on a floured board and knead it, adding a little flour if necessary, for about 5 to 8 minutes or until it is smooth and elastic. Form the dough into a ball and place it in a large clean bowl that has been coated with the remaining tablespoon of olive oil. Cover with a plate or with plastic wrap and place the bowl in a warm place for about 45 minutes to 1 hour, or until the dough has doubled in bulk. When the dough has doubled, punch it down with your fists and break it into 3 balls.

Knead one ball of dough at a time on a floured board for one minute, working in a little more flour if the dough seems sticky. Use the palm of your hand to flatten the ball into a round circle about 1 inch thick. Hold the circle in your hands and stretch the dough by turning the circle and pulling your hands apart gently at the same time. Then spread the dough out on a floured board and pat it smooth. Roll the dough with the rolling pin from the center to the far edge until there is a 10-inch circle. Place the dough on a well oiled 10-inch round baking pan and push the dough evenly with your fingers until it is stretched to cover the bottom of the pan. The edges of the pizza should be slightly thicker than the middle. Knead, stretch, and roll the rest of the dough into 2 more pizzas.

Pizza Margherita
Tomato and Mozzarella Pizza

1 cup pizza sauce
1 cup diced mozzarella cheese
Salt
Freshly ground black pepper

6 to 8 fresh basil leaves, finely
  chopped
2 to 3 tablespoons olive oil
4 tablespoons freshly grated
Parmesan cheese

Pour 1 cup of the pizza sauce over the dough in the pizza pan and spread it with a pastry brush or the back of a spoon. Place the diced mozzarella on top of the sauce, season with salt and pepper and sprinkle with the chopped basil. Dribble the olive oil over the pizza and sprinkle it with the Parmesan cheese.

Bake the pizza on the lowest shelf of a preheated 500° F. oven for 10 minutes, or until the crust is lightly browned and the filling is bubbling. Serve at once, otherwise it will toughen as it cools.

Pizza alle Salsicce
Sausage Pizza

2 Italian style sausages
1 cup pizza sauce
1 cup diced mozzarella cheese

3 tablespoons grated Parmesan
  cheese
2 tablespoons olive oil

Remove the casing from the sausages and crumble the meat into small pieces.

Sauté the crumbled sausages in a small skillet for about 5 minutes over medium-high heat, or until the meat begins to color.

Pour the pizza sauce over the prepared pizza dough and spread it evenly. Add the diced mozzarella on top and then sprinkle the cooked sausages over the pizza. Sprinkle the Parmesan cheese and the olive oil over the pizza and bake in a preheated 500° F. oven for 10 minutes, or until the cheese bubbles and starts to turn golden.

Pizza ai Funghi
Mushroom Pizza

1 pound mushrooms, champignon
  (white) or crimini (brown)
1/4 cup olive oil
3 garlic cloves, crushed
2 tablespoons fresh finely chopped
  parsley

1/2 teaspoon salt
1/2 teaspoon freshly ground black
  pepper
1 cup pizza sauce
3 tablespoons freshly grated
  Parmesan cheese

Wipe the mushrooms with a damp cloth, slice the caps thinly and discard the stems.

Place the olive oil and crushed garlic in a medium skillet. Sauté over medium-high heat, until the garlic starts to brown, then discard it. Add the sliced mushrooms and chopped parsley and season with salt and pepper. Sauté, stirring occasionally, for about 10 minutes, or until most of the liquid has evaporated.

Pour the pizza sauce over the prepared pizza dough and spread it evenly. Spread the mushrooms over the sauce and sprinkle it with the Parmesan cheese. Bake the pizza in a preheated 500° F. oven until the topping is bubbling and the crust is golden in color, about 10 minutes.

Insalata di Arugula e Indivia
Salad of Arugula and Endive

Serves 6

4 medium heads Belgian endive
2 large bunches arugula
6 small red radishes
1/4 cup extra virgin olive oil

2 tablespoons fresh lemon juice
1/2 teaspoon salt
1/2 teaspoon freshly ground black
  pepper

Rinse and pat dry the endive, arugula, and radishes. Cut the endive into 1/2-inch wide strips. Remove the stems from the arugula and break the leaves into bite-size pieces. Cut the radishes into very thin rounds. Place the endive, arugula, and radishes into a salad bowl. Make the dressing by mixing together the olive oil and lemon juice and season with salt and pepper. Pour the dressing over the salad just before serving.

Granita di Fragole
Strawberry Ice

Serves 6

1 cup water
1/2 cup sugar
2 cups fresh ripe strawberries,
pureed

2 tablespoons lemon juice
6 fresh mint sprigs

Bring the water and sugar to a boil in a large saucepan over medium heat, stirring until the sugar dissolves. When the sugar and water begins to boil, let the mixture cook for 5 minutes, then immediately remove the pan from the heat and let the syrup cool to room temperature. Stir in the pureed strawberries and lemon juice. Pour the mixture into an ice-cube tray with the divider. Freeze the strawberry ice for 3 to 4 hours. Remove the cubes and crush them in an ice crusher or blender. Then return the ice to the freezer.

When ready to serve pour some of the ice into individual glass containers and serve with a sprig of mint.

Note If using frozen strawberries instead of fresh ones, reduce the sugar for the syrup to 1/4 cup.

Other flavored ices are prepared in a similar manner.

Orange Ice

2 cups water
3/4 cup water

1 cup orange juice
Juice of one lemon

Coffee Ice

1 cup water
1/2 cup sugar

2 cups strong expresso coffee

Follow the same procedure as for the strawberries ice.

PUGLIA

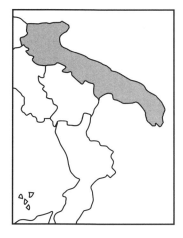

Puglia is the extreme south-eastern part of Italy. Along the Adriatic Sea it is the heel of the Italian boot. Puglia's narrow coastline with high steep cliffs is the longest in Italy. Over the centuries the waters of Puglia have provided its population with an infinite supply of a variety of fish.

Due to Puglia's proximity to Greece, its peoples have cultural ties to that country. Much of Puglia's fish cookery evolved from Greek recipes, especially the many fish soups. Puglia's cuisine is based on local seasonal vegetables combined primarily with fish and pasta.

When Italians think of food they usually think of pasta, meat, and vegetables, in that order. In Puglia this food relationship is reversed, because vegetables are produced in such vast quantities that they are the most important item of the local cuisine.

Puglia's good soil and Mediterranean climate with abundant sunshine are very conducive to agriculture. Some of the finest vegetables of Italy are cultivated in this region, including artichokes, arugula, fava beans, cauliflower, broccoli, onions, fennel, peppers, eggplant, red and savoy cabbage. The region is famous for its tomatoes.

When my husband and I visited Puglia and its capital Bari, we saw field-after-field of fava beans growing in between rows of olive trees, interspersed with beautiful wild poppies. The picturesque patches of the wide variety of vegetables frequently make the landscape look like a quilted blanket. These vegetables give a variety of flavors and colors to the traditional cuisine of Puglia. The vegetables are frequently mixed with different shapes of pasta, some of which are unique to Puglia.

At one time Puglia was known as a region of sheep farming, but now the pastures have become fields of grain, vegetables, and sugar beets. Bari, the capitol city, has flour mills, pasta factories, and olive oil refineries. Bari's province is a major producer of olive oil, wine, vegetables, and fruit.

The cooking of Puglia is simple, however, some dishes take more effort than others in their preparation. Fava beans with chicory, tomato bruschetta (toasted bread), orecchiette (a type of pasta) with green vegetables, stuffed eggplant and bell peppers, are all classic dishes of Puglia. Meals often are centered around one main dish with several ingredients cooked together, such as fish with potatoes, pasta with meat, or lamb and peppers .

The people of Puglia love their pasta and probably consume the most pasta of any of the Italian regions. Noodles, lasagna, *orecchiette*, small gnocchi, *laganelle* (small stuffed lasagna), and macaroni are favorites. Each is prepared in many different ways. A local type of pasta dough is also used to make all kinds of pizza, *calzone* (stuffed dough) and small pies. The traditional *calzone Pugliese* has a filling of tomatoes, onion, olives, anchovies, capers, and parsley.

Some of the popular pasta dishes include *orecchiette*, which is an ear-shaped pasta made by pressing the dough with the thumb,. It is cooked with broccoli, pancetta, garlic, anchovies, olive oil, and hot pepper. *Orecchiette ai tre colori* (of the three colors of the Italian flag - red, white, and green) is made with tomatoes, cheese and ruchetta (similar to arugula), a locally grown herb. *Orecchiette con cime e acciuga* is cooked with turnip tops and anchovies.

The meat sauce used in making *ragu*, a sauce for pasta, is often made with horse meat. The people of Puglia prefer it to beef or lamb because of its slightly sweet taste. For this dish, regardless of whether horse meat or beef is used, the meat is cut into thin slices and covered with pancetta, a slice of pecorino cheese and some parsley and garlic. The meat then is rolled up, tied with kitchen string, and cooked in a tomato sauce with a little wine. When the dish is ready to serve, the sauce is first served with the pasta and then the small bundles of meat are served as a main course with some vegetables.

Lampascuini alla vetrettese is a local dish based on a wild onion (*lampascuini*) that grows in Puglia. The dish consists of a puree of the wild onion with vinegar. This mixture is spread on bread as an antipasto. Although the wild *lampascuini* is bitter, the bitterness is removed by soaking the onions for 48 hours in cold water or by blanching them. The onions can also be baked or boiled and used in a salad or they can be stewed with wine and tomatoes.

Soups are very common fare in Puglia, especially in the winter. *Maritate alla foggiana* (means married) is a soup using a combination of vegetables, meat and bacon — a pleasant marriage. Another popular soup is *minestra di castrato* made with mutton and vegetables.

The waters off of Puglia contain many species of fish and shellfish. While most seafood is harvested from the sea, some is cultivated in inland ponds and between piers in structures that resemble glass houses. Oysters and other mollusks are grown in the Gulf of Taranto. Many oysters and even the small octopuses are eaten raw with only a squeeze of lemon juice, olive oil, and pepper.

One of the traditional fish dishes of Puglia is *orata alla pugliese*. It consists of gilthead (a Mediterranean white fish with flaky flesh) cooked with potatoes, pecorino cheese, parsley and olive oil. *Orata alla San Nicola*, a dish named after the patron saint of Bari, is prepared with fish that is marinated in oil and lemon juice, and then broiled.

Other Puglia fish dishes are *sgombri all'aceto*, mackerel in vinegar, and *alici recanate*, a type of anchovy tart. Fish soups, stuffed mussels, and squid stew are cooked by the people of Puglia in many different ways. Mussels are frequently used in soups. They are also served au gratin, fried, or in a sauce to top polenta.

Lamb is the most popular meat in Puglia. Beef is rarely consumed because the pasture land of Puglia is not good for feeding cattle, but sheep and goats can feed on the small herbs and bushes of these pastures. Usually the lamb is larded before it is roasted or grilled. It is traditionally flavored with rosemary and sage. Lamb is also prepared in fricassees. This is a casserole-type dish to which egg yolks beaten with lemon juice are added at the end of the cooking time.

Cheese also plays an important role in the cooking of this region. Mozzarella, Scamorza, *provole di bufala*, fresh ricotta, caciocavallo, ricotta salata (salted ricotta), and pecorino are all local cheeses used to flavor a myriad of dishes. Many of these cheeses can be enjoyed by themselves.

Fresh fruit is often eaten at the end of a meal. The desserts of Puglia are similar and prepared in much the same way as those of other nearby regions. Two of the best known desserts of Puglia are pastries. *Carteddate* is made with flour, oil, white wine and honey. *Zeppole di San Giuseppe* are doughnuts made with flour, sweet wine, sugar, olive oil, and honey.

Frittelle di ricotta are ricotta fritters made with ricotta cheese, breadcrumbs, eggs, sugar, milk and then fried in oil. Another dessert is *bocconotti* which is a baked sweet ravioli. The dough of this ravioli is stuffed with custard and then the small ravioli are baked in the oven.

Fruit and almond orchards, olive groves, and vineyards are found in Puglia. The Puglia region is the largest producer of wine and olive oil in Italy. The region is known as the wine cellar of Italy. Although Puglia produces a large variety of wines, most of its wines are used for blending and improving other Italian wines. The addition of these Puglia bulk wines adds body and high alcoholic content.

Wines

Among the best Puglia wines are: Aleatico di Puglia, a sweet red wine and Locorotondo, a dry and delicate white wine. Two of the most well-known producers of wine in Puglia are: Castel del Monte which features reds, whites and roses and Copertino which makes only red and rose wines.

Unique rooftops of Alberobello, a town in southern Puglia.
Photo courtesy of Frank Spadarella.

Cena di Famiglia
Family Dinner

Serves 6

Bruschetta al Pomodoro
Tomato Toasted Bread

Penne e Broccoletti
Penne and Broccoli

Pesce alla Marinara
Fish in Tomato Sauce

Zucchini Fritti Impanati
Fried Zucchini

Cicoria e Radicchio con Arugula
Chicory and Radicchio with Arugula

Coppettte di Crema
Vanilla Bean Custard

Caffè
Coffee

Family Dinner

Italian families get together for dinner at least once a week. For the Italians, family dinners are joyous occasions where food and wine are enjoyed. These dinners are also opportunities for the family members to exchange news of the latest happenings and to gossip. For me these dinners are also an opportunity to serve the various dishes which members of my family enjoy. I try to plan the menus of my family dinners around the food preferences of my family and the availability of seasonal ingredients.

For this menu I have chosen some of the favorites I serve to my children and grandchildren when they visit us.

Tomato toasted bread starts the dinner as an antipasto. The penne pasta with broccoli florets is an unusual, colorful, and tasty dish. For the entrée I used sea bass cooked in tomato sauce. When served with fried zucchini the combination makes a colorful, but light main course.

My family loves salads. This salad, is a combination of chicory, radicchio, and arugula, and provides a palate cleanser before the dessert of vanilla bean custard.

Preparations

You can do most of the preparations for this dinner in the afternoon and then finish cooking just before dinner. Toast the bread for the antipasto early in the afternoon and when the bread is cool, place the slices in a plastic bag. Prepare the tomato, onions and cut the anchovies. Then place them in separate dishes in the refrigerator. Assemble the appetizer just before dinner.

Also in the afternoon rinse and cut the broccoli for the pasta. Chop the bacon, garlic, and anchovy fillets. In the evening, while the pasta and broccoli are boiling, sauté the bacon, garlic and anchovies. Drain the pasta and broccoli and dress them with the sauce.

Make the sauce for the fish in the afternoon and reheat it that evening. Cook the fish about 15 minutes before dinner. Cut the zucchini early in the day, measure the flour and place it on aluminum foil, beat the eggs in a bowl and refrigerate them. Fry the zucchini just before dinner and keep it warm.

Clean and cut the salad ingredients in the morning or even the day before, place them in a plastic bag and refrigerate. Make the dressing and set it aside. The vanilla bean custard dessert can be made a day ahead and refrigerated.

Bruschetta al Pomodoro
Tomato Toasted Bread

Serves 6

This toasted bread with tomatoes is a traditional shepherds' and peasants' lunch that has now become a fashionable appetizer.

12 (1/4 inch thick) slices of coarse
   bread
2 garlic cloves
Salt and fresh ground black pepper
Extra virgin olive oil

3 large ripe tomatoes, coarsely
   chopped
1 small sweet onion, chopped
6 anchovy fillets, cut in half

Toast the bread slices until golden in color on both sides in the oven or over a grill.

Rub one side of each bread slice with garlic, then sprinkle with salt and pepper and olive oil.

Cover each slice with some of the chopped tomatoes. Then sprinkle them with a little chopped onion and place half an anchovy fillet on top.

Penne e Broccoletti
Penne and Broccoli

Serves 6

4 tablespoons olive oil
2 ounces bacon, finely chopped
3 garlic cloves, finely chopped
1/4 teaspoon hot pepper flakes
4 packed in oil anchovy fillets,
   drained and mashed
1 pound penne rigate

1 pound broccoli tips cut into
   florets, stems peeled and sliced
1/3 cup freshly grated pecorino
   romano cheese
1/4 cup freshly grated Parmesan
   cheese
Salt and freshly ground pepper

Heat oil in a small saucepan over medium heat. Add the bacon, garlic, pepper flakes and anchovies and sauté until the garlic starts to color, about 2 minutes. Cook the penne in boiling salted water, stirring once in a while, until the pasta begins to soften, about 8 minutes. Add the broccoli to the pasta and cook until the pasta is tender, but al dente, about 3 minutes. Drain and transfer pasta and broccoli to a large heated serving bowl.

Pour the bacon-anchovy mixture over the pasta. Add the 2 cheeses and mix thoroughly. Add salt and pepper, if desired. Serve while hot.

Pesce alla Marinara
Fish in Tomato Sauce

Serves 6

3 garlic cloves, finely chopped
5 tablespoons olive oil
5 medium tomatoes, peeled, seeded, and chopped or 2 cups chopped canned Italian tomatoes
1/2 cup sliced black olives
1 cup dry white wine
Salt

1/2 teaspoon dried oregano
1/4 teaspoon chili pepper
1/2 teaspoon freshly ground black pepper
3 pounds sea bass, halibut, or cod, cut into 6 steaks
3 tablespoons fresh chopped parsley

In a deep skillet, large enough to accommodate the 6 fish steaks, sauté the garlic in the olive oil over medium heat for a few minutes. Add the chopped tomatoes, olives, and wine. Season with salt, oregano, and chili and black pepper, and cook for about 10 minutes, stirring often. Place the fish steaks in the skillet and cook, covered, over low heat until the fish is done about 15 minutes, depending on the thickness of the fish steaks. Just before serving, sprinkle parsley on top of fish and sauce.

Zucchini Fritti Impanati
Fried Zucchini

Serves 6

6 medium zucchini
1 cup all-purpose flour
2 large eggs
1/2 teaspoon salt

1/2 teaspoon freshly ground black
  pepper
1/2 cup olive oil or enough olive oil
  for frying

Scrub the zucchini under cold running water. Cut off and discard both ends of the zucchini. Then cut them lengthwise into 1-inch slices.

Place the flour on a piece of aluminum foil. Beat the eggs with the salt and pepper in a bowl. Dip the zucchini slices first in the flour, them in the beaten eggs and then again in the flour. Heat the oil in a large skillet. When the oil is hot, add the zucchini slices. Cook over medium-high heat until golden brown on both sides. (This may have to be done in 2 batches.) Remove the zucchini slices from the oil and drain them on paper towels. Serve hot with the entree.

Cicoria e Radicchio con Arugula
Chicory and Radicchio with Arugula

Serves 6

Chicory is curly endive. Both the flavor of chicory and radicchio are a little bitter but combined with arugula the combination makes an appetizing salad. If curly endive is not available, substitute 2 heads of Belgian endive.

1 bunch of curly endive
2 medium heads radicchio, core
  removed
1 large bunch Arugula, stems
  removed

5 tablespoons extra virgin olive oil
Juice of 1 lemon
1/2 teaspoon salt
1/2 teaspoon freshly ground black
  pepper

Wash and dry the salad greens. Cut the chicory and the radicchio into strips and mix with the Arugula in a large salad bowl. Make the dressing by mixing the olive oil and lemon juice, then season with salt and pepper. Pour the dressing over the salad just before serving.

Coppette di Crema
Vanilla Bean Custard

Serves 6

This dessert can be made a day ahead and refrigerated.

2 cups whole milk	*4 egg yolks*
1 (1/4-inch) sliver of lemon peel	*1/3 cup sugar*
1 1/2 teaspoons vanilla extract	

Place the milk, lemon peel and vanilla extract in a saucepan and simmer over low heat for about 4 minutes, . Remove the saucepan from the heat and set it aside.

Beat the egg yolks with the sugar in a medium bowl, until creamy and foamy. Little by little pour the hot milk into the egg mixture, stirring constantly with a wooden spoon to prevent the eggs from curdling. Pour the mixture into the top of a double boiler and cook over hot water, stirring constantly with a wooden spoon, until the milk is very creamy.

Preheat the oven to 350° F. Pour 1 inch of lukewarm water in a roasting pan which is large enough to hold 6 ramekins. Spoon the cream mixture into 6 ramekins and place them into the prepared roasting pan. Then place the pan in the preheated oven. Bake for about 40 minutes or until a knife inserted in the center comes out clean.

Remove the pan from the oven and let the ramekins cool for 30 minutes. Then refrigerate the custards for at least one hour before unmolding onto a serving dish. Serve with a favorite biscotti.

Optional Sprinkle nutmeg on top of custard.

Una Speciale Occasione
A Special Occasion

Serves 6

Antipasto di Melanzane
Antipasto of Eggplants

Orecchiette con Ragu
Orecchiette with Sauce

Braciolette
Meat Rolls

Cicoria e Fava
Chicory and Broad Beans

Frittelle di Ricotta
Ricotta Fritters

Caffè
Coffee

A Special Occasion

In Puglia, as in this country, special occasions call for a celebration — a dinner with friends. In addition to holidays and birthdays, a special occasion can celebrate news of taking a long vacation, the acquisition of a new home, or starting a new career. Recently friends of ours bought a new home, which called for a get-together and celebration. For this dinner I added some special touches — one of my best china service, flowers for the dining table, plus a bottle of good champagne cooling in the refrigerator.

This five course meal begins with an eggplant appetizer, seasoned with an oil dressing and herbs, and served with slices of coarse Italian bread. The pasta with tomato sauce is a light, piquant second course. The sauce for the pasta comes from the sauce for the meat rolls, making it one preparation for two courses.

The simple-to-prepare meat rolls make an elegant entree. Fava beans combined with chicory, a typical Puglia dish, is a light accompaniment for the meat. Crispy and creamy ricotta fritters end this special occasion dinner.

Preparations

Several items on this menu can be prepared ahead. You need to make the antipasto of eggplant in the morning so that the flavors will meld. Set the dish aside until time to serve.

The meat rolls with the sauce can be made the day before and refrigerated, then reheated on the evening of the party. Boil the fava beans early in the afternoon and puree them. Also boil the chicory at this time and squeeze out the excess water.

On the evening of the party warm the sauce with the meat rolls and keep it simmering while you cook the pasta. Heat the fava puree in a small saucepan and also heat the chicory. Just before serving, drizzle the oil over both of them.

The ricotta fritters cannot be fried ahead of time, but the batter can be prepared early in the afternoon and refrigerated. Remove the batter from the refrigerator one hour before you are going to make the fritters, so that the batter will be at room temperature. Fry the fritters immediately after serving after-dinner coffee to your guests.

Antipasto di Melanzane
Antipasto of Eggplants

Serves 6

4 large eggplants, thinly sliced
Salt
1/2 cup or more olive oil
2 teaspoons freshly ground black
   pepper

3 to 4 garlic cloves, finely chopped
2 sprigs fresh mint, finely chopped
2 sprigs fresh oregano, finely
   chopped
1 tablespoon wine vinegar

Sprinkle the eggplant slices with salt and let them drain in a colander for 20 minutes to remove the bitter juice. Then rinse the eggplant slices and pat them dry with paper towels. Brush the eggplant slices lightly with a little olive oil and grill them over charcoal or under the broiler until they are lightly browned, turning them over once.

Place the cooked eggplant on a serving platter and sprinkle with pepper, garlic, mint, oregano and then sprinkle with the vinegar. Then drizzle with the olive oil. In order for the eggplant to absorb the dressing, make this dish hours before serving and keep it at room temperature. Serve with slices of coarse Italian bread.

Orecchiette con Braciolette
Pasta with Meat Rolls

Serves 6

In Puglia women still make their pasta at home. This is very unusual because most of the Italians now buy dry pasta. Orecchiette (little ears) are the symbol of the Puglia region. This pasta is eaten almost everyday and prepared differently in each village. Typically the sauce for this pasta contains vegetables, beans, legumes, and different types of meat.

Orecchiette, imported from Italy, may be purchased in grocery stores or Italian delicatessens. If you cannot find the orecchiette pasta use pasta shells.

2 1/2 pounds beef sirloin, cut into 12
   thin slices
Salt and freshly ground pepper
12 thin slices pancetta, cut into two
   pieces each
2 cups pecorino cheese, 1 1/2 cups
   cut in slivers and 1/2 cup grated
5 garlic cloves, 3 finely chopped, 2
   cut in half

1/2 cup fresh chopped parsley
1/4 cup extra virgin olive oil
1 medium onion, finely chopped
4 cups canned Italian tomatoes
   with their juice
1 cup dry red wine
1 pound orecchiette pasta or shell
   pasta

Have the butcher cut the meat in 12 thin slices. Pound each slice with the flat side of a meat clever until very thin. Season the slices with salt and pepper.

Place 1 slice of pancetta, cut in 2 pieces on each slice of beef. Then scatter a few slivers of pecorino cheese, some chopped garlic, and parsley over each slice. Roll up each meat slice into a small roll and tie it with kitchen string or secure it with a wooden pick.

Heat the olive oil in a Dutch oven over medium heat, add the meat rolls and brown them, turning them several times for about 5 to 7 minutes. Remove the meat rolls from the pan and set them aside.

Add the chopped onions to the Dutch oven and sauté over medium heat until the onions are transparent about 2 minutes. Add the chopped tomatoes, season with a little salt and pepper, and stir. Place the meat rolls back into the pan with the tomato sauce, add the red wine, and cook covered over low heat for about 1 hour or until the sauce starts to thicken and the meat rolls are tender.

Boil the orecchiette pasta or shells in plenty of boiling salted water for 7 minutes or until cooked, but still al dente. Drain the pasta thoroughly, place it on a large heated platter, pour a sufficient amount of the sauce over the pasta to moisten it, and then sprinkle with grated cheese and mix thoroughly.

Remove the meat rolls out from the sauce, and cut the string or remove the wooden picks. Place the meat rolls back into the sauce to keep them hot until ready to serve. Serve the Orecchiette or shell as the first course and then the meat rolls for the entree.

Cicoria e Fava
Chicory and Broad Beans

Serves 6

This dish of fava and chicory is the most well-known of all the dishes of the Puglia region.

1 pound dried or fresh fava beans
2 medium onions, chopped
2 celery stalks, chopped
2 medium potatoes, peeled and cut
    into 1 1/2-inch pieces
Salt

2 heads curly endive or large heads
    of chicory
Freshly ground black pepper
1/2 cup extra virgin olive oil
1 red onion, optional

If using dried fava beans, soak them overnight in cold water. Peel them before you put them in a large pan with fresh water to cover by 3 inches.

If using fresh fava beans, shell them and place them into a large pan with cold water to cover by 3 inches. Add the chopped onions, celery, and potatoes. Bring to a boil and cook slowly over low heat for about 1 hour. Add salt during the last 15 minutes of cooking. Place the cooked fava mixture into a bowl and mash it with a fork. Set the mixture aside.

Wash and trim the chicory or endive and cut it into branches. Place them in boiling salted water over medium-high heat for 10 to 12 minutes or until they are tender. Drain the endive thoroughly and squeeze out the excess water.

If serving the red onion with this dish, peel it and slice it very thin. Place the slices in cold water for about 1 hour and then dry them on paper towel.

When ready to serve gently heat the fava puree in a small saucepan. Place the fava puree on a heated plate and mound the hot cooked endive next to it. Season both with salt and fresh black pepper and drizzle some extra virgin olive oil over both. If using the sliced onions, place some on the plate.

When eating this dish take some of everything and put them together to make a mouthful.

This dish can be served hot or at room temperature. It may be made ahead, but not refrigerated. Do not add the oil until ready to serve.

Frittelle di Ricotta
Ricotta Fritters

Makes 10 to 13 fritters, depending on their size

1 1/2 cups whole-milk ricotta, well drained
2 cups soft bread crumbs (not stale)
1/2 cup milk for soaking
1/3 cup sugar
2 extra large egg yolks, beaten

Grated rind of 1 orange
1/3 cup olive oil, for frying
2/3 cup all-purpose flour
2 extra large eggs, beaten
Confectioner's sugar, for garnish

Press the ricotta cheese through a sieve and then place it in a glass bowl. Soak the bread crumbs in milk in a small bowl and then squeeze them dry. Add the sugar, beaten egg yolks, and grated orange rind to the ricotta. Then add the bread crumbs and mix well to form a smooth, thick batter.

Heat olive oil in a deep skillet for frying over medium heat. Using a large serving spoon scoop up some of the ricotta mixture to form an egg-shaped fritter. Lightly flour the fritters first, then use a pastry brush to brush them with the beaten eggs. When the oil is very hot, fry the fritters until golden in color, about 1 minute. Place the fritters on a serving platter lined with paper towels to absorb excess oil. When all the fritters are on the platter, remove the paper towels and sprinkle them with some confectioner's sugar. Serve while hot. The texture of the fritters should be very crusty outside and very creamy inside.

To make this fritters even better tasting, add some Grand Marnier to the fritters batter or serve them with some vanilla ice cream.

Basilicata

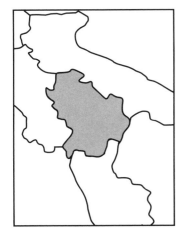

Considered to be the poorest region of Italy, Basilicata has little agriculture or industry. However, one of the ingredients of its cuisine, the hot pepper, has become a major component of Basilicata cooking, as it has throughout southern Italy. Many varieties of peppers, ranging from mild to hot, are grown and used in the region. Most of the dishes of Basilicata, from soup to roasts and vegetables, however, contain *peperocino* (red pepper), usually the hot variety.

Geographically Basilicata is the instep of the Italian boot. It borders the Ionian and Tyrrhenian Seas. The region, whose history can be traced back to the times of the Caesars, used to be called Lucania and its people are still known as Lucani.

Basilicata is almost entirely mountainous with slopes rising from the sea. Originally the Lucani built their towns on high ground, far from the sea to shelter themselves from the Turkish pirates. Because of the rugged terrain, poor soils, cold winters, hot, dry summers, and the difficulty of irrigation, the products of the land are scarce. Some tomatoes, strawberries, almonds, and figs are cultivated. Very few sheep and goats are pastured in the mountains. Thus each family raises a pig and depends mainly on pork for its meat source.

The day that the pig is killed, the family has a great feast. All kinds of *salumi* (cured pork products) — sausages, salami, prosciutto, *capocollo* (cured pork shoulder) — and lard are produced from this pig. Lard, together with olive oil, is the fat used for local cooking.

The Lucani make a well-known sausage called *luganega*, which is famous all over Italy. This long, thin, smoked or dry-cured sausage has been made since Roman times. It is usually eaten when it is fresh, and is prepared grilled, fried, or stewed with vegetables. Another *salumi* is *soppressata*, a large oval sausage that is seasoned with ginger and is sometimes preserved in oil.

Every part of the pig is used in Basilicata, even the blood which is the prime ingredient in *sanguinaccio*, a black pudding made in the shape of a cake or sausage. *Pezzente*, which means beggar, is a sausage made with the butcher's leftovers from his shop and this is sometimes mixed with bits of sheep and kid.

In Basilicata bread used to be made with coarser wheat flour then today's bread and it was made in the traditional shape of a cartwheel. This bread was called *panella* and was very large. The women usually made this bread once a week and brought it to the bakery for baking, because very few homes had even a primitive outdoor oven to accommodate this large bread. It kept well for the whole week. Now bread is seldom made at home, but pasta still is.

The pasta of Basilicata is coarse and made with wheat-flour and water. It is fashioned in many different shapes including fusilli, lasagna, and *cavatieddi*, a pasta shaped like small mussel shells. When meat is available, the dressing for the pasta is a *ragu* made with small pieces of pork or sheep. It is called *ntruppic* meaning obstacles. Then chili pepper fried in oil and salted ricotta cheese is added. The salted ricotta cheese is the local specialty of Basilicata.

Because of the shortage of locally-produced meat, the Lucani cooks prepare many vegetable dishes to take the place of meat. Usually they are cooked in the oven and mixed with herbs, chili pepper, and olive oil. Broad beans and lentils are used in soups and pasta. *Pepperonata*, is Basilicata's best-known vegetable dish. It is a stew of sweet peppers and tomatoes flavored with lots of chili peppers and mixed with chunks of pork meat, when available. Since there is little meat, often not even enough to make soup, pasta is served as the first course as well as the second course.

Although Basilicata faces two seas, the Ionian and the Tyrrhenian, it has no seaports. It is the only region that does not have a traditional fish dish, but the Lucani people created one for themselves called *Baccala*. *Baccala* consists of salt cod (from northern Europe) and potatoes in layers seasoned with oil, oregano, garlic, and chili pepper. which is then baked in the oven.

Many of the cheeses produced in the other southern regions are also made in Basilicata. However, they are typically aged longer for a stronger flavor. Even the local ricotta, *ricotta forte*, has a strong flavor and a pungent aroma.

Desserts are eaten even less in Basilicata than in other regions. *Panzarotti* is a fried or baked pastry with a filling of pureed chick peas flavored with chocolate, sugar, and cinnamon. *Panzarotti* is eaten hot fresh from the stove and sprinkled with powdered sugar. Occasionally *Panzarotti* is baked, then dipped in honey while still hot but then eaten cold.

Wines

Basilicata's best wine is Aglianico del Vulture, a dry red wine served with roasts. The grapes for this wine are of ancient Greek origin. Moscato de Vulture, a delicate sparkling wine, and Malvasia del Vulture are dessert wines. The grapes for these wines are grown in volcanic soil at an elevation of about 2,000 feet on the slopes of the extinct volcano Mount Vulture.

Men chatting.
Photo courtesy of Frank Spadrella

Weekend in Montagna
Mountain Weekend

Serves 4

Pollo alla Potentina
Chicken Potentina Style

Patate con Diavolicchio
Potatoes with Hot Peppers

Cappelle di Funghi al Forno
Roasted Mushrooms Caps

Insalata di Cetrioli
Cucumber Salad

Copete
Almond Cookies

Caffe
Coffee

Mountain Weekend

Friday night

Many of us like to get away for an occasional weekend in the mountains. In many parts of the United States, as in Italy, the mountains offer many opportunities for a relaxing weekend.

Some of the typical mountain cuisine of Italy can be found in the isolated communities of the rugged, beautiful mountains of Basilicata.

For a weekend in the mountains, I planned this and the following menu based on the food of Basilicata. The accent of hot peppers, typical of the region, is used in several dishes.

The chicken cooked with onions, wine, hot pepper flakes, tomatoes, and parsley has a piquant aroma and taste. Boiled potatoes with a dressing of oil, garlic, pepper, and parsley accompanies the chicken. Also served with the chicken are roasted mushrooms seasoned with parsley, garlic, peppers, and oregano — a dish to please any mushroom lover.

The cucumber salad is a refreshing interlude after this tasty meal. Almond cookies with a glass of dessert or sparkling wine finish the meal. Fresh fruit or ice cream are optional accompaniments.

Preparations

To enhance the enjoyment of a retreat to a mountain weekend, some of the dishes may be prepared ahead.

The chicken recipe can be prepared several days ahead. However, cook the chicken only 15 minutes instead of the 30 indicated in the recipe after having added the tomato sauce, parsley, and basil. Cool the chicken, then refrigerate it in a plastic container with a cover. At the mountain destination, reheat the chicken and finish cooking it.

The potatoes need to be boiled on the evening of the dinner. The chopped parsley and crushed garlic can be prepared at home, placed in airtight containers and refrigerated. Before going away for the weekend, clean the mushrooms, remove the stems and then place the mushrooms in a plastic bag and refrigerate. For the mushroom caps, chop the parsley and garlic and place them in a small bowl. Add the bread crumbs, salt, pepper, oregano and olive oil. Cover the bowl and refrigerate. If it is a warm day, transport all of the refrigerated items in a cooler.

As the salad takes little time to assemble, make it before dinner.

Bake the cookies days ahead and place them in an air-tight container. Purchase a sparkling wine to drink with the almond cookies.

Pollo alla Potentina
Chicken Potentina Style

Serves 4

1 (2 1/2 to 3 pound) chicken
2 tablespoons olive oil
1 onion, thinly sliced
1 cup dry white wine
1/4 teaspoon hot crushed red pepper
    flakes
1 cup chopped fresh ripe tomatoes

or 1 cup canned chopped Italian
    tomatoes
2 tablespoons fresh chopped parsley
1 large tablespoon fresh chopped
    basil
1 teaspoon salt

Cut the chicken into pieces, remove any extra fat, rinse under cold water, and pat dry with paper towels.

Heat the olive oil in a large casserole or Dutch oven over medium heat. Add the sliced onion and the chicken pieces and sauté until lightly browned. While sautéing add the white wine a little at a time. Add the pepper flakes and continue cooking until the wine has completely evaporated about 15 minutes. Then add the chopped tomatoes, parsley and basil and season with salt and mix.

Cover the casserole and cook over medium heat for about 30 minutes or until the chicken is done, turning the chicken occasionally during the cooking. Add a little water or chicken broth, if necessary.

Serve the chicken with the pan juices, some potatoes and one portabello mushroom per person.

Patate con Diavolicchio
Potatoes with Hot Peppers

Serves 4

Diavolicchio is the name given to chili peppers of the Basilicata region. It is the most frequently used flavoring in the cooking of Basilicata and Abruzzi. These chili peppers are used both fresh and dried.

In the country, the doorways and balconies of the farmhouses are hung with chains or ropes of red chilies drying in the sun. When the chilies are dry they are brought inside to the kitchen where they are hung during the winter months and used daily.

2 large potatoes	*1/4 teaspoon crushed red pepper*
4 tablespoons extra virgin olive oil	*flakes*
2 garlic cloves, crushed	*1/2 teaspoon salt*
1 small hot chili pepper, chopped, or	*2 tablespoons fresh finely chopped*
	parsley

In a saucepan with salted water boil the potatoes with their skins over medium heat for about 20 to 30 minutes or until done.

When the potatoes are cooked, remove them from the saucepan and let them cool. Peel the potatoes, slice them and place them on a heated platter.

Heat the oil in a small skillet over medium heat. Add the crushed garlic and chopped chili peppers or hot pepper flakes and cook until the garlic starts to color. Discard the garlic and remove the skillet from heat. Pour the chili-oil mixture over the sliced potatoes and sprinkle with the salt and chopped parsley. Serve the potatoes with the cooked chicken.

Cappelle di Funghi al Forno
Roasted Mushroom Caps

Serves 4

In Basilicata porcini mushrooms are used to make this dish. Since fresh porcini are not readily available in this country, substitute portabello mushrooms or any other large-capped cultivated mushroom.

4 medium flat portabello mush-
    rooms, stems removed, or 8 small
    flat mushrooms, stems removed
3 tablespoons finely chopped parsley
3 garlic cloves, finely chopped
2 tablespoons bread crumbs
1/2 teaspoon salt

1/2 teaspoon dried crushed hot
    pepper flakes
3 tablespoons extra virgin olive oil
1/2 teaspoon crushed dried oregano
4 tablespoons extra virgin olive oil,
for roasting

Wipe the mushrooms gently with a damp cloth and set them aside.

Place the parsley, garlic, bread crumbs, salt and hot pepper flakes in a small bowl. Add 3 tablespoons of oil and mix all the ingredients together. Add the oregano and mix again.

Oil a large baking sheet with 1 tablespoon of oil and spread it all over the bottom of the baking sheet with a piece of paper towel.

Place the mushrooms with the stem side up on the baking sheet. Spread the parsley mixture evenly over the cavity of each mushroom. Sprinkle about 1 tablespoon of oil over each mushroom, if the mushrooms are large. Use 1 teaspoon of oil if the mushrooms are small. Place the baking sheet in a preheated 400° F. oven for about 10 minutes.

Serve the mushrooms hot with the chicken and potatoes.

Food Note

Almond trees flourish throughout southern Italy and almonds are used in many dishes, including entrees.

Insalata di Cetrioli
Cucumber Salad

Serves 4

2 large cucumbers
6 small red radishes
1/2 teaspoon salt

1/4 teaspoon freshly ground black
  pepper
4 tablespoons extra virgin olive oil
1 tablespoons red wine vinegar

    Peel the cucumbers and slice them into 1/4-inch rounds. Place the sliced cucumber into a salad bowl. Rinse and scrub the radishes, but do not peel them. Cut them into very thin slices and add them to the bowl. Season the cucumber mixture with salt and pepper, olive oil and vinegar. Toss thoroughly and serve.

Copete
Almond Cookies

Yields about 2 dozen cookies

3/4 cup blanched almonds
2 egg whites
1/8 teaspoon cream of tartar

3/4 cup sugar
1/2 teaspoon ground cinnamon
1/2 cup confectioner's sugar

    Toast the almonds for 5 to 8 minutes in a preheated 350° F. oven. Cool the almonds and grind them finely.

    Beat the egg whites until foamy. Add the cream of tartar and beat until softly whipped. Add the sugar and cinnamon powder slowly in a thin stream, beating until the mixture is stiff. Beat in the confectioner's sugar, then slowly fold in the almonds until the mixture is well blended.

    Line a cookie sheet with parchment paper. Use a soup spoon to form mounds of the almond mixture on the cookie sheet, keeping the mounds apart from each other, for they will expand as they bake. Place the baking sheet in a preheated 350°°F. oven for about 15 minutes. Remove the cookies from the oven and let them cool on a wire rack.

    These almond cookies are crunchy and crumbly on the outside, but soft and moist on the inside. These cookies can be stored in an air tight container in a cool dry place and will last for up to 10 days. Serve the cookies with a glass of sparkling wine or dessert wine.

Weekend in Montagna
Mountain Weekend

Serves 6

Bucatini con Acciughe
Bucatini Pasta with Anchovies

Salsicce Arroste
Roasted Sausages

Patate al Forno con Cipolle e Pomodori
Baked Potatoes with Onions and Tomatoes

Insalata alla Lucana
Salad Lucana Style

Torta d'Arance
Orange Cake

Caffe
Coffee

Mountain Weekend

Saturday Night

On the second evening of an enjoyable weekend in the mountains a simple dinner is ideal after a day of strenuous skiing or hiking. While simple, this dinner can be an extremely enjoyable one.

A very unusual pasta with a savory sauce starts this meal. Mashed anchovies, garlic, parsley and olive oil are combined with bread crumbs, then tossed with bucatini for a unique flavor and crunchy texture. Bucatini, similar to spaghetti but with a hollow center, is ideal for this sauce as sauces adhere well to this type of pasta.

For the main course sausages are roasted on the grill. Grilling the sausages adds to the informality of the meal. Sliced potatoes with onions and tomatoes and topped with pecorino cheese baked in the oven make a flavorful accompaniment to the sausages.

A mixed salad with a dressing of scallions, garlic, and pepper provides a light interlude and a palate cleanser.

An orange cake with a refreshing citrus flavor ends this meal.

Preparations

The sauce for the bucatini pasta has to be made while the pasta is boiling. It is quick to prepare, and the dish can be assembled in a few minutes.

However, the night before leaving on your trip prepare the chopped parsley, place it in a plastic container, and refrigerate.

The purchased sausages need no preparation.

The potato casserole can also be prepared the night before leaving. Assemble the potatoes with the onion and tomatoes, then cover with plastic wrap, and refrigerate. Before serving, bake the casserole in the oven.

Rinse the butter lettuce and pat it dry. Also rinse the scallions, yellow pepper, and celery stalk, place in plastic bags, and refrigerate. Before dinner, cut all of the salad ingredients and make the dressing.

Make the orange cake a day before leaving and refrigerate it. Whip the cream just before serving.

Bucatini con Acciughe
Bucatini with Anchovies

Serves 6

Bucatini are thick spaghetti with a hollow center. They are not as large in diameter as macaroni. If bucatini are unavailable substitute a very thick spaghetti.

1 (2 ounce) can anchovies, well
    drained, bones removed
1/2 cup olive oil
2 garlic cloves, crushed

1/2 teaspoon chopped chili pepper
    flakes
1 cup bread crumbs
2 tablespoons fresh chopped parsley
1 pound bucatini or thick spaghetti

Cut the anchovies into small pieces.

Heat the olive oil in a skillet over medium heat. Add the crushed garlic, chili pepper, and chopped anchovies. Stir and cook until the anchovies are dissolved and the garlic starts to brown. Discard the garlic.

Boil the pasta in salted water until tender but still firm. When the pasta is almost done, stir the bread crumbs and parsley into the anchovy sauce and let the mixture cook for a few minutes.

Drain the pasta and place it in a warm bowl. Pour the anchovy sauce over the pasta, stir thoroughly, and serve,

Salsicce Arroste
Roasted Sausages

Serves 6

The traditional sausage used for this dish is luganega, a very long, thin, pure-pork sausage which is made of pure pork. It is also called *salsiccia a metro* (sausage by the meter) because it is traditionally sold by length not by weight. Luganega sausage was known in Basilicata in Roman times. Now this sausage is more popular in northern Italy. Luganega is usually grilled or fried.

If using the luganega sausages, cut them into six 6-inch lengths and roll each length into a coil., securing each coil with a toothpick.

Wrap each coil separately in a dampened piece wax paper or foil, and roast them in the ashes of a barbecue fire. However, the more readily available Italian sausages may be used in this recipe.

6 regular Italian sausages	*6 slices coarse Italian bread*

Prick the skin of each sausage with a fork in several spots. Place the sausages on a hot barbecue and cook them for about 5 minutes on each side. When cooked, remove them from the fire and place each sausage on a piece of toasted bread that has been grilled on the fire while the sausages were cooking.

Serve the cooked sausages with a large scoop of the baked potato casserole.

Patate al Forno con Cipolle e Pomodori
Baked Potatoes with Onions and Tomatoes

Serves 6

2 pounds potatoes	*1/2 cup freshly grated pecorino*
1 pound onions	*cheese*
1 pound ripe tomatoes	*1 cup bread crumbs moistened with*
Salt	*1/2 cup water*
8 tablespoons olive oil	

Peel, rinse, and slice the potatoes into 1/4-inch thick slices, and pat dry with paper towels. Cut the onions into thin slices. Blanch the tomatoes in boiling water for 1 to 2 minutes. Then peel the tomatoes, squeeze out the seeds, and chop the tomatoes in pieces.

Place 2 tablespoons of oil in an oven proof casserole and spread the oil in the bottom of the dish. Arrange a layer of sliced potatoes in the bottom of the casserole. Cover the potatoes with some sliced onions and a layer of tomatoes. Sprinkle with salt and 2 tablespoons of oil. Continue in this manner making 2 more layers. Sprinkle the last layer with grated pecorino cheese and the moistened bread crumbs. Cover the casserole with foil and place it in a preheated 375° F. oven for 1 hour.

After 50 minutes, remove the foil from the casserole and bake another 10 minutes. The top should be crisp and golden in color.

Scoop some of the potato mixture into individual dishes and serve with the roasted sausages.

Insalata alla Lucana
Salad Lucana Style

Serves 6

2 heads butter lettuce
1 large carrot, shredded
2 scallions, thinly sliced
1 celery stalk, thinly sliced
1 yellow pepper, cut into strips
1/4 cup extra virgin olive oil

2 garlic cloves, crushed
1 hot chili pepper, coarsely chopped
  or 1/4 teaspoon hot red chili
  pepper flakes
1/2 teaspoon salt

Rinse the lettuce and discard outer leaves. Pat the leaves dry with paper towels and break them into pieces. Place the lettuce into a large bowl with the carrot, scallions, celery and pepper.

Heat the olive oil in a small saucepan over medium heat, and sauté the garlic cloves and the chili pepper, until the garlic starts to color. Discard the garlic and pour the hot oil mixture over the salad. Then sprinkle with salt and toss the salad quickly and serve.

Food Note

When garlic is called for in a recipe, always use fresh garlic. Do not use garlic flakes or powder as the taste is quite different.

Torta d'Arance
Orange Cake

Serves 8

6 egg yolks, room temperature
5 tablespoons unsalted butter, room
    temperature
1 cup sugar
3 tablespoons orange juice
Rind of 1/2 orange, finely grated

1/3 cup ground almonds
3/4 cup all purpose flour
1 teaspoon baking powder
6 egg whites
Dash of salt

In a bowl beat the egg yolks, butter, sugar and orange juice together until well mixed. Add the grated orange rind, grounded almonds, flour, and baking powder. Mix until smooth, adding a little orange juice if needed.

Beat the egg whites with the salt in a bowl until they hold stiff peaks. Gently fold the egg whites into the egg yolk mixture. Slowly pour the batter into an ungreased parchment-lined 9 and 1/2-inch spring form pan. Bake in a preheated 350° F. degree oven for 50 minutes or until a wire cake tester inserted in the center comes out clean.

Topping

1 egg
1 egg yolk
1/2 cup sugar
2 tablespoons potato flour or all
    purpose flour
Rind of 1/2 orange, finely grated

Juice of 4 large oranges or 1 cup
    frozen concentrated orange juice,
    thawed
Juice of 1/2 orange
1 tablespoon rum
1 cup whipping cream

Place the whole egg, egg yolk, sugar, flour, orange rind and orange juice of 4 oranges in a small saucepan over medium heat. Stir constantly with a wooden spoon until creamy and the sugar is dissolved.

Slice the orange cake horizontally into 2 equal parts. In a small bowl mix the juice of 1/2 an orange and the rum. Spread this mixture with a pastry brush on both cut halves of the cake. Spread the orange cream topping over one half of the cake. Place the two halves together and then spread the remaining cream topping over the cake..

To serve, whip the cream, and slice the cake into wedges. Serve a slice of orange cake with a spoonful of whipped cream per person.

CALABRIA

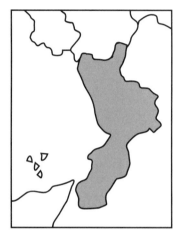

The food of Calabria reflects the season and the simple life of its inhabitants. Calabrian cooking is based on what is available — fish along the seacoast, lamb and goat meat in the mountains, along with home-grown vegetables.

Calabria, the toe of the Italian boot and the southern-most region of the Italian peninsula, is very beautiful. The Tyrrhenian and Ionian seas surround Calabria on three sides — east, south, and west. Calabria is divided from Sicily by the Straits of Messina, which has a minimum width of 3 kilometers.

The region is the terminus of the Appennine Mountains. An important area of Calabria is the Sila Plateau which is rich in water, making it conducive to agriculture, particularly the cultivation of vegetables. This plateau also has many forests and is scattered with chestnut groves. There are also many species of mushrooms and game, such as quail, pheasant, hare, partridge and woodcock on the plateau.

The climate varies in Calabria — warm, almost tropical along the coast and cool in the mountains with rain and snow in winter. Calabria, generally, receives the most rain of all the southern regions.

Citrus trees are cultivated along the coast, especially near Reggio Calabria, the capital of the region. Calabria has the largest production of citrons and bergamots in Italy. In fact, bergamots, which are similar to large lemons, are exclusively grown in Calabria. The taste of the fruit is very acidic and is used as a base ingredient in the manufacture of many types of perfumes.

Oranges and grapefruits are also abundant in Calabria. There is a species of orange that grows only in Calabria,. It ripens late in the season at the beginning of spring and is called, appropriately enough, *arancia Calabria*. Calabria is also known for its sweet tomatoes and figs.

The Calabrian cuisine is based on three ingredients — grain, grapes, and olives. Grains provide the basis for a number of unique local breads and pastas. Huge round loaves of bread are still baked by housewives. The loaves are so large that they are baked in enormous community ovens. Each housewife uses a type of wooden branding iron to identify her loaves. Some of these branding irons are quite intricately carved and have become treasured antiques.

There is also a special bread in Calabria called *scanata*. It is made with boiled potatoes and flour. The people of Lecce make two unusual types of bread: *pane purecasiu* is served with a sauce of oil, onion, and tomatoes, and *puccia* is made with black olives. Another specialty of Calabria is a unique bread called, *pitta*, meaning "painted" because the bread is colored with such ingredients as tomatoes, sardines, and olives. *Pizza Calabrese con tonno e pomodoro*, another ,specialty is made with tuna and tomatoes and *pizza di patate* is made with potato.

In Calabria pasta is traditionally served with a vegetable or pork sauce. Chili peppers, the most popular seasoning in Calabria, are frequently used as a seasoning for these sauces. Calabria is known for *lasagne imbottite cotte al forno*, a rich baked lasagna. Another famous Calabrian pasta dish is *pasta ammudicato*, which consists of noodles with anchovies, bread crumbs, and chili sauce.

Eggplant is the most important vegetable grown in Calabria and the people have created many recipes for it. It is used in soups and in *agrodolce*, which is a sweet and sour sauce. Every village has its own special eggplant recipe

Some of the most popular eggplant dishes are: *melanzane alla cariatese* — eggplant stuffed with salted anchovies, bread crumbs, capers, black olives and garlic; *melanzane al funghetto* — eggplant sautéed in olive oil with garlic and parsley; *melanzanse fritte* — eggplant that has been sliced, coated in egg and bread crumbs and then fried; and *melanzane alla parmigiana* — eggplant with tomatoes, mozzarella, Parmesan, and hard boiled eggs. There are even eggplant recipes containing chocolate.

Calabria provides a third of the national production of olive oil. Therefore, Calabrians use local olive oil to season eggplant simply cooked on the grill. Peppers and mushrooms are often also grilled and sprinkled with Calabrese olive oil.

Pork is the most popular meat in Calabria. It is used in pork *ragu*, which is flavored with chili peppers. Pork is also used to make all kinds of *salumi* and sausages. *Soppressata* and *capocollo* are well-known *salumi* from Calabria.

Pecorino, made from sheep's milk, is the best known cheese of Calabria. It is primarily made for local consumption by families who raise sheep .

The sea around Calabria is abundant in fish, especially tuna, swordfish, sardines, and anchovies. Some are exported either fresh, frozen or preserved in salt.

Fish dishes are often seasoned with dried and ground chili peppers. Calabrian cuisine includes many excellent fish soups, such as *zuppa di pesce alla gallipolina*, a fish chowder that can be traced to an old Spartan recipe. *Cozze alla marinara* is a mussel soup made with ginger and vinegar, while *zuppa di pesce alla brindisina* is made with fish and eels.

Many of Calabrian desserts are fried and then covered with honey. Some of the most popular are fried gnocchi and sweets of different shapes which are Arab in origin. Most the sweets are made only on special occasions.

Mostaccioli are small cakes that are made in Calabria and its surrounding regions. The cake dough contains honey, almonds, citron peel, and spices moistened with wine. The dough is rolled out, cut, and after baking covered with chocolate icing. The Calabresi sometimes cut the dough into squares but mostly the *mostaccioli* are cut into the shape of horses, fish and hearts, even shapes of men and women.

Wines

Calabria produces heavy wines with a high alcohol content and very vivid colors. The production of wine in this region is modest. These wines, however, pair well with the spicy food of the local cooking.

The best wines from Calabria are Donnici, Pollino, and Savuto. These three red wines are highly alcoholic with a fresh taste of wild berries. Esaro Bianco is frequently served with fish and Greco di Gerage, a soft sweet wine, is served with dessert and pastries.

Cirò, the only famous wine of Calabria, was once offered to the Olympic athletes. It is still available today to the Italian athletes. The red Cirò is rich and velvety and the white wine, which is made from the Greco grapes, is young and fresh. There is also a Rosè Cirò.

Harvest time. Photo courtesy of Frank Spadarella.

Un Pranzo di Domenica
A Sunday Dinner

Serves 6

Minestra di Verdure
Vegetable Soup

Costolette d'Agnello
Lamb Chops

Patate al Forno
Oven Potatoes

Fichi al Cioccolato
Stuffed Figs in Chocolate

Caffe
Coffee

A Sunday Dinner

Italians love the weekend, especially Sunday, as they do not have to go to work. Many enjoy going on long drives or inviting friends that live far away for a visit. Sometimes friends will call to say that they are coming, but most of the time they prefer their visit to be a surprise.

My mother used to tell me to always be prepared for unexpected guests on the weekend, just as she was always prepared. She would have one chicken and one rabbit cleaned, cut, and ready to cook in case friends arrived.

My "spur of the moment" Sunday dinner starts with a vegetable soup, which is rich in vitamins and flavor. The main course is lamb chops flavored with a unique sauce of red bell peppers and olives. The flavor of the accompanying potatoes are enhanced with pecorino cheese. Figs stuffed with almonds and candied peel and liberally covered with chocolate syrup are a rich and grand finish to this meal.

Preparations

The vegetable soup can be prepared several days ahead, except for the pasta, and then refrigerated.

The morning of the dinner, boil the pasta until al dente and drain it. Then put the pasta in cold water to stop the cooking process and thoroughly drain again. Remove the soup from the refrigerator, place it in a large saucepan and add the pasta. Reheat the soup at serving time and add the grated cheese.

The tomato sauce with the onions, peppers, and olives can be made in the morning. Cook it completely and then refrigerate. That evening reheat the sauce, fry the lamb chops, and add them to the sauce for a few minutes.

Also prepare the potatoes early in the day and cook them. Reheat the dish before serving dinner.

Depending on your preference, the dessert can be made in the morning or early afternoon. Stuff the figs and bake them. Then set them aside to cool completely.

Minestra di Verdure
Vegetable Soup

Serves 10

1/4 cup olive oil
3 slices pancetta, cut into small
   pieces
1 medium onion, coarsely chopped
4 celery stalks, sliced
3 carrots, cut into 1/4 inch rounds
1 clove garlic, finely chopped
2 tablespoons chopped parsley
1 pound cabbage, cut into thin
   strips

1 pound broccoli, cut into florets,
   tender stems sliced
2 medium potatoes, peeled and diced
3 teaspoons salt
1 teaspoon ground black pepper
1/2 pound pasta shells
1/2 cup freshly grated pecorino
   cheese
3 large chicken bouillon cubes,
   optional

Place the olive oil in a large stock pot over medium heat oil and when hot add the pancetta pieces. Cook them until the bacon starts to wilt. Add the onion, celery, carrots, garlic and parsley and sauté over high heat for 2 minutes, stirring often.

Add the cabbage, broccoli and potatoes and season with salt and pepper. Then add just enough water to cover all of the vegetables. Cover the stock pot and cook slowly over low heat for 40 to 45 minutes.

Cook the pasta shells in boiling salted water until al dente. Drain thoroughly and add to vegetable soup. Add the pecorino cheese to the soup and mix well. Serve immediately with some extra cheese on the side, if desired.

Note This recipe will serve about 10 people. Any leftovers may be reheated. The use of bouillon cubes is optional, but add to the flavor of the soup.

Costolette d'Agnello alla Calabrese
Lamb Chops Calabrese Style

Serves 6

This dish is a specialty of the town of Cosenza.

12 rib lamb chops with long bone
    left in place
1/2 teaspoon salt
1/2 teaspoon freshly ground black
    pepper
4 tablespoons olive oil
1 onion, finely chopped
2 large red bell peppers, cut into
    thin strips

1 cup ripe tomatoes, peeled and
    chopped
2 tablespoons capers, drained
1 cup green olives with pits, left
    whole
3 tablespoons fresh parsley,
coarsely chopped

Ask your butcher to cut the lamb chops so that the rib bones are left long. Season the chops with salt and pepper on both sides. Heat 2 tablespoons of the olive oil in a large skillet over medium-high heat, until very hot. Add the chops and fry them on each side for 1 minute, searing them well. Then remove the chops to a heated platter. The chops should be well browned outside, but pink inside.

Heat the remaining 2 tablespoons olive oil in another skillet. Add the chopped onion and the bell peppers and sauté over medium heat, until the onion is limp and translucent. Then add the chopped tomatoes, capers, green olives, and chopped parsley. Season with salt and pepper, stir thoroughly, and cook for 10 minutes, stirring once in a while.

Add the cooked chops and their juices to the vegetable-tomato mixture in the skillet and let them sit over extremely low heat for a few minutes. Adjust seasoning, if desired, and serve immediately while very hot. Serve 2 lamb chops per person with some of the olives, peppers, and tomatoes.

Patate al Forno
Oven Potatoes

Serves 6

    In Calabria chopped tomatoes are frequently placed over the sliced potatoes. I eliminated the tomatoes as the lamb chops in this menu have a tomato base. However, 2 large, peeled and chopped tomatoes may be layered with the potatoes. If doing so, reduce the water to 3/4 cup as the tomatoes will emit moisture.

4 large baking potatoes
6 to 8 tablespoons virgin olive oil
1 1/2 cups freshly grated pecorino
   cheese

Salt, freshly ground black pepper
3/4 cup fresh bread crumbs
1 cup water

    Peel the potatoes and sliced them into 1/4-inch thick slices. Grease a baking pan with 2 tablespoons of the olive oil and arrange a layer of the potato slices over the bottom of the pan. Sprinkle some pecorino cheese, salt, pepper, and a little olive oil over the potatoes. Continue layering in this manner until all of the potatoes and cheese are used up. Pour the water over the potatoes and finish with a layer of bread crumbs that have been moistened with a little water.

    Cover the pan with aluminum foil and bake in a preheated 375° F, oven for 40 minutes. Remove the foil and bake for another 20 more minutes or until the potatoes are tender and the bread crumbs are crisp and golden brown.

Fichi al Cioccolato
Stuffed Figs in Chocolate

Serves 6

6 large figs, fresh or dried
1/2 cup toasted walnuts, finely
   chopped
1/2 cup toasted almonds, finely
   chopped
1/2 cup diced candied orange peel

2 cloves, finely mashed or
   1/8 teaspoon ground cloves
4 squares bitter chocolate
3/4 cup sugar
3 tablespoons Amaretto liqueur

Wash the figs, drain and pat them dry with paper towels. With a sharp knife cut the figs open down one side. Place the chopped walnuts, almonds, candied orange peel, and the mashed cloves in a small bowl. Stuff each fig with the nut mixture and press them closed again. Arrange the figs on a baking sheet and bake them in a preheated 350° F, for 15 minutes, or until the figs have turned slightly darker.

In a small saucepan melt the chocolate with the sugar and Amaretto liqueur over medium heat.

As soon as the figs come out of the oven, place them on a platter and pour the melted chocolate syrup over them. Let the figs sit until the chocolate is set and dry. Serve the figs with a glass of white or red wine.

Note If large figs are not available, use small one and allow 2 figs per person. Increase the chocolate to 5 squares. The rest of the ingredients remain the same.

Una Semplice Cena
A Simple Dinner

Serves 6

Macheroni alla Calabrese
Macaroni Calabria-Style

Involtini di Maiale alla Calabrese
Stuffed Pork Rolls Calabria-Style

Zucchine Gratinate
Zucchini with Cheese

Torta di Frutta Secca
Fruit Cake

Caffè
Coffee

A Simple Dinner

Once in a while we want to enjoy a simple meal — a meal that does not take much preparation, and one in which a number of items can be prepared ahead of time. We still want it to be tasty and delicious.

The Calabria-style sauce for the pasta includes prosciutto to give it a very slight smoky flavor. The red pepper flakes give it a touch of sharpness.

Salami, pancetta, and cheese are used as a stuffing for thin slices of pork loin for the entree. This flavorful dish is served with a mild zucchini casserole to complement the pork.

Almonds, hazelnuts, and figs are combined in an unusual fruit-cake to end this simple but wonderful dinner.

Preparations

To avoid last minute preparations for this dinner, prepare the sauce for the macaroni in the morning and reheat it before cooking the pasta just before dinner. The sauce may also be made a day ahead and refrigerated.

Prepare the entree in the morning. Pound the pork slices, stuff and roll them, secure with a toothpick, and refrigerate. When ready to cook bring the pork rolls to room temperature before grilling or broiling them.

The zucchini casserole can also be made in the morning. Fry the zucchini, make the sauce, and put the two together in a casserole. Then set it aside. Add the sliced mozzarella and oil in the evening, and then place the casserole in the oven to warm and melt the cheese while the pork rolls are cooking on the grill.

The fruit cake can be made days ahead and refrigerated. Bring it to room temperature before serving.

Maccheroni alla Calabrese
Macaroni Calabria-Style

Serves 6

1/4 cup olive oil
1 medium onion, finely chopped
1/2 teaspoon dried red pepper flakes
1/4 pound prosciutto ham (3/4 cup
   cut into small cubes)
2 tablespoons chopped fresh parsley
1 tablespoon chopped fresh basil
1 garlic clove, finely chopped

3 cups canned chopped Italian
   tomatoes with their juice
1/2 teaspoon salt
1/2 teaspoon freshly ground black
   pepper
1 pound macaroni pasta
1/3 cup grated pecorino or
   caciocavallo cheese

Heat the olive oil in a large skillet over medium heat. Add the chopped onion and red pepper flakes and sauté until the onions are limp. Add the chopped prosciutto, parsley, basil and chopped garlic. Mix thoroughly and continue cooking for 2 minutes, then add the chopped tomatoes, and season with salt and pepper. Cook over medium heat for 30 minutes, stirring occasionally.

Bring a large saucepan of salted water to a boil, add the macaroni and cook until al dente. Drain the pasta well, place in a bowl, and add just a little of the sauce.

Place a layer of the macaroni on a preheated serving dish, sprinkle generously with grated pecorino cheese and add some more sauce. Continue making layers of macaroni, cheese, and sauce until all of the ingredients are used up. Serve immediately while still very hot.

Involtini di Maiale alla Calabrese
Stuffed Pork Rolls Calabria-Style

Serves 6

12 slices of pork, cut from the loin
12 slices pancetta, thinly cut
6 slices pecorino, provolone or
   caciocavallo cheese, sliced thin.
   then cut in half

12 slices salami, sliced thin and
   chopped
Salt
Freshly ground black pepper
4 to 6 tablespoons virgin olive oil

Pound each slice of pork with the flat side of a meat cleaver between two pieces of plastic wrap until the meat is thin and flat. Place a slice place of pancetta, half a slice of cheese and some chopped salami on each slice of meat. Season with little salt and pepper, then roll up the meat into rolls and secure each with a toothpick.

Brush the rolls with olive oil and put them on a grill over a medium hot fire. Grill the rolls until they are golden brown, or cook them under a hot broiler turning them often. (The pork rolls take about 10 minutes to cook. They need to be turned often so they do not burn.) When the pork rolls are cooked, sprinkle a little salt and pepper on each and place them on a heated platter. Serve immediately with the zucchini casserole. Serve 2 rolls per person.

Zucchine Gratinatte
Zucchini with Cheese

Serves 6

6 medium zucchini
6 tablespoons all purpose flour
1/2 cup olive oil for frying
Salt
3 tablespoons olive oil for sauce
2 pounds ripe peeled tomatoes or

3 cups canned Italian tomatoes
with juice, coarsely chopped
1/2 teaspoon freshly ground black
pepper
1/2 pound mozzarella cheese, sliced
thin

Wash the zucchini, trim the ends, and slice them lengthwise. Dredge the slices in the flour.

In a large frying pan heat the 1/2 cup of oil over medium-high heat. Add a few of the zucchini and fry until golden brown. Fry a few slices at a time so that they do not overlap. Remove the zucchini slices from the pan with a perforated spoon and place them on paper towels. Then sprinkle them with some salt.

Press the chopped tomatoes and their juices through a sieve. Heat 3 tablespoons of oil in a large baker over medium heat. Add the tomato pulp, salt, and pepper, and cook for 20 minutes, stirring once in a while.

Add the fried zucchini slices to the tomato sauce. Simmer for 5 minutes, remove from heat, and cover the mixture with the sliced mozzarella. Sprinkle a little olive oil over the top and bake in a preheated 400° F. oven for about 5 minutes, or long enough for the cheese to melt and begin to change color. Serve while hot.

Torta di Frutta Secca
Fruit Cake

Serves 6 to 8

1/3 cup almonds
1 cup hazelnuts
3/4 cup dry figs
3 squares bitter chocolate, ground
1 1/4 cups all purpose flour

4 teaspoons baking powder
3 eggs
2/3 cup sugar
3/4 cup diced candied peel

Grease and lightly flour a 9-inch springform pan.

Blanch the almonds in boiling water, when slightly cool, peel them. Place them in a 350° F. oven for a few minutes to dry out. Then chop them finely in the food processor.

Toast the hazelnuts in a 350° F. oven for 10 minutes, Then remove the outer skin and chop them. Remove the stems from the figs and finely chop them.

In a small bowl, sift the flour together with the baking powder. Beat the eggs in a large bowl, add the sugar and beat together until the eggs are light and fluffy, Add the almonds, hazelnuts, figs, chocolate, candied peel to the egg mixture. Then add the flour and beat lightly until the batter is well blended.

Pour the batter into the prepared pan and bake in a preheated 350° F. oven for 45 minutes or until the cake springs back lightly when touched near the center. Cool the cake on a wire rack, then remove it from the pan, and let it cool completely before serving. To keep the cake for a longer period of time, store it in the refrigerator.

SICILY

Sicily is a varied land with snow on volcanic Mt. Etna, fields of wheat, sterile sand dunes, and large cities. The island's many days of burning sun gives one the feeling of being in the tropics. It is spectacularly beautiful with mountains, silvery beaches, and abounds in Greek temples and Baroque churches. Sicily is the largest of the Mediterranean islands.

Sicily is surrounded by water — in the north by the Tyrrhenian Sea, in the east by the Ionian Sea, and in the south by the Mediterranean Sea. Since Sicily is surrounded by water, fishing is very important. Tuna, swordfish, sardines, anchovies, and shellfish are the predominant fish of Sicily.

The island has a Mediterranean climate with mild winters and very hot summers. The predominating wind is from south-east. Coming from Africa, it crosses the Mediterranean Sea and picks up humidity, making the atmosphere very hot and sultry.

The origins of Sicilian cooking are varied since the island was dominated successively by Greeks, Phoenicians, Romans, Arabs, Normans, French, and Spaniards. From all of these ethnic groups the Sicilians learned new cooking skills and improved upon them. The Arabs were the most influential in bringing new foods and methods of cooking to Sicily.

Sugar, spices, eggplant, spinach, apricots, and almonds came with the Arabs. They also taught Sicilians how to preserve fish and meat, how to dry and candy fruit, how to make sorbets, and other sweets.

The Sicilian cuisine is primarily based on pasta, fish, and vegetables. Pasta is served mainly with sauces based on fish and vegetables. Swordfish and tuna are usually grilled and often served with *salmoriglio,* a lemon and oil dressing that is very delicate and brings out the flavor of the fish. Meat is not eaten frequently. It is mostly used in sausages which are the basis of many pasta dishes. Although most Sicilian dishes are made from simple ingredients, they are very sophisticated and often quite rich.

Sicilian cooking is not known for hors d'oeuvres. The Sicilians prefer to start a meal with seafood, olives, anchovies, and snails. However, today, the restaurants and trattoria have tables laden with a rich variety of hors d'oeuvres.

When my husband and I visited Sicily we tried many different antipasti. Our favorite was *carpaccio di pesce spada a vela,* which means "raw swordfish like a sail." It is cut paper thin served with arugula, olive oil, lemon juice, salt, and black pepper. The freshness and mild flavor of the swordfish paired well with the peppery arugula to make a great combination and an unbelievable antipasto.

Rice is practically unknown in Sicily although it was here that rice was introduced to Italy by the Arabs. *Arancini di riso*, "little oranges of rice," is a traditional Sicilian snack and is one of the few Sicilian rice dishes.

Butter is not used in Sicilian cooking, as milk is used for making cheese, which is essential for flavoring pasta. The cheeses used for grating are very tasty: the salty incanestrato, the piacentino, made with pepper and the best known cheese, caciocavallo.

The desserts of Sicily are known for their variety and richness. The most famous are *cassata* and *cannoli*, a cylindrical-shaped pastry filled with sweetened ricotta and candied fruit. *Cassata* is a sponge cake that is filled with flavored ricotta and candied fruit peels.

Ice cream and sorbet were brought to Sicily by the Arabs. They are made from local fruits, primarily citrus. Oranges, lemons, mandarin, clementines, and grapefruit are in abundance on the island of Sicily.

Wines

The best wine in Sicily is Corvo, a white wine from the province of Palermo. It pairs well with fish. Capo Bianco is recommended with broiled or grilled swordfish. Zibibbo, a muscat favored by Sicilians, is made from well-ripened grapes and comes from the island of Pantelleria, off the African coast. Many other excellent Sicilian wines are produced locally.

The most famous wine is Marsala, made in the western part of Sicily. It is available sweet or dry. The best Marsala is Marsala Vergine, pale amber in color and very dry.

Marsala is very versatile. It makes a good aperitif when chilled, can served with dessert, and is used in cooking. It is also good served as an after-dinner drink.

Roman Theater, Taormina, Sicily.
Photo courtesy of Frank Spadarella

Una Cena d'Estate
A Summer Dinner

Serves 6

Spaghetti alla Siciliana
Spaghetti Sicilian Style

Grigliata di Pesce Spada al Salmoriglio
Grilled Swordfish with Salmoriglio Sauce

Fagiolini Verde all'Olio e Limone
Green Beans in Olive Oil and Lemon

Patate con Zafferano
Potatoes with Saffron

Sorbetto al Limone
Lemon Sorbet

Caffè
Coffee

A Summer Dinner

My husband and I had a fantastic visit to the island of Sicily. We enjoyed tasting and eating typical Sicilian foods, along with some sightseeing. After this trip I found it difficult to put together only two menus from all the wonderful dishes that we tasted.

The Spaghetti Sicilian Style has a little bite to it. A wonderful spicy taste adds complexity to the dish.

The mildness of the grilled swordfish is enhanced by the herbs of the accompanying sauce. The potatoes, flavored with saffron, oregano, garlic, and parsley make a perfect side dish. Steamed green beans with a lemon-olive oil sauce complete the entree.

A light lemon sorbet concludes this dinner.

Preparations

This dinner is quick to prepare. You do not need to do a great deal of preparation ahead of time.

Only the Sicilian sauce for the spaghetti can conveniently be prepared ahead of time. Make it several days ahead and store in the refrigerator. Before serving, warm up the sauce while the pasta is cooking.

In mid-afternoon marinate the swordfish and place it in the refrigerator. Late in the afternoon make the sauce for the fish. Before serving that evening, broil or barbecue the fish and rewarm the sauce.

In the late afternoon cook the string beans until al dente. Drain them and keep at room temperature. Just before serving dinner place the beans in the skillet with the oil and heat them. Then add the lemon juice and parsley and season the beans with salt and pepper. You may prepare the potatoes 30 minutes before dinner and cook them for only 20 minutes, instead of the 30 minutes called for in the recipe. Leave the potatoes on the burner but turn off the heat. The potatoes will finish cooking in the warm pot while the first course is being enjoyed.

The lemon sorbet can be made a day ahead and frozen. Half an hour before guests are to arrive place the sorbet in a blender with the egg white. Blend the mixture and then freeze it again. Scoop the sorbet out when ready to serve.

Spaghetti alla Siciliana
Spaghetti Sicilian Style

Serves 6

1 large (1 to 1 1/4 pounds) eggplant
Salt
2 sweet yellow or red bell peppers
6 large ripe tomatoes or 4 cups
    canned Italian peeled tomatoes
    with their juice, finely chopped
1/2 cup olive oil
2 large garlic cloves, crushed but
    left in one piece
4 anchovy fillets, finely chopped

1/2 cup brine cured black olive
    (kalamata), pitted and chopped
    coarsely
4 teaspoons capers, drained
4 large sprigs fresh basil, finely
    chopped
1/2 teaspoon freshly ground black
    pepper
1 pound spaghetti
1/3 cup freshly grated Pecorino
    Romano cheese

Rinse and cut the eggplant into small cubes and place it in a colander. Sprinkle with salt and let stand for 20 minutes to drain off bitter juices. Rinse the eggplant under cold water and dry with paper towels.

Char the peppers under the broiler or over gas until their skins are burnt and blistered on all sides. Place them in a brown paper bag and let stand for 10 minutes. Peel the skins off the peppers and cut them in half, discarding the cores and seeds. Cut the peppers into thin strips.

Blanch the tomatoes in a pot of boiling water for a few seconds to loosen the skins. Drain, peel the tomatoes, then cut them in half and squeeze out the seeds. Chop the tomatoes and set aside.

Heat olive oil in a medium saucepan over medium-high heat and sauté the cloves garlic until brown, then discard them. Add the cubed eggplant and sauté until it begins to brown, about 10 minutes. Add the strips of pepper and sauté until the peppers are softened.

Add the chopped anchovies and stir for 3 to 4 minutes. Add the chopped olives, capers and basil. Then add the chopped tomatoes, reduce heat to medium and simmer until the sauce starts to thicken, about 10 to 15 minutes. Season with salt and pepper, if needed.

Boil the spaghetti in a large pot of boiling salted water until al dente. Drain and transfer the pasta to a large serving bowl. Spoon the sauce over the pasta, sprinkle with cheese, and toss. Serve immediately.

Note The sauce can be made several days ahead. Cover and refrigerate. Before using, rewarm over low heat.

Grigliata di Pesce Spada al Salmoriglio
Grilled Swordfish with Salmoriglio Sauce

Serves 6

The Sicilians prepare swordfish in many ways. It is found in abundance in the Strait of Messina.

The word *salmoriglio* (in Sicilian *sammurigghiu*) means "brine. However, this translation is not appropriate for the mild taste and texture of this blend of olive oil, lemon juice, garlic, and herbs. The fish that is usually served with Salmoriglio Sauce is swordfish or tuna. This sauce is poured over the fish after it is grilled or broiled. This sauce is also served with young lamb.

Marinade for swordfish

1/2 cup olive oil	Juice of 2 lemons
1 small onion, chopped	1/4 cup dry white wine
1 bay leaf	6 (6 to 7 ounce) swordfish fillets,
Salt	each about 1 inch thick
1 teaspoon whole peppercorns	

Place the oil, onion, bay leaf, salt, peppercorns, lemon juice and white wine in a large casserole. Stir thoroughly, and add the swordfish fillets, turning them in the marinade to coat them on all sides. Set aside for two hours in the refrigerator..

Sauce for the swordfish

!/2 cup extra virgin olive oil	1 tablespoon dried oregano
Juice of 1 lemon	1/4 teaspoon crushed hot red pepper
2 tablespoons hot water	flakes
4 tablespoons chopped fresh parsley	Salt and pepper
3 garlic cloves, finely chopped	2 long rosemary strips, for basting

This recipe can be prepared on a barbecue or under a broiler. Preheat barbecue or broiler to medium-high heat.

Whisk the olive oil in top of a double boiler, over simmering water until the oil is heated. Gradually whisk in the lemon juice, then the 2 tablespoons hot water. Add the chopped parsley, garlic cloves, oregano, and pepper flakes and cook the sauce 5 minutes to blend the flavors, whisking often. Season with salt and pepper and remove from heat.

Remove the swordfish fillets from the marinade and grill or broil them over a hot fire until cooked through, about 5 minutes per side. While cooking dip the rosemary sprigs into the sauce and baste the swordfish with the sauce. Continue basting once more while cooking the fish.

Transfer the fish to a preheated platter and spoon the remaining sauce over the fish and serve immediately.

Fagiolini Verde all'Olio e Limone
Green Beans in Olive Oil and Lemon

Serves 6

1 1/2 pounds small green beans
1 tablespoon coarse salt
4 tablespoons olive oil
Juice of 1 lemon

1 teaspoon ground pepper
2 tablespoons chopped fresh Italian
   parsley

Remove tips and any strings from the beans and rinse them in cold water.

Bring 8 cups of salted water to a boil over high heat. Place the beans in the water, bring the water back to a boil and then boil the beans for 6 minutes. Drain the beans and place them in a large bowl. Add the olive oil, lemon juice, and then sprinkle with pepper and parsley. Taste if additional salt is needed. Serve the beans immediately.

Note If not serving the beans immediately keep them in the colander or on a towel after draining them. Just before serving place the beans in a skillet with the oil and heat them over medium heat, mixing often. When the beans are hot, add the lemon juice and parsley just before serving.

Patate con Zafferano
Potatoes with Saffron

Serves 6

Potatoes play an important role in Italian cooking -- roasted, fried, boiled, or pureed. They are used as an appetizer in potato salads and fritters. Potatoes are also an important ingredient in soups, such as minestrone, and in gnocchi (dumplings). Potatoes are traditionally served with boiled meats or fish. This potato dish is flavored with saffron, which is widely used in Sicilian cooking.

2 pounds potatoes, peeled and cut
   into 2-inch cubes
2 garlic cloves, finely chopped
2 tablespoons finely chopped fresh
   Italian parsley
1/3 cup extra virgin olive oil
1/2 teaspoon salt

1/2 teaspoon freshly ground black
   pepper
2 teaspoons dry oregano
1/4 teaspoon saffron or 1 sachet
saffron powder dissolved in 1/2 cup
   warm water

Place the cubed potatoes in a bowl of cold water. Heat the olive oil in a heavy medium-size saucepan, add the chopped garlic and parsley and sauté over medium heat for 1 minute. Drain the potatoes and add them to the pan. Mix well and season with the salt and pepper. Add the oregano, mix again, and cook for 5 minutes. Then add the warm saffron water, cover the saucepan and cook for about 30 minutes. The potatoes should be done and the water absorbed. Serve immediately.

Sorbetto al Limone

Lemon Sorbet

Serves 6

Sicily is famous for its wonderful, large, fragrant, juicy lemons. In Sicily lemon sorbet is usually served after a fish dinner. It may also be served halfway through a meal as a palate cleanser.

1 cup water
1 cup sugar
3 cups fresh squeezed lemon juice

1 egg white
6 fresh mint leaves

Pour the water into a medium-size saucepan, add the sugar and mix well with a wooden spoon until the sugar had dissolved. Place the pan over medium heat and boil gently for 5 minutes. Add the lemon juice, mix thoroughly and let the mixture cool. Then transfer it into a glass bowl and place the bowl in the freezer until the sorbet is frozen.

Keep the sorbet frozen until a half an hour before dinner. Then place it in a blender with the egg white and blend it until it resembles snow. Transfer the sorbet to a container and place it in the freezer for about 1 to 2 hours or until ready to serve dessert. Scoop the sorbet into glasses and garnish with a fresh mint leaf.

Una Cena d'Inverno
A Winter Dinner

Serves 6

Penne con Pistacio
Penne Pasta with Pistachios

Tonno Arrosto con Verdure
Roasted Tuna with Vegetables

Insalata di Arance
Orange Salad

Torta di Noci
Walnut Torte

Caffè
Coffee

A Winter Dinner

Although this menu is traditionally a Sicilian winter menu, it can be enjoyed anytime of the year.

The penne with pistachio sauce is a very unusual dish with a wonderful flavor. It is typically Sicilian as it is made with nuts grown on the island at the foot of Mt. Etna.

The tuna roasted with the different vegetables is a mild and very colorful entree. The citrus flavor of the orange salad combined with the scallions and chopped parsley is a very refreshing palate cleanser after the fish dish.

The walnut torte is a very simple dessert, decorated only with confectioner's sugar sprinkled on top. It can be enjoyed with a glass of Marsala or Muscatel wine, for which Sicily is noted.

Preparations

This menu is very easy to make and many items may be prepared ahead of time.

However, the penne pasta with the pistachio sauce needs to be made the evening of your dinner. In the morning you can chop the onion and coarsely chop the pistachio nuts and set them aside. In the evening, while the pasta is boiling make the sauce and then combine the sauce with the pasta after it is cooked.

The roasted tuna can be partially prepared ahead-of-time. The vegetables can be sautéed in the afternoon. Prior to the arrival of your guests, place the vegetables in a casserole, add the tuna steaks and cook them in the oven for 30 minutes.

In the afternoon prepare the orange salad by peeling the oranges, removing the pith, and slicing them. Place the orange slices in a bowl, cover, and refrigerate. Chop the parsley and onion and set aside. Assemble the salad in the evening and toss with olive oil, salt, and pepper.

Make the walnut torte several days ahead, cover and refrigerate. Bring the torte to room temperature before sprinkling with confectioner's sugar. Then slice into wedges and serve.

Penne con Pistacio
Penne Pasta with Pistachios

Serves 6 to 8 as a first course

4 tablespoons unsalted butter
3 tablespoons extra virgin olive oil
1 medium onion, finely chopped
1 1/2 cups coarsely ground pistachio
   nuts

1 1/2 cups whipping cream
Freshly ground black pepper
1 pound penne pasta
1/3 cup freshly grated Parmesan
   cheese

Bring water to a boil in a large pot.

In the meantime, place the butter and oil in a medium skillet over medium heat. Add the chopped onion and sauté until the onion is translucent, about 5 minutes. Then stir in the ground pistachios and sauté them for about 2 minutes. Add the cream and season with pepper, to taste. Bring the cream to a boil and then simmer the sauce until thickened, about 5 minutes.

When the water is boiling, add salt and the pasta and cook until al dente. Drain and add the pasta to the skillet with the cream sauce, mixing well to coat the pasta with the sauce. Sprinkle with Parmesan cheese, mix again, and then serve immediately

Tonno Arrosto con Verdure
Roasted Tuna with Vegetables

Serves 6

1 (1 1/4 to 1 1/2 pound) eggplant
1 large red bell pepper
1 large yellow bell pepper
1 large green bell pepper
6 scallions, cut into rounds slices
1 medium red onion, cut into
   medium-size pieces

3 sprigs of thyme
10 whole peppercorns
1/2 teaspoon salt
8 tablespoons extra virgin olive oil
2 small limes, cut into thin slices
6 thick tuna steaks (about 3
   pounds)

Rinse the egg plant, cut it into medium pieces, sprinkle with salt and leave in a colander to drain off the bitter juices.

Rinse the rest of the vegetables under cold running water, pat them dry, and cut them into medium-size pieces. Use a mortar to grind together the thyme, with the peppercorns and salt.

Heat 2 tablespoons of the olive oil in a large skillet and sauté the eggplant over medium heat, until it starts to color, about 10 minutes. Drain the eggplant on paper towels, then place it in a bowl.

Add another 2 tablespoons of oil to the skillet. Then add the red, yellow, green bell peppers, the scallions, and onion and sauté over medium-high heat, for 10 minutes, stirring often. Season with salt and combine the vegetables with the eggplant. Add the sliced lime to the vegetables.

Place a third of the vegetables in a large ovenproof casserole spreading them evenly on the bottom. Season the tuna on both sides with the ground thyme mixture and place the tuna in the middle of the casserole. Place the rest of the vegetables around the tuna and drizzle the remaining oil over the tuna pieces.

Place the casserole in a preheated of 350° F. oven for 30 minutes. Serve one piece of tuna per person accompanied by cooked vegetables and the accumulated juices. Serve immediately.

Insalata di Arance
Orange Salad

Serves 6

This orange salad may also be served with boiled meats and with meats that have a high fat content.

6 oranges
2 tablespoon fresh chopped parsley
1 scallion, white part only, finely
* chopped*

4 tablespoons extra virgin olive oil
1/4 teaspoon salt
1/2 teaspoon freshly ground black
* pepper*

Peel the oranges, taking care to remove all the white pith. Cut the oranges into 1/2-inch thick round slices and pick out the seeds. Place the orange slices in a salad bowl. Add the chopped parsley and onion and pour the olive oil over the oranges. Season with salt and pepper and toss gently to mix well.

Let the salad sit for 10 minutes before serving.

Torta di Noci
Walnut Torte

Serves 6 to 8

Many Sicilian dessert are based on different nuts, such as almonds, pistachios, and walnuts. In this torte, which is different from other Sicilian walnut tortes, the walnuts are ground. They are combined with fine bread crumbs which are used in place of flour.

3/4 cup walnuts
1 1/4 cups sugar
1/2 teaspoon ground cinnamon
1/8 teaspoon ground cloves
1/2 cup very fine unseasoned bread crumbs
Grated peel of 1/2 lemon
2 extra-large eggs

4 extra-large eggs, separated
6 tablespoons unsalted butter, at room temperature
1/3 cup very fine unseasoned bread crumbs
1 tablespoon sugar
2 tablespoons confectioner's sugar

Place the shelled walnuts and 1/4 cup of the sugar into the bowl of a food processor and finely grind the nuts. Then add the cinnamon, cloves, 1/2 cup bread crumbs and the lemon peel and process until finely ground.

Place the remaining 1 cup of sugar, the 2 extra large eggs, 4 egg yolks and 4 tablespoons butter in a electric mixer bowl and mix thoroughly with an electric mixer until the eggs are almost whipped. Little by little, add the ground walnut mixture, then add the 1/3 cup of bread crumbs. Mix again and continue mixing for 5 minutes.

Grease the bottom and sides a 9-inch cake pan with the remaining 2 tablespoons of butter. Sprinkle the sides of the pan with some bread crumbs and place a piece of parchment paper on the bottom of the pan and butter it.

Beat the 4 egg whites until soft peak form and then gently fold them into the batter. Pour the batter into the prepared pan and even the top with a spatula. Bake the torte in a preheated 375°F. oven for 20 minutes. After that time, sprinkle the tablespoon of sugar evenly over the top and bake for another 20 minutes or until it is firm to the touch.

Remove the cake from the oven and place it on a rack to cool for 1/2 hour. Gently remove the tortefrom the pan onto a round dish and let it cool completely.

Before serving the walnut torte sprinkle the confectioner's sugar over it. Slice the torte into wedges and serve.

SARDINIA

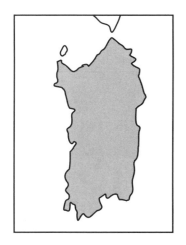

The island of Sardinia is located west of Italy in the Mediterranean Sea. It faces the Tyrrhenian Sea and the straits of Bonifacio, which separate it from the island of Corsica, a political entity of France.

Sardinia, is the second largest island in the Mediterranean Sea and the third largest region of Italy, after Sicily and Piedmonte. It is a region of Italy very different from all the others. Many of the cities have a Spanish atmosphere because the Spanish dominated Sardinia for four centuries (approximately from 800 to 1200 A.D.) Sardinia has areas of rocky grasslands with wild flowers where sheep graze. There are many cork trees, olive trees, palm tree, pine trees. The island also has an abundance of wild game, including deer and boar.

Sardinian winters are mild near the coast, moderate in the center of the island, and very cold on the high mountains. The summers are very dry and hot. Very little rain falls in autumn and spring.

Over the centuries Sardinia was invaded by the Phoenicians, Arabs, Spaniards, Romans and the inhabitants of the Italian mainland from Piedmont. Although fairly close to the Italian mainland, Sardinians have kept apart from the inhabitants of the mainland. They have upheld their own traditions, which are a mixture of Roman, Arab, Spanish, and Italian cultures.

There are two types of cooking in Sardinia, one from the coastal area and the other from the mountainous interior. The cooking of Sardinia was influenced by the Mediterranean cultures, which at one time or another occupied the island. For example: the Arabs introduced *cascasa* to Sardinia. The Arabs call it *cuscus*.

Many of the invaders of Sardinia remained on the island. They taught the inhabitants how to prepare fish stew and how to cook swordfish, tuna, shell fish and many of the other fish that abound in the sea surrounding the island. Two fish dishes of Spanish heritage are: *cassola*, a highly spiced fish soup named for the pot in which it is cooked, and *scabecciu*, or pickled fish.

The Sardinians adopted the Genoese name *burrida* for their fish stew although it is not prepared in the typical Genoese fashion. *Bottarga*, another Sardinian fish specialty is made with gray mullet roe or tuna roe. It is usually sliced very thin and served as an appetizer with olive oil and lemon juice. The use of tuna in this dish is a Sicilian influence.

Basically the Sardinian people are not people of the sea. Thus most of the fishing is done by descendants of invaders who have settled there and brought their fish recipes with them.

Traditional food is based on products of the land rather than the sea. Cheese, milk, and roasted meat are the mainstays of Sardinian cuisine. They are usually eaten with bread.

Bread is very important to the Sardinians. Special breads are made for special occasions. These breads are shaped in different ways and sizes — from thick loaves to paper-thin flat breads called *carta da musica*, sheet music. The *carta da musica* is a thin crisp bread sprinkled with salt and olive oil and is always served at the beginning of a meal.

Women bake bread while the men cook the meat out of doors. Kid, lamb, or piglet is usually roasted whole on the spit. All of the meats are flavored with local herbs, such as mint, myrtle, and other more locally grown herbs. Sardinia is rich in game. Wild boar, partridge, quail, and blackbirds are cooked on the spit with rosemary and other herbs.

Pork, besides being roasted, is also used to make *salumi* and *salsicce* (cold cuts and sausages). A Sardinian favorite is prosciutto made from wild boar. This prosciutto is very lean and very tasty. Sausages are spiced with wild fennel and chili peppers and flavored with vinegar and/or garlic. They are eaten raw or cut up in a sauce for pasta.

Cheese is very important in this pastoral community. Pecorino Sardo, a hard cheese made from sheeps' milk, is well known throughout Italy and is exported all over the world. Ricotta is prepared fresh, salted for grating for pasta, or smoked. Goat cheeses are also fresh and seasoned.

An abundance of fruits and nuts grow on Sardinia. Figs and many of the nuts — almonds, hazelnuts, walnuts — are used to make sweets.

The people of Sardinia were divided in two groups — the shepherds and farmers living in the center of Sardinia and the fishermen living along the coast. Most of the fishermen prepare their fish whole. This is considered to be the best way to cook fish because it keeps the fish completely intact. The fish are usually roasted over an open fire to conserve the taste and flavor.

The shepherds at one time used to cook the meat inside the ground in a hole with branches of herbs and glowing embers beneath and above the meat. This type of cooking is called *su caraxiu*. It is said that the shepherds were the first to use this method of cooking, because once in a while they would steal animals from among themselves. To hide the stolen meat while it was cooking, they would bury the food and have burning fire on top. Strange and unusual ways of cooking are characteristic of the people from Sardinia.

The *aragosta* (lobster) is found around the coast of Sardinia, but it differs from our true lobster, as it is smaller and has no claws. In Sardinia, *aragosta*, is usually eaten cold with olive oil and lemon juice or split in half and grilled.

Bread has always been the staple of shepherds' and farmers' tables and is never thrown away. It keeps well for the shepherds during the long months that they are gone from their homes. Bread is also used in many dishes, such as soups and lasagna.

Sardinian sweets are usually small in size and are eaten accompanied by a glass of sweet wine. Many of the sweets contain ricotta, honey, and cheese. Sweets are not eaten every day, but are reserved for specialfamily and community occasions.

In the past, sweets were present only in a few ceremonies. The first dessert of the year was *su pistiddi* prepared for the St. Antonio holiday. It consisted of two layers of dough flavored with lemon and orange peel. *Sas wrilletas* is a braided pastry that is dunked in honey. Another sweet, *sas cattas*, is fried fritters. A traditional sweet for carnival festival is *seadas*, which consists of two layers that are fried and then covered with honey or sugar.

Wines

Sardinia has its share of great wines. There is the Malvasia of Cagliari and the famous, sherry-like Vernaccia of Oristano. The white wines pair well with fish, especially lobster. Other good wines are Cannonou di Sardegna, a full-bodied red wine and Verimentino di Gallura, a white wine that is frequently served with antipasti.

Excellent dessert wines like moscato (muscatel) are produced throughout the island. They are both red and white and range from sweet to dry. Some are fortified.

Castel Sardo Fishing Harbor. Photo Courtsey of Rick Small.

Una Cena d'Estate
A Summer Dinner

Serves 6

Conchiglie Rigate con Verdure e Limone
Shell Pasta with Vegetables and Lemon

Costolette d'Agnello con Ciliege
Lamb Chops with Cherries

Spinaci Saltati
Sautéed Spinach

Patate con Prezzemolo
Potatoes with Parsley

Dolce di Ricotta
Ricotta Dessert

Caffè
Coffee

A Summer Dinner

In choosing this Sardinian menu, I, like many cooks in Sardinia, took advantage of the fresh vegetables for the pasta dish. The small shell pasta served with the chopped vegetables and lemon peel, is a very light and refreshing start for this summer menu.

The unique combination of lamb chops cooked with fresh cherries makes a rich entree. It is served with sautéed spinach, which adds color and a contrasting flavor. The mild boiled potatoes pair well with the lamb and the sauce. Sardinians, like most Italians, typically eat some type of potato with the entree, either boiled, roasted or fried.

A light baked ricotta dessert with citrus and honey flavors, similar to a cheesecake, ends the meal.

Preparations

To avoid last minute preparations for this dinner you can make the vegetable sauce for the pasta in the morning and that evening reheat it just before dinner while the pasta is cooking.

In the morning, prepare the lamb chops by removing the fat. Remove the pit from the cherries and chop them. Also in the morning, rinse the spinach, remove the stems, and break the leaves into pieces. Cook the spinach until tender and squeeze out any liquid. Place the spinach in a bowl, cover, and refrigerate. Clean the garlic for the spinach and set aside, covered. That evening cook the spinach and garlic in olive oil.

In the afternoon, clean the potatoes, place them in a large saucepan with a sufficient amount of cold water to cover them well and set aside. Boil the potatoes forty-five minutes before your company is due to arrive, drain, and set them aside to cool. When cooled enough to handle, peel the potatoes and place them on a platter. Do not slice them until you are ready to serve dinner. They will stay warmer if not cut ahead. When ready, slice the potatoes and season them with salt and pepper. Sprinkle oil and parsley over the potatoes and serve.

The lamb chops can be cooked just before your company is due to arrive. Sauté the lamb chops, remove them, make the sauce, and place the lamb chops back in the skillet and remove from heat. Finish cooking the chops in their sauce just before dinner.

Make the ricotta dessert a day ahead to let the orange juice and honey flavors penetrate the baked ricotta. Refrigerate the dessert until time to serve it.

Conchiglie Rigate con Verdure e Limone
Shell Pasta with Vegetables and Lemon

Serves 6

Shell pasta is very similar in shape to Malloreddus, a specialty of the island of Sardinia. The Malloreddus are a very old kind of local pasta made with corn flour and saffron. The name also refers to a small gnocchi made with durum wheat and water, flavored with saffron.

3 tablespoons olive oil
6 tablespoons unsalted butter
1 bunch (6) scallions, white and
    green part finely chopped
2 celery stalks, finely chopped
1 small carrot, finely chopped
1 garlic clove, finely chopped
Peel of 1/2 lemon, cut into very thin
    slivers
2 medium fresh tomatoes, seeds
    removed and cut into small cubes
1/4 teaspoon salt
1/4 teaspoon freshly ground pepper
2 tablespoons chopped fresh parsley
1 pound small shells pasta
1/3 cup fresh grated pecorino or
    Romano cheese

Heat the oil and 4 tablespoons of the butter in a skillet over medium heat. Add the chopped scallions, and sauté 1 minute. Add the chopped celery and carrots and sauté 1 minute. Then add the garlic and lemon peel and sauté for another minute, stirring constantly. Add the cubed tomatoes, stir and sauté for 1 more minute. Season with the salt and pepper and stir thoroughly. Add the chopped parsley, mix, and sauté 1 more minute.

While the vegetables are sautéing, bring a pot of water to a boil and add 1 tablespoon of salt and the pasta. Cook, uncovered, over high heat until the pasta is tender but firm to the bite, al dente. Drain the pasta and add it to the skillet with the vegetables. Add the cheese and the remaining 2 tablespoons of butter and mix again over low heat. Taste and adjust seasoning, if needed, and serve at once.

Costolette D'Agnello con Ciliege
Lamb Chops with Cherries

Serves 6

1/3 cup all-purpose flour
12 lamb chops
1/4 cup olive oil
3/4 cup fresh or canned pitted Bing
  cherries, chopped
1 cup dry white wine

4 teaspoons instant beef bouillon
  diluted in 1/2 cup hot water
1/2 teaspoon salt
1/2 teaspoon freshly ground black
  pepper
12 cherries with stems for garnish

Flour the lamb chops and shake off any excess. Heat the oil in a large skillet over medium-high heat. Add the lamb chops and brown them on both sides for about 5 minutes. Remove the lamb chops and place them on a plate. Add the chopped cherries and white wine to the skillet and stir over high heat to dissolve any meat particles attached to the bottom of the skillet. When the wine is reduced by half, about 3 to 4 minutes, add the diluted beef bouillon and mix well.

Return the lamb chops and their juice to the skillet. Reduce the heat to medium and mix until the lamb is well coated with the sauce and cooked, about 5 minutes. The cooking time varies depending on the thickness of the chops and the desired doneness.

Season the lamb chops with salt and pepper and mix well. Serve at once with 2 lambs chops and some sauce for each serving. Garnish each serving with 2 cherries with stems, some sautéed spinach and boiled potatoes.

Spinaci Saltati
Sautéed Spinach

Serves 6

2 pounds fresh spinach
Salt
2 large garlic cloves, halved
2 tablespoons extra virgin olive oil

1/2 teaspoon ground black pepper
2 tablespoons freshly squeezed
   lemon juice

Wash the spinach in several changes of water. Remove the stems and tear the leaves into pieces. Place the wet leaves into a saucepan with a little salt. Do not add any water. Cover the pan and cook the spinach over medium heat until tender, about 2 to 3 minutes. Drain and squeeze the spinach as dry as possible.

In a frying pan, combine the garlic and oil and cook over medium heat until the garlic turns golden, about 2 to 3 minutes. Remove and discard the garlic. Add the spinach and cook, tossing with a fork, over low heat for 5 minutes. Season with salt and pepper and the lemon juice, and serve while hot with the lamb chops.

Patate con Prezzemolo
Potatoes with Parsley

Serves 6

2 pounds medium new potatoes,
   unpeeled
1/2 teaspoon salt

1/2 teaspoon freshly ground black
   pepper
1/3 cup extra virgin olive oil
2 tablespoons chopped fresh parsley

Place the potatoes in a large saucepan and generously cover them with cold water. Bring the water to a boil, cover, and cook over medium heat for about 25 to 30 minutes, or until cooked, but still firm.

Drain the potatoes and peel them as soon as they are cool enough to handle. Slice the potatoes into 2/3-inch thick rounds. Place the potatoes flat on a large platter and season with salt and pepper. Sprinkle oil and chopped parsley evenly over the potatoes. Serve some of the potatoes with each serving of lamb chops.

Dolce di Ricotta
Ricotta Dessert

Serves 6

Ricotta is one of the famous cooking cheese of Italy. Many of the regions have special ricotta desserts for festive occasions.

1 1/2 cups ricotta
3/4 cup almonds, peeled and finely
    chopped
2 drops almond extract
1 cup clear honey

3 eggs
1 tablespoon butter
2 tablespoons fine bread crumbs
Juice of 1 orange

Place the ricotta, almonds, almond extract, 1/2 cup of the honey and the eggs into the bowl of a food processor and mix until blended. Grease a 10-inch cake pan with the butter and dust it with the bread crumbs, then pour in the ricotta mixture. Bake in a preheated 400° F. oven for about 45 minutes or until the mixture is firm to the touch and the top is golden brown. Let it cool for a while and then remove from the pan..

Beat the orange juice into the remaining 1/2 cup honey and then pour over the ricotta dessert. Let sit for 1 hour and then refrigerate.

Serve the dessert cold. It is even better the following day.

Una Cena d'Inverno
A Winter Dinner

Serves 6

Spaghetti con Agliata 'Azada'
Spaghetti with Garlic Sauce

Favata
Sardinian Bean and Pork Stew

Pere e Formaggio
Pears and Cheese

Torta di Mandorle
Almond Cake

Caffè
Coffee

A Winter Dinner

This menu is ideally served in the winter when it is cold, windy, raining, or snowing outside and you are sitting by a lit fire with good friends and good wine to drink. While most satisfying as a winter meal, this Sardinian menu is good served any time of the year.

The menu is easy to prepare and consists of dishes that can be made ahead of time. The meal is hearty, filling, robust, and satisfying.

I chose the spaghetti with the garlic sauce, because I wanted a simple pasta to precede the pork stew, which is a very rich dish.

The pork stew consists of spareribs, sausage, and bacon cooked together slowly with celery, fennel, and cabbage. It is an interesting combination of flavors.

My choice for dessert is fresh pears and cheese to refresh the palate after the savory stew. The pears are mild and sweet and eaten together with the strong pecorino cheese, they make a pleasing combination. The pears tame the sharp flavor of the cheese. Italians frequently end a meal with fruit and cheese. The production of cheese is very important to the pastoral areas of Sardinia.

A light almond cake ends this hearty meal. Almonds are grown in Sardinia and are often used in desserts, especially cookies and cakes.

Preparations

Many items in this menu can be prepared ahead to make your winter entertaining easier.

In the morning remove the skins of the garlic cloves and rinse the parsley for the spaghetti sauce. That evening, while the pasta is cooking, sauté the garlic mixture and combine it with the cooked pasta.

The pork and bean stew can be made two days ahead, refrigerated, and reheated that evening.

The pears cannot be sliced ahead of time because they will turn dark in color. They can, however, be sliced quickly that evening before serving. You can slice the cheese in the morning or during the day. Wrap the cheese slices in plastic wrap and refrigerate.

The almond cake can be made early in the afternoon. Sprinkle it with the confectioner's sugar just before serving.

Spaghetti con Agliata "Azada"
Spaghetti with Garlic Sauce

Serves 6

The secret of this dish is in the preparation of the garlic sauce. In this sauce recipe the garlic is sautéed quickly over low heat so that it will not brown.

3 garlic cloves
1 cup fresh parsley leaves
1 dried hot red chili pepper or
   1/2 teaspoon crushed hot red
   pepper flakes

1/2 cup extra virgin olive oil
1/2 teaspoon salt
1 pound spaghetti
1/2 cup grated pecorino cheese

Place the garlic, parsley, and chili pepper in the bowl of a food processor and finely chop them (or chop by hand). Then place this mixture in a small saucepan and add the oil and salt.

Boil the spaghetti in boiling salted water until al dente.

While the spaghetti is cooking, sauté the garlic mixture over low heat for 2 to 3 minutes. Do not let the garlic change color. Drain the pasta, place it in a warm dish, and toss it with the sauce and the pecorino cheese. Serve immediately.

Favata
Sardinian Bean and Pork Stew

Serves 6

This recipe is a typical dish served in the winter in Sardinia. When made two or three days ahead, it is even more tasty.

There are different varieties of fennel, some are bitter and some are sweet. It is a very popular vegetable in Sardinia and in Italy. Fennel is not hard to find in this country. In this recipe sweet fennel is used.

1 1/2 pound dried fava beans (lima or butter beans)
1/2 cup olive oil
2 pounds pork spareribs, cut into 4 pieces
6 Italian pork sausages, strings removed
1/2 pound lean bacon, in one piece
1 large onion, thinly sliced
2 celery stalks, thinly sliced

2 fennel bulbs with leaves, thinly sliced
1/2 head Savoy cabbage, shredded
2 garlic cloves, finely chopped
2 large tomatoes, peeled and chopped
1/2 teaspoon salt
1/2 teaspoon freshly ground black pepper

Soak the beans in lukewarm water overnight.

Heat the oil in a Dutch oven over medium heat. Add the pork ribs and sausage and sauté until golden in color. Add the drained beans and cover with 6 to 8 cups of hot water, making sure the mixture is well covered because the beans will absorb water. Add the bacon, onions, celery, fennel, cabbage, garlic and tomatoes. Season with salt and pepper and mix thoroughly.

Cook slowly, uncovered, over low heat for two hours, stirring once in a while. If more liquid is needed, add some hot water and continue cooking until the meat is tender and almost to the point of being overcooked,

When the meat is cooked, remove the pork and divide it into ribs. Remove the bacon and cut it into small pieces. Return both to the pan and reheat when ready to serve. Serve the pork stew very hot with slices of crusty Italian bread.

A variation is to toast the slices of bread. Then place one slice of bread in the bottom of each serving dish and cover it with the hot pork stew.

Pere e Formaggio
Pears and Cheese

Serves 6

3 large pears   *1/2 pound Pecorino Sardo cheese*

Wash, core and halve the pears lengthwise. Cut six slices of pecorino cheese.

Serve half a sliced pear with one slice of cheese per person, with some bread.

Torta di Mandorle
Almond Cake

Serves 6 to 8

4 large eggs, separated   *1/2 teaspoon baking powder*
1/2 cup plus 3 tablespoons sugar   *Grated peel of 1 lemon*
1/2 cup almonds, blanched, finely   *Butter for greasing pan*
   chopped   *Flour for dusting pan*
1/2 cup all-purpose flour   *Confectioner's sugar*

In a medium size bowl beat the egg yolks with the sugar until light and creamy. Add the finely chopped almonds, flour, baking powder and grated lemon peel and mix thoroughly. Beat the egg whites until stiff peaks form and gently fold them into the cake batter. Butter and flour a 10-inch round cake pan and pour in the cake batter. Place the cake pan in a preheated 350° F. oven and bake for about 35 minutes.

The cake is done when a tooth pick inserted into the center of the cake comes out clean. Remove from the oven, let cool and then remove cake from pan and let cool on a wire rack. Place the cooled cake on a serving dish and sprinkle the cake generously with confectioner's sugar.

Bibliography

Numerous books were consulted in writing this book. The following ones were especially helpful.

Alberini, Massimo. Antica Cucina Veneziana. Italy: Edizioni Piemme, 1990.

Balzano, Raffaele. Sardegna a Tavola. Albia, Italy: Edizione R. Balzano, 1994.

Bibi, Bruno. Codice Della Cucina Ligure. Milano, Italy: Il Secolo XIX, 1990.

Boni, Ida. Italian Regional Cooking. New York: Crown Publishers, Inc., 1977.

Butazzi, Grazietta. Toscana in Bocca. Palermo, Italy: Editrice de Il Vespro, 1977.

Corsi, Guglielma. Un Secolo di Cucina Umbria. Assisi, Italy: Edizioni Porziuncola, 1986.

Del Conte, Anna. Gastgronomy of Italy. New York: Prentice Hall Press, 1987.

Dolcino, Esther e Michelangelo. Le Ricette Liguri per Tutte le Occasioni. Genova, Italy: Nuova Editrice Genovese, 1990.

Fabris, Ida. Le Ricette della Mia Cucina Marchigiana Umbra e Abruzzese. Firenze, Italy: Edizioni del Riccio, 1997.

Feslikenian, Franco. Cucina e Vini del Lazio. Milano, Italy: U. Mursia & C., 1973.

Lanari, Giancarlo. Ricette Tradizionali di Basilicata. Potenza, Italy: Comitato Basilicata 1990.

Landra, Laura e Margherita. Cucina Regionale. Milano, Italy: Giovanni De Vecchi Editore, 1990.

Mallo, Beppe. La Cucina delle Regioni d'Italia Calabria e Lucania. Bologna, Italy: Edizioni Mida, 1989.

Ortusi, Pellegrino. La Scienza in Cucina e L'Arte di Mangiar Bene. San Casciano Firenze, Italy: Sperlin & Kupfer Editori, 1991.

Pedrotti, Walter. La Cucina di Trento. Verona, Italy: Edizioni La Libreria di Demetra, 1994.

Petroni, Paolo. Il Libro della Vera Cucina Emiliana. Firenze, Italy: Casa Editrice Bonechi, 1978.

Pizzetta, Silvano. Regioni D'Italia. Milano, Italy: Arnolda Mondadori Editore, 1983.

Roden, Claudia. The Good Food of Italy. New York: Alfred A. Knopf, 1990.

Salda, Anna Gossetti, ed. Le Ricette Regionali Italiane. Milano: Casa Editrice Solares, 1967.

Santini, Aldo. La Cucina Toscana. Livorno, Italy: Editoriale Il Tirreno, 1990.

Santolini, Antonella. La Cucina delle Regioni D'Italia Roma. Bologna, Italy: Edizioni Mida, 1989.

Tropea, Ivana. Le Licette della Mia Cucina Romana. Firenze, Italy: Edizioni del Riccio, 1977.

Recipe Index

Index   334